ALL THE NEWS THAT'S FIT TO CLICK

All the News That's Fit to Click

HOW METRICS ARE TRANSFORMING THE WORK OF JOURNALISTS

CAITLIN PETRE

PRINCETON UNIVERSITY PRESS

PRINCETON & OXFORD

Published by Princeton University Press
41 William Street, Princeton, New Jersey 08540
6 Oxford Street, Woodstock, Oxfordshire OX20 1TR

press.princeton.edu

Library of Congress Cataloging-in-Publication Data

Names: Petre, Caitlin, author.
Title: All the news that's fit to click : how metrics are transforming the work of journalists / Caitlin Petre.
Description: Princeton : Princeton University Press, [2021] | Includes bibliographical references and index.
Identifiers: LCCN 2021018399 (print) | LCCN 2021018400 (ebook) | ISBN 9780691177649 (hardback) | ISBN 9780691228754 (ebook)
Subjects: LCSH: Web usage mining in journalism—United States. | Online journalism—United States. | News audiences—United States. | Journalism—Technological innovations—United States. | BISAC: SOCIAL SCIENCE / Media Studies | COMPUTERS / Data Science / Data Analytics
Classification: LCC PN4784.W43 P48 2021 (print) | LCC PN4784.W43 (ebook) | DDC 070.4/30285—dc23
LC record available at https://lccn.loc.gov/2021018399
LC ebook record available at https://lccn.loc.gov/2021018400

British Library Cataloging-in-Publication Data is available

Editorial: Meagan Levinson and Jacqueline Delaney
Production Editorial: Mark Bellis
Jacket Design: Layla Mac Rory
Production: Erin Suydam
Publicity: Kate Hensley and Kathryn Stevens

This book has been composed in Arno

Printed on acid-free paper. ∞

Printed in the United States of America

10 9 8 7 6 5 4 3 2 1

For my parents

CONTENTS

ALL THE NEWS THAT'S FIT TO CLICK

Introduction

IN EARLY 2011, the website *Business Insider* published a leaked copy of "The Aol Way," a 58-slide PowerPoint presentation that outlined Aol's strategy for producing profitable media content in the digital age. The purpose of the slide deck was to train editorial staff at Aol's numerous online media properties—including the politics site *Politics Daily*, the celebrity gossip site *PopEater*, and the technology blogs *TechCrunch* and *Engadget*—on their parent company's editorial vision and approach.

The slides made clear that Aol's management saw journalism as a type of work that could be almost entirely rationalized. Decisions and actions that previously had been left to journalists' discretion were now to be standardized in order to maximize web traffic—and, therefore, advertising revenue. The slides instructed editors to consider four factors when deciding which topics to cover: traffic potential (i.e., editors' estimate, with the help of an algorithmic prediction tool, of how many pageviews each "piece of content" would generate); profit potential (the estimated amount of money a piece of content would cost to produce versus how much advertising revenue it was likely to bring in); turnaround time; and, finally, "editorial integrity." Headlines were to include as many newsy keywords as possible to increase their chances of appearing high in search engine results, the slides explained; content should always be delivered in the "most addictive" format possible to maximize audience attention. Writers were expected to write five to ten stories per day, each of which should "be profitable" and generate at least 7,000 pageviews (a marked increase from the company's then-average of 1,500). One memorable slide instructed journalists to "use editorial judgment & insight to determine production. [For example], if 'Macaulay Culkin' & 'Mila Kunis' are trending because they broke up → write story about Macaulay Culkin and Mila Kunis."[1] Argue as journalists might (and have) over what constitutes "editorial judgment," there could be little disagreement that Aol was stretching the definition of the term to the point of absurdity.

"The Aol Way" was received with a mixture of astonishment, derision, and horror in journalism circles. A writer for *TechCrunch* called the document "a 58-page death warrant for journalists and the practice of journalism at Aol";[2] a *Fortune* writer disparaged it as a "desperate" attempt to "squeez[e] out as much profit as possible from each 'piece of content,' regardless of its quality."[3] One Aol journalist who was quoted anonymously in the *Business Insider* story called joining the company "the worst career move I've ever made." Many journalists worried that something akin to "The Aol Way" would soon be widely taken up in the news industry. A writer for the tech site *Venturebeat* noted that while his editorial colleagues were doing a "happy dance" that they didn't work for Aol, their relief may have been premature: "my boss . . . reports that he's taking copious notes."[4]

To these journalists, "The Aol Way" represented a new type of managerial interference in editorial work. Yet in advocating for relentless metrics-driven content optimization, Aol was in fact taking a page out of a century-old managerial playbook. In 1911, a mechanical engineer named Frederick Winslow Taylor published a book called *The Principles of Scientific Management*, in which he put forth a new approach to maximizing the efficiency of factory work. Taylor exhorted managers to pay close attention to the *labor process*—the way work is organized and carried out. According to Taylorism, managers should approach the shop floor with the same spirit of empirical inquiry and methodological rigor with which a scientist conducts experiments in a laboratory. Taylor encouraged managers to conduct "time studies," in which they would break down a particular task (say, loading ingots of iron onto a railway car) into the smallest possible component parts and painstakingly hone the most efficient way to complete each one. Once he has discovered and implemented the optimal labor process, the scientific manager assigns workers to each mini-task and supervises them to ensure that work is carried out exactly as directed.

Taylor's approach served to accomplish two ends: first, to increase the efficiency and output of the labor process (and thereby raise profits); and second, to deskill workers by transforming their craft knowledge and abilities into a series of systematized steps that could be carried out by workers who were in essence interchangeable and therefore easily replaceable. Under Taylorism, managers are responsible for conception and planning of the labor process, while workers merely execute it.[5]

The basic tenets of Taylorism spread through U.S. industrial work in the first half of the twentieth century and, later, into clerical, retail, and service work. Yet creative and knowledge workers—put simply, those whose work centers on the production, communication, and circulation of knowledge and cultural products—remained relatively insulated from scientific management tactics during this period. There are several reasons for this. First, the ability to collect and analyze relevant data on these workers' performance was comparatively limited. Second, creative and knowledge work were thought to require a higher degree of autonomy in the labor process in order to produce quality outputs. Finally, these workers typically enjoyed greater cultural and material resources than other groups, which could be mobilized to resist data-driven performance evaluation and labor discipline.[6]

Yet the layer of insulation between creative and knowledge workers and metrics-driven forms of labor discipline is now wearing thin.[7] Digital metrics are increasingly infiltrating processes of cultural production in the music, TV, film, and book publishing industries, as well as many types of labor typically conceptualized as knowledge work, such as medicine, political campaigning, and urban planning. The growing role of metrics in these fields has prompted heated debate: big data enthusiasts predict that metrics will render knowledge work more effective, efficient, and democratic;[8] skeptics worry that metrics will undermine professional judgment and artistic creativity, with dire results.[9] Their differences notwithstanding, both sides agree that metrics are becoming more influential in the knowledge workplace. Still, we know surprisingly little about exactly what *kind* of influence are they having. To discover that, we must examine metrics in situ: how are they produced, interpreted, and put to use by social actors, and with what implications for the future of knowledge work?

This book sets out to answer that question, via a close look at the role of metrics in U.S. digital journalism. The contemporary commercial news media confronts several challenges that, taken together, suggest that the journalism labor process is a prime candidate for a radical metrics-driven transformation. The biggest problems are economic: deregulation in the 1990s led to a wave of corporate consolidation in the news business that has continued largely unchecked—if not at times actively encouraged—by the Federal Communications Commission.[10] Meanwhile, as large technology platforms like Google and Facebook have become a primary mode of news distribution as well as the dominant force in the online advertising business, many news organizations have seen their revenues plummet. The combination of corporate consolidation and platform dominance has led to fewer and smaller newsrooms, especially at the local level, and a more concentrated media land-scape.[11] As "The Aol Way" so vividly demonstrated, corporate news organ-izations facing slim-to-nonexistent profit margins may seek to intensify labor discipline by placing a growing emphasis on performance metrics.

Cultural challenges have accompanied the economic ones—namely, grow-ing skepticism and distrust toward the news media on the part of the American public.[12] Even before President Trump's highly publicized attacks on the profes-sional news media, the number of Americans who expressed "a great deal" or "quite a lot" of trust in newspapers and television news dropped ten percentage points from 2006 to 2016.[13] This, too, seems to point toward a bigger role for audience metrics in the production of journalism: as historian Theodore Porter has argued, professions facing external criticism and a lack of public trust are likely to adopt standardized quantitative approaches to their work.[14]

If media companies have increasing motivations to integrate metrics into their editorial operations, they also have many more technological tools with which to so. In the digital age, journalism has experienced a rapid proliferation of data about audiences' online behavior in the form of web metrics (some-times also referred to as analytics).[15] Today's news organizations use tools that track audiences' behavior on websites to see how many readers navigate to a particular story, comment on it, email it to a friend, or share it on a social media platform. Analytics tools tally not only pageviews, sometimes also known as "hits" or "clicks," which measure the number of times a particular web page has been visited, but also unique visitors (or "uniques"), which is an approximate measure of the number of distinct people who visit a page or site within a given period, usually thirty days.[16] Real-time analytics "dashboards" also provide data on "scroll depth" (how far readers typically scroll down on a particular page) and "engaged time" (how long they spend looking at con-tent, on average). Data on referral sources (where on the internet a site's read-ers are coming from) and social media shares is also widely available. All told, the increase in audience-tracking affordances has been so dramatic that one newsroom analyst called it a "revolution in audience analytics."[17]

This book explores how this "revolution" is reshaping editorial working con-ditions, newsroom power dynamics, and journalists' relationship to and experi-ence of their work. Put simply: What does the explosion of audience metrics mean for journalism as a form of *labor*? To answer this question, I draw on a mix of ethnographic observation and in-depth interviews conducted over a period of four years at three sites: Chartbeat, a web analytics company that specializes in metrics for newsrooms; the *New York Times*, an organization that is working to reconcile its storied print past with the work rhythms, technologies, and economic challenges of digital journalism; and Gawker Media, a then-independent online media company that owned a network of popular blogs.

Although a substantial body of research has addressed the role of audience metrics in journalism, surprisingly little of this scholarship explicitly analyzes metrics as a form of labor discipline that shapes both the organization and lived experience of journalistic work under capitalism.[18] One stream of existing research has sought to determine if and how newsroom metrics have changed the content and presentation of news.[19] Another stream has investigated the impact of metrics on journalists' norms, values, and practices.[20] While this work at times mentions the use of metrics as a managerial tactic and form of employee performance evaluation, rarely has this been the main focus.[21]

Yet journalism is not only a set of practices. It is also a form of labor—one that has become increasingly casualized and precarious in an era of rapid technological development, technology platforms' dominance over digital advertising and media distribution, and the virtually unchecked consolidation of commercial media companies.[22] Journalists' working conditions have moral significance not only in and of themselves but also because they shape the quality of the news. Following cultural sociologists David Hesmondhalgh and Sarah Baker, we can reasonably assume that "bad work"—that is, work that is boring, insecure, isolating, excessive, and poorly compensated—is more likely to produce low-quality cultural products, while the opposite is true of "good work"—that is, work that is fairly compensated, secure, interesting, and autonomous.[23] A central premise of this book is that to understand the impact of metrics on contemporary journalism and news, as well as what the proliferation of metrics means for other forms of knowledge work, we must look closely at how the data interacts with newsroom working conditions and power dynamics.

To that end, this book examines the role of newsroom metrics in reshaping the journalistic labor process. Embarking on this study, the topic presented what struck me as an interesting puzzle. On the one hand, a long line of social science thinkers dating back to Max Weber have analyzed quantification as a rationalizing and disciplining force that can remake social realities just as much as it measures them.[24] In the case of journalism, by providing granular, up-to-the-second data about how audiences are responding to news content, metrics seem likely to disempower journalists as workers in two ways. First, much as Taylorism systematically deskills craft workers by separating the conception and high-level planning of work (which becomes the exclusive province of managers) from its rote execution, metrics threaten to strip journalists of the ability to set the news agenda using their specialized sense of editorial judgment. In other words, as "The Aol Way" illustrated, metrics could facilitate a regime of scientific management in which journalists are reduced from expert arbiters of newsworthiness to mere executors tasked with unquestioningly following the dictates of quantified representations of audience popularity. Second, insofar as metrics are collectively understood to represent audience attention—and, therefore, advertising and subscription revenue—they are an intrusion of commercial considerations into the newsroom. By installing analytics dashboards, management is arguably taking a sledgehammer to the "wall" between editorial and business operations that has long been central to the notion of journalistic independence and professionalism.[25]

On the other hand, decades of research in sociology, communication, and science and technology studies have shown that the introduction of a new technology rarely produces dramatic social change all on its own. Rather, the impact of new technologies depends on how they are used in particular social, economic, political, and organizational contexts.[26] In the workplace, technologically facilitated managerial regimes require both coercion *and* consent if they are to fundamentally change the labor process.[27] This may be especially true when quantitative tools of labor discipline are implemented in knowledge-work fields. As Hesmondhalgh and Baker write: "Workers in these *relatively* powerful and high-status forms of [professional and craft] work often have a very uneasy relationship with managers, and greater power in relation to management than many other workers."[28] Journalists' liminal professional status and the beleaguered state of the news business notwithstanding, news workers seem relatively empowered to resist scientific management tactics and the metrics-driven devaluation of their labor. The pages that follow are animated by this tension: between the known power of metrics to discipline and rationalize social behavior on one hand, and the indeterminate effects of new technologies on the other.

The Argument

In this book, I argue that newsroom metrics are a powerful form of managerial surveillance and discipline. Via a habit-forming, game-like user interface, analytics dashboards like Chartbeat extract increased productivity from rank-and-file journalists and can intensify competitive dynamics between them. However, in order to succeed commercially, analytics products must not simply discipline journalists' work but also gain their trust and acceptance. Newsroom analytics companies do this by making technological and rhetorical concessions to journalists' autonomy. Unlike the Taylorist manager's stopwatch to which they are sometimes compared, tools like Chartbeat are designed and marketed to forge strong emotional attachments directly with journalists, perform deference to their sense of editorial expertise, and profess allegiance to their professional norms. Such tactics facilitate metrics-driven labor discipline, insofar as they help forestall newsroom resistance against metrics.

Yet even as analytics tools function as a powerful form of labor discipline, they also represent a new patch of terrain on which newsroom power struggles unfold. Because analytics tools must leave room for the (limited) exercise of journalistic judgment, they are interpretively ambiguous technological artifacts: that is, it's often unclear what the data *means* or what should be done with it. While journalists become fixated on metrics, they also strategically *use* the numbers' ambiguous meaning to pursue their own strategic goals and even, at times, gain a measure of leverage over management. In sum, the ambiguity of newsroom metrics makes journalists more likely to consent to the rationalization of their labor while also ensuring that this rationalization proceeds only fitfully and remains incomplete.

In making this argument, I am informed by and seek to build upon three areas of scholarly research: the literature from communication and media studies on what is variously called knowledge work, media work, and cultural labor; the sociology of quantification and rationalization; and literature on metrics and the labor process. The next sections will briefly discuss each of these, in order to build the conceptual and theoretical foundations of what's to come.

The Management of Knowledge Work and Creative Labor

While this book focuses closely on the case of journalism, I also aim to provide a framework for thinking about the relationship between metrics and labor in other forms of knowledge work. Drawing on the scholarship of Vincent Mosco and Catherine McKercher, I conceptualize knowledge work as "the labor of those who handle, distribute, and convey information and knowledge"[29] and who, crucially, are typically understood to require the opportunity to exercise independent judgment in order to successfully carry out their work.[30] Under this definition fall librarians, writers, artists, researchers, doctors, lawyers, teachers, journalists, and many others.

Knowledge work is a contested concept. Some argue that by defining only certain occupations as knowledge work, we elide the ways in which *all* types of work in capitalism (1) occur under the same basic relations of production, and (2) require the possession and communication of particular kinds of knowledge and information.[31] While these critiques have validity, there is still value in treating knowledge-work occupations, as defined above, as a distinct object of analysis. Whether or not what is commonly characterized as "knowledge work" *is* in fact meaningfully different from other types of work in terms of the degree or kind of knowledge required to perform it, there exists a widespread cultural understanding that knowledge workers require a measure of aesthetic and/or professional autonomy to produce what is expected of them. Thus there is an expectation (especially among workers in and adjacent to these occupations) that so-called knowledge work be managed differently from other forms of labor.

Other scholars have criticized the concept of knowledge work as too broad to adequately analyze fields of cultural production. This group favors narrower alternatives such as creative labor, media work, cultural labor, and cultural work, which foreground the "specific importance of *culture*, of *mediated communication*, and of the *content* of communication products" with their unique "ability to shape and influence societies."[32] Yet in terms of labor process, cultural production under capitalism presents a dilemma for managers similar to that of knowledge work: the logic of capital accumulation demands a labor process that is rationalized and standardized, but the economic value of these cultural producers' outputs derives, at least in part, from their originality, unpredictability, and ineffable aesthetic sensibility.

Cultural producers are therefore understood to require some degree of autonomy in how they carry out their work.[33] Managers in these industries must continually navigate the "art-commerce relation," in which "artistic desires for creative autonomy and independence exist in uneasy tension with capitalist imperatives of profit-generation and controlled accumulation."[34] Given that explicitly coercive management tactics are likely to inspire resistance among cultural workers—and, in stifling creativity, may prove counterproductive for the goal of creating profitable cultural products—managers rely on subtler forms of labor discipline, sometimes called "creative" or "soft" management. These include instilling an entrepreneurial sensibility in workers such that they assume and individualize the risks inherent in cultural production[35] and offering managerial directives as mere "guidelines" or suggestions.[36]

Where do journalists fit into this picture? On the one hand, journalists actively produce "social meaning" in a way that positions them as cultural workers. And like other cultural workers, journalists create discrete *products*, which may make their work more likely to be mechanized and standardized than that of professionals, like doctors, who provide an intangible *service*.[37] However, journalists differ from artistic-creative workers in a key respect: they "occupy jobs centered on the construction and dissemination of what might be called interpretive information or knowledge" rather than aesthetic or artistic products.[38] Whereas individual creativity and self-expression are idealized in artistic fields, journalism's occupational ideology prizes considered judgment—the ability to quickly absorb, adjudicate between, and publicly communicate complex and conflicting sources of information. Furthermore, journalism is an anomalous case of cultural production in that its practitioners operate according to a set of normative, rather than artistic, commitments. As media scholar Mike Ananny puts it, "Unlike artistic fields of cultural production, the press—ideally and principally—pursues its autonomy in order to advance *public* interests."[39]

Therefore, while artistic workers seek *aesthetic* autonomy, journalists primarily seek *professional* autonomy—the ability to practice newswork according to a set of collective normative values and with relative insulation from political actors and the market.[40] Yet because the U.S. press is heavily commercialized, many of the management tensions and challenges are the same as those found in other forms of industrial cultural production. If aesthetic cultural work is defined by the art-commerce relation, we might say that journalism is characterized by the *democracy*-commerce relation.

In sum, placing journalism within the category of knowledge work captures the ways in which journalists are similar to *both* creative/artistic workers *and* professional workers. Indeed, the fact that journalists, perhaps uniquely, span the boundary between these two groups makes them an optimal case through which to examine the impact of metrics on knowledge work. To do so, I draw on a body of historical and sociological literature on the social determinants and impacts of quantification.

Numbers and Rationalization in the Modern World

A foundational insight of social science is that quantification—what we count and how we go about counting it—profoundly shapes the social world. Max Weber argued that the modern era was defined by a numbers-driven rationalization of the social order, in which political, economic, and cultural life are rendered increasingly calculable and predictable via measurement innovations like double-entry bookkeeping and government censuses. In a rationalized world, all forms of coordinated human action and decision making become increasingly standardized.

Weber contended that rationalization had substantial benefits, such as allowing humans to exert greater control over the natural world and facilitating more meritocratic forms of social life. Yet he also believed that rationalization posed a dangerous threat to humans' autonomy and sense of meaning. As more elements of human life were reduced to numbers, and premodern ways of understanding the world were displaced by modern science, technology, and capitalism, Weber worried that people would become disenchanted. A fully rationalized world may be more efficient, but it is ultimately oppressive—trapping us in what Weber famously referred to as the iron cage.[41]

Subsequent scholarship has carried forward Weber's work on rationalization, examining how numbers shape how people understand the social world and act within it. Just as some types of speech are also *actions* that produce real-world effects (such as when a wedding officiant pronounces a couple married or a gambler places a bet), producing and communicating numbers can also be a form of consequential social action.[42]

Numbers do two things in particular that are relevant to our purposes in this book. First, numbers *commensurate*: they take two or more qualitatively different entities and render them comparable by applying to each a single numerical standard. In other words, commensuration "unites objects by encompassing them under a shared cognitive system. . . . Difference or similarity is expressed as magnitude, as an interval on a metric, a precise matter of more or less."[43] Grades, college rankings, and prices are all forms of commensuration—as are newsroom metrics. While numerical rankings tend to take on an air of objectivity and straightforwardness, commensuration is in fact labor-intensive. It takes a good deal of cognitive work to figure out which entities should be considered commensurable in the first place and how they stack up against one another on a particular metric. For this reason, commensuration can also be controversial, especially when it is seen as biased, failing to consider relevant context, or otherwise inappropriate. In such cases, commensuration may be contested—as when, for example, a student complains to a professor about a grade.

As the disgruntled student example illustrates, those on the receiving end of quantitative performance evaluation are rarely passive or static. It is difficult to publicly measure something or someone without changing it or them in some way. Thus a second thing that evaluative numbers do in the social world is elicit a response from the people and organizations they measure. Scholars call this phenomenon *reactivity*. In their in-depth study of the effects of yearly law school rankings, Wendy Espeland and Michael Sauder found that schools adjusted their admissions criteria and financial aid priorities in an attempt to improve their rank, largely to the detriment of their educational mission.[44] In this instance, the reactivity was unintentional: *U.S. News & World Report*, the magazine that published the rankings, originally envisioned them as a resource for prospective law students (and a way to boost circulation), not as a means to reform legal education. In other cases, evaluative measures are deliberately designed to be reactive, and specifically to prompt those being measured to modify their behavior in some way. Workplace performance metrics generally fall into this category, as do wearable activity monitors like the Fitbit.

While much sociological work on quantification emphasizes its power to remake the social world, some scholars have pointed out that rationalization is not actually a straightforward or linear process. Organizations may appear to adopt rationalized procedures, but these changes are often only ceremonial. In many cases, organizational actors *claim* to follow the official standardized rules in an effort to seem legitimate and efficient while continuing to carry out their day-to-day work just as they have always done it.[45] Relatedly, as a professional field becomes increasingly structured and defined, organizations within it start to mimic each other by adopting rationalized rules—not necessarily because such rules and procedures actually make organizations more effective, but because they are a way to manage uncertainty.[46] These studies suggest that while modern organizations face great pressure to *appear* rational, they may not actually conduct their affairs in a rationalized way—and, even if they do, rationalization may not streamline their operations in quite the way Weber predicted. In addition, the same metrics can take on different meanings (and thus produce dramatically different effects) depending on institutional context.[47]

These nuanced findings notwithstanding, numbers-driven rationalization continues to be alternately romanticized and condemned in the so-called era of "big data."[48] As ever-larger swaths of the social and natural world are rendered into digital data via networked technologies, big data enthusiasts have predicted that analytics will increasingly supplant biased forms of human judgment and decision making, leading to fairer, smarter, more profitable outcomes for society.[49] Others worry about the power of performance metrics to "deskill" workers, diminish people's autonomy, and otherwise disempower them.[50]

Metrics, Deskilling, and the Capitalist Labor Process

The 1970s brought renewed sociological attention to the labor process among Marxian scholars. In his classic 1974 book *Labor and Monopoly Capital*, Harry Braverman analyzed Taylorism as a form of management that systematically "deskills" workers by eliminating from their jobs any opportunity for the exercise of specialized knowledge, judgment, or substantive skill. The result, Braverman argued, is that ever more knowledge and power become consolidated in the hands of management.[51] Braverman argued that because it is a fundamental part of capitalist control over labor, deskilling would not be limited to assembly line manufacturing, service, and clerical work but would increasingly occur in the "middle layers" of employment, including nurses, teachers, engineers, accountants, technicians, "petty managers," and, we might add, journalists.[52]

Other scholars have added nuance to Braverman's analysis by shifting the analytical focus from the actions of management to the subjectivity of the worker. In his classic ethnography of a factory shop floor, sociologist Michael Burawoy emphasized the importance of worker consent—as opposed to managerial coercion—in the smooth functioning of the capitalist labor process. In the machine shop Burawoy studied as a participant-observer, workers played a game in which they competed against each other to "make out," or produce output at a rate considerably higher than the management-set quota, but not *so* high that management increased the quota. While workers who exceeded the quota earned a small bonus, the main appeal of making out was not the money but rather that doing so mitigated the tedium of the job and was a way to earn the respect of one's coworkers. While workers thus had their own psychological and social motivations to make out, the shop-floor game led them to work harder than they otherwise would have, making them willing participants in the intensification of their own exploitation.[53]

In short, Burawoy agreed with Braverman that the logic of capitalism requires that work become progressively more rote and less skilled. Yet he offered an important amendment to Braverman's thesis: deskilling must leave *some* space for workers to make choices and exercise agency, lest they channel their feelings of frustration, boredom, and disempowerment into open rebellion against management. While these worker choices do not fundamentally alter the economic relationships of capitalism, they are nonetheless meaningful and worthy of analytical attention.

Whether shop-floor games and informal forms of worker resistance—such as complaining and work slowdowns—genuinely subvert managerial interests or, by contrast, inadvertently serve them by acting as a "safety valve" that forestalls more impactful forms of rebellion is a lingering question.[54] Yet some scholars have persuasively argued that this kind of either/or framing is too reductive to capture of the complexity of the capitalist labor process. Instead, managerial control and worker resistance are best understood as having a dialectical relationship: workers have agency that allows them to meaningfully resist managerial dictates in various ways, but management will continually work to co-opt and domesticate workers' oppositional behaviors.

The chapters that follow will show how the concept of a dialectic between managerial control and worker autonomy is useful for understanding the case of metrics in newsrooms. Chartbeat's real-time newsroom metrics facilitate a regime of managerial surveillance and discipline that makes Frederick Taylor's stopwatch seem almost quaint by comparison. Yet journalists possess professional status, ample reserves of cultural capital, and a highly visible public platform—resources they can mobilize to resist metrics-driven performance evaluation if they choose to do so. For this reason, earning the trust and acceptance of rank-and-file journalists was crucial if Chartbeat was ever going to become fully institutionalized in newsrooms, but it also presented a formidable challenge. Indeed, we will see that Chartbeat expended considerable effort to win over journalists via its marketing pitch and the user-experience design of its signature newsroom analytics tool.

Chartbeat's strategy paid off handsomely: journalists became fixated on trying to increase their traffic numbers, despite reservations many of them voiced about incorporating metrics into their editorial work. In the process, they pushed themselves to work ever harder in a way that served managerial interests more than their own, even in the absence of direct or explicit coercion. Perhaps unsurprisingly, given its effectiveness as a booster of worker productivity, Chartbeat has become a fixture in newsrooms in the United States and around the world.

However, this is not a simple story of managerial domination. In order to secure journalists' consent to metrics-driven monitoring, Chartbeat incorporated ambiguity into its newsroom analytics tool, leaving space for the limited exercise of editorial judgment. These design decisions in turn enabled journalists to leverage metrics in unexpected ways that at times empowered them relative to management.

The Study: Exploring Metrics at Chartbeat, the *New York Times*, and Gawker Media

At the outset of this research, I had two major exploratory questions. First, how is a newsroom analytics tool produced?[55] These products are not, after all, fully formed entities that descend upon newsrooms from on high. Rather, analytics tools are technological artifacts whose particular features and affor-dances are the outcome of negotiations among a diverse set of stakeholders, including product designers, engineers, marketers, media company executives, newsroom data analysts, and journalists. Analytics tools are, in other words, the outcome of a *social process* that has significant consequences for the future of journalism, but had never been closely investigated.[56]

To understand the social process that produces newsroom analytics, I knew I would need to see the inner workings of an analytics company up close, and Chartbeat soon emerged as an optimal case study. At the time of its founding in 2009, Chartbeat was the first web analytics company to specialize in audi-ence data specifically intended for use by journalists in newsrooms. (Rivals, like Google Analytics, offered tools that originally had been designed for use in e-commerce or advertising sales.) Other start-ups soon began to emulate Chartbeat's newsroom-centered approach, but by then Chartbeat's products had saturated the news industry. By the time my research there began in August 2013, Chartbeat's tools had been taken up by more than 50,000 news-rooms in the United States and more than 60 additional countries.[57]

Chartbeat specialized in "real-time" web analytics, which told newsrooms how many people were visiting their websites at that moment and what they were doing during their visits. The company's signature tool was the Chartbeat Publishing dashboard, a multicolored full-screen display that showed news organizations a wide range of metrics about their audiences: how many visi-tors were currently on each particular article page (aka concurrent visitors, as Chartbeat called them), the average amount of time they had been there, which internet sites referred them, how often they visited, where in the world they were located, what percentage of them were looking at the site on mobile phones, and much more. Chartbeat was also known for the Big Board, which ranked a news site's stories according to concurrent visitors and was designed to be displayed on a newsroom wall.

From August 2013 through January 2014, I spent time as a "fly on the wall" in Chartbeat's office, located in the Union Square neighborhood of New York City. Fortuitously, my time there coincided with a period in which the com-pany was in the process of designing and launching a new version of the Chart-beat Publishing dashboard (referred to internally as CPB2). I was able to wit-ness much of this process take place. During my fieldwork, I observed internal meetings, product-testing sessions, and client trainings and meetings. I was also given a spare desk in the middle of Chartbeat's open office where I was able to hang out for hours at a time, observing the rhythms of daily office life.

In addition, I conducted 22 interviews and in-depth conversations with 16 employees who worked on a range of teams across the company.

The second question I set out to answer was this: How are analytics interpreted and put to use in actual newsrooms? Here I took a comparative approach to choosing case studies. I selected two news organizations that both subscribed to Chartbeat but differed from each other in many other significant dimensions: the *New York Times* and Gawker Media. Choosing two newsrooms that both used the same analytics tool but were otherwise quite dissimilar enabled me to see how factors like newsroom structure, organizational history and culture, business strategy, level of prestige, and journalistic style affect the way an analytics tool is taken up.

The *New York Times* is arguably the emblematic "legacy" news publication in the United States. It is one of the country's oldest papers and has been majority-owned by a single family, the Ochs Sulzbergers, for over a century. Yet the *Times*'s unmatched prestige did not protect it from the turmoil roiling the news industry in the early twenty-first century. During the primary period of my research, 2011–15, the paper was struggling to reconcile its print-era revenue models and work routines with what journalism scholar Nikki Usher has called the "emergent news values" of the digital age, such as immediacy, interactivity, and participation.[58]

The *Times*'s approach to metrics reflected this ambivalence and uneasiness. The newspaper was a long-time Chartbeat client, but top editors were reluctant to integrate it—or any analytics tool—into the editorial workflow. Rather than subscribe to Chartbeat Publishing, which was Chartbeat's most sophisticated analytics tool and the one used by most of its high-profile clients, the *Times* subscribed only to Chartbeat "Basic," a less expensive, stripped-down version of the tool that was typically used by much smaller news organizations and blogs. As later chapters will discuss in more detail, *Times* newsroom managers also carefully restricted access to metrics within the newsroom, such that editors and select digital staffers had access to audience data while reporters did not.

As a result, my interviewees at the *Times* had wildly different exposure to metrics depending on where they were situated in the newsroom hierarchy. Some were deeply immersed in metrics on a daily basis, while others had never so much as laid eyes on Chartbeat (one prospective interviewee professed never to have heard of it). I conducted 25 interviews with 22 newsroom staffers at the *Times*, including reporters, editors, columnists, web producers, and newsroom operations staff. While I was not permitted to conduct sustained ethnographic observation at the *Times*, many of my interviews took place within the newsroom, which allowed me to develop a sense of the physical space and atmosphere.

If the *Times* is the paradigmatic legacy media organization, Gawker Media was the paradigmatic digital upstart. Founded in 2002 by entrepreneur Nick Denton, Gawker was a network of blogs on a range of subjects, the best known of which were *Gawker* (the company's flagship site, which focused on politics, media, and celebrity gossip), *Jezebel* (women's issues and feminism), *Deadspin* (sports), and *Gizmodo* (technology). While Gawker was mainly known for its "core" sites (in addition to the ones just listed, these included sites that covered science fiction, video games, self-help tips, and automobiles), the Gawker universe extended far beyond such titles to encompass a sprawling network of blogs—many penned by unpaid contributors—that were hosted on Kinja, the company's content-management system and publishing platform. (To limit unwieldy terminology, I use the term Gawker without italics as shorthand for Gawker Media; the blog of the same name will be referred to as *Gawker* in italics.)

By the mid-aughts, Gawker sites had become famous for their snarky tone and gleeful disregard for traditional journalistic norms, such as objectivity and the prohibition on paying for scoops. But perhaps the most notable way in which Gawker deviated from the customs of legacy journalism was its unabashed reliance on quantitative performance measures to evaluate stories, sites, and editorial staff.

Indeed, there was arguably no contemporary media organization more strongly associated with a metrics-driven editorial culture than Gawker. In sharp contrast to the *Times*, all Gawker writers and editors had access to Chartbeat, as well as another analytics tool called Quantcast. On the floor of Gawker's offices where editorial staffers worked, screens displaying metrics were positioned such that it was nearly impossible for writers and editors to avoid passing by them when they walked to the office kitchen and bathroom, or entered or exited the stairwell leading to the street. Denton had also implemented a variety of pay-for-performance systems over the years, in which writers were compensated based partly on the traffic their posts generated.

From February to August 2014, I observed internal meetings at Gawker, analyzed the company's internal memos, and interviewed 28 staff members inhabiting a variety of roles, including site leads, editors, writers, editorial fellows, and editorial and business-side executives. I also spent five days virtually "sitting in" on the online group chats of two of Gawker's sites.

Doing Slow Research in a Fast-Changing Field

Ethnographic research is something that can't be rushed. It takes time to get to know a place, its people, its rhythms. It takes time to earn subjects' trust and be granted a window into their lived experience. It takes time to write detailed field notes, transcribe interviews, and analyze the hundreds of pages of resulting text. Perhaps most importantly, it takes deep, unhurried reflection to make *sense* of what one has seen, heard, and read—to think through what the findings tell us not just about the research sites but also about the broader social world of which they are a part.

And yet, while all this time is passing, research sites stubbornly refuse to hold still—perhaps especially if they are digital technology or media companies. The technologies, organizational landscape, and economic realities of the contemporary news industry continue to change at a dizzying speed, and the firms I studied were no exception. In the years since I completed the research for this book, Gawker was bankrupted by a lawsuit and has since passed through multiple owners, the *Times* rolled out metrics more widely in its newsroom, most significantly by investing in the development of Stela, an internal analytics tool, and Chartbeat went through a major staff expansion, a subsequent staff contraction, a rebranding exercise, and a change in the CEO. Some of these shifts are highly relevant to the questions I take up in this book, others only tangentially so. The concluding chapter addresses these changes in more depth and offers some thoughts on their significance for the arguments I make in these pages.

For now, I will simply say that the ever-changing nature of the digital media industry field site need not be a liability. In fact it can be an asset, to the extent that it forces the researcher to pull their thinking to a higher level of abstraction and, in doing so, increase the analytical rigor and richness of the work. As my sites continued to change after I left the field, I was repeatedly pushed to reconsider the age-old question "what is this a case of?"—"this" being not only the particular organizations I studied but also the particular time period during which I studied them. I had no choice but to identify the broader, deeper themes that would not be rendered irrelevant by the latest newsroom restructuring or the launch of a new technological tool.

This book is, like all ethnographic research, a snapshot—but it's not a random one. It reveals a moment in the development of digital media when metrics were thoroughly institutionalized in some newsrooms (like Gawker) and still working their way into others (like the *Times*). If our goal is to understand exactly *how* tools of rationalization and labor discipline become entrenched in knowledge workplaces, and with what consequences, we could hardly hope for a better picture at which to look.

Plan of the Book

The book contains seven chapters. Chapter 1 continues to lay the foundation for what is to come: I examine journalism's normative and empirical specificities as a case, and argue that journalists' working conditions and labor process deserve more scholarly attention than they typically receive. I then provide an overview of the institutional context and history of the three sites I studied for this book, with particular focus on where they fit into the broader journalism field in the United States.

The remainder of the book is divided into three parts. Part I takes a close look at the kind of "user experience," to borrow a term from the tech industry, that analytics tools create for journalists. Chapter 2 argues that real-time newsroom analytics tools are designed to be habit-forming by mimicking key features of addictive games. This game-like user experience extracted increased productivity from journalists by making them feel they were locked in a relentless competition against their coworkers and themselves to achieve ever-higher metrics.

Although many journalists found Chartbeat addictive, it could also feel tedious, demoralizing, and meaningless. Some Chartbeat staffers worried that these negative feelings might inspire resistance to the tool, which would in turn pose problems for the analytics company's ability to sign and retain clients. Thus chapter 3 examines how Chartbeat sought to make metrics feel unthreatening and meaningful to journalists—by professing allegiance to journalistic values, performing deference to journalistic judgment, and including design elements that tapped into ideas of magic, mystery, and transcendence.

If part 1 focuses on the experience of using tools like Chartbeat, part 2 explores how journalists interpret the data. Chapter 4 details the ways in which, despite their reputation for dictating clear takeaways, metrics are interpretively ambiguous in three ways: it is often unclear what the data mean, why articles get the traffic they do, and which actions should be taken based on metrics. Chapter 5 illustrates how, in the face of this ambiguity, journalists seek to draw firm, if at times seemingly arbitrary, symbolic boundaries between legitimate and illegitimate uses of metrics. Drawing on concepts from social anthropology and the sociology of work, I argue that some forms and uses of audience data become categorized as "clean"—that is, they harness the potential of metrics while containing the threat to journalism's professional identity—while others are categorized as "dirty" or contaminating.

Part 3 of the book examines how metrics interact with existing newsroom hierarchies and managerial regimes. Chapter 6 explains when, how, and why editors restricted access to some metrics and strategically invoked others in the process of managing journalistic labor. Chapter 7 explores the ways in which newsroom metrics intersected with journalists' diverging perceptions of professional autonomy at the *New York Times* and Gawker, as well as the material consequences of these intersections.

After summarizing the book's main arguments, the conclusion discusses how each field site has changed since my research ended and offers thoughts on how these changes speak to the book's claims. In the conclusion I also consider the implications of my findings for other forms of knowledge work facing an influx of digital metrics. Finally, appendix A provides insight about the process by which I obtained access to my field sites and the methods I employed while in the field; appendix B offers a detailed guide to the Chartbeat Publishing analytics dashboard.

1

Digital Journalism: Putting
the Case in Context

JOURNALISM IS AN illuminating case through which to examine a much broader social phenomenon: what happens when a long-established knowledge-work field faces an influx of digital performance metrics. Still, journalism has a number of unique features that must be attended to if we are to make sense of it as a case. To that end, this chapter has three aims. First, I lay a foundation for the argument to come by exploring journalism's normative and empirical specificities as a form of knowledge production, especially with regard to the field's conception of professional autonomy and its understanding of news audiences. Second, I make the case that journalists' working conditions and labor process deserve far more analytical attention than they typically receive. Finally, I provide an overview of the institutional context and history of the three sites I studied for this book, with a particular focus on where they fit into the broader U.S. journalism landscape.

A Field in Flux: Tensions over Journalists'
Autonomy and Audiences

All mediated forms of culture—from music to television to books—are "carriers of meaning" that influence how we understand the social world.[1] Journalism is among the most powerful cultural industries in this regard—not for nothing has it been called "the primary sense-making practice of modernity."[2] It is mainly through news consumption that many of us encounter political leaders and other powerful figures, cultivate a sense of empathy (or antipathy) toward people in different life circumstances, learn about and contextualize contemporary events that are outside our immediate, observable environs, and develop a sense of the crucial issues animating public life. The press is also expected to operate as an essential check on powerful individuals and institutions in government and the corporate sector.[3]

For these reasons, few would dispute that a robust press is a necessary condition for democratic self-governance—and in the United States, the press enjoys unique cultural and constitutional protections on the basis of that premise.[4] But what *is* a thriving press, exactly? What kinds of material, political, and cultural conditions are necessary to ensure that journalists can do their jobs in the way that democracy needs them to?

Many of the prevailing answers to these questions—among journalists and scholars alike—revolve around the concept of professional autonomy: put simply, the notion that "journalists should be left alone to do their work" with minimal outside interference.[5] Much of journalism history in the United States can be understood as the profession's ongoing efforts to establish independence from the state and the market, both of which are generally viewed as corrupting influences on editorial freedom and journalistic integrity.[6] A range of established journalistic norms and practices, such as refusing gifts, denying sources quote approval, and establishing a "wall" between the editorial and business sides of news organizations, stem from efforts to maintain autonomy.

Yet the very notion of journalistic autonomy contains within it a contradiction, because journalism is an inherently outward-facing profession. The practice of reporting relies on journalists' access to interviews, tips, and documents from a range of external sources. And journalism requires an audience to fulfill its civic mission to inform, communicate with, and facilitate a democratic public. As journalism scholar Michael Schudson puts it in an essay pointedly titled "Autonomy from What?": "What keeps journalism alive, changing, and growing is the public nature of journalists' work, the nonautonomous environment of their work, the fact that they are daily or weekly exposed to the disappointment and criticism of their sources (in the political field) and their public (whose disapproval may be demonstrated economically as readers cancel their subscriptions or viewers change channels)."[7] Similarly, Mike Ananny argues that press freedom is not simply freedom from all external influences on journalistic practice. Rather, press freedom is better understood as the particular configuration of "separations [from] and dependencies [on]" states, markets, and audiences.[8]

The tensions embedded within the concept of journalistic autonomy have long been apparent in journalists' ambivalent and conflicted relationship to audiences—and, nowadays, metrics. In the print era, data about audiences was comparatively sparse: newspaper and magazine journalists had measures such as circulation figures (which could be further broken down into subscription rates and newsstand sales), market research (usually consisting of the results from audience surveys, interviews, and focus groups), and reader feedback like letters to the editor, but such information was piecemeal.[9]

Print-era journalists tended to be skeptical or even hostile toward even this limited information about their audiences. Instead, they preferred to make editorial decisions based on their own intuitive "news judgment" and the opinions of their newsroom peers and supervisors. As sociologist Herbert Gans wrote in an oft-quoted passage from his classic newsroom ethnography *Deciding What's News*, journalists "had little knowledge about the actual audience and rejected feedback from it. Although they had a vague image of the audience, they paid little attention to it; instead, they filmed and wrote for their superiors and for themselves, assuming . . . that what interested them would interest the audience."[10]

As many journalism scholars have argued, print-era journalists rejected audience research because doing so was one of the only means to protect their always-tenuous professional status. Sociologist Andrew Abbott has characterized professions as "somewhat exclusive groups of individuals applying somewhat abstract knowledge to particular cases."[11] Although it is commonly categorized as a profession, journalism has long struggled to comfortably inhabit this definition. Even before the rise of the internet helped shift institutional gatekeeping power away from news organizations and toward technology platforms, journalists had difficulty establishing themselves as a "somewhat exclusive group of individuals." Indeed, while paradigmatic professions such as medicine and law rely on strict licensing requirements to limit entry into the profession, the First Amendment prohibits U.S. journalism from establishing any such thing. Nor can journalists lay a strong claim to jurisdiction over a form of abstract knowledge. As journalism scholar Matt Carlson has argued, "abstraction makes for bad journalism. Clarity, especially in the explanation of complex topics, makes for good journalism."[12] The accessibility of journalistic language is helpful for informing the public, but it also renders journalists' claims to specialized expertise potentially suspect.

In the absence of a structural closure mechanism that limits entry into the profession or a repertoire of abstract knowledge, journalists create and maintain boundaries around their profession by "doing things a certain way and privileging certain rationales for those actions."[13] In the United States, journalists' "way of doing things" encompasses a wide range of work rituals and rhythms, behavioral rules (governing, for instance, relationships to sources), specialized lingo, norms such as objectivity, and stylistic conventions. Crucially, the opinions and assessments of other journalists—rather than outsiders—typically hold the most weight when considering whether the job has been done well or not.[14] Seen through this lens, journalists' disinterest in or even outright rejection of audience data and feedback is hardly surprising: such a posture was foundational to journalists' understanding of themselves as autonomous professionals.

Still, a question remains: Why did managers allow it? After all, in a heavily commercialized media system like that of the United States, most journalists are employed by for-profit companies.[15] A handful of exceptions aside, the corporations that employ journalists rely on audiences for revenue—directly, in the form of subscriptions and newsstand sales, and indirectly, in the form of advertising revenue that is bought and sold based on the size and demographics of the audience.

The audience-dependent nature of these revenue sources might lead us to expect that media company managers would have had little patience for journalists' historic lack of interest in audiences. Yet there are two reasons why, despite the centrality of the audience to the business model of commercial journalism, rank-and-file journalists historically have faced little managerial pressure to tailor their editorial agenda to audience desires. First, until recently, newspapers and magazines enjoyed extremely high operating margins. In the pre-internet era, print news organizations benefited handsomely from scarcity, because the high up-front costs of producing and distributing news limited the number of competitors. These companies were essentially guaranteed a steady stream of revenue from both paying audiences and advertisers looking to reach prospective customers. Profits reached a high point in the 1980s, when publishers joked that newspapers were a business in which "even the brain dead could make money." By the late 1990s, when signs of economic trouble in the industry were clearly visible on the horizon, newspaper companies still averaged an operating margin of 19.5 percent, with some companies reaching margins in the high 20s or 30s.[16] With the status quo delivering such large returns, there was little reason to enforce rationalized forms of labor discipline that would have almost certainly inspired resistance among journalists.

Journalists' long-time disinterest in audiences was also tolerated for a second reason: like other cultural workers, journalists were thought to require autonomy at the point of production in order to create a successful product. This shared understanding of journalistic work led supervisors to take what scholars of media work have called a "soft" or "creative" managerial approach, in which "the manager's role is to facilitate rather than to dominate."[17] In addition, editors, the newsroom actors who take the most direct supervisory role in managing journalists in day-to-day work, usually started out as rank-and-file journalists themselves. As such, editors tend to identify with journalists more readily than with business-side executives and newspaper owners.[18] As we will see in later chapters, editors also often perceive metrics as a threat to their *own* managerial authority and their privileged position atop the newsroom hierarchy.

In sum, a unique and fragile mix of factors contributed to the journalistic disinterest in audience feedback in favor of the "self-referential" approach that persisted through much of the twentieth century: journalists' desire to shore up their shaky professional status, a shared cultural belief in the necessity of some measure of journalistic autonomy, a group of managers—editors—who were disinclined to mobilize metrics as a tool of labor discipline, and high profit margins in the news business that reduced the pressure on them to do so. Some of these factors still hold true or have even intensified in the twenty-first century: for example, in the age when digital networked technologies have lowered barriers to entry to media production, it has become even more difficult for journalists to claim they are a "somewhat exclusive" group.[19]

However, one major factor *has* changed: the high profit margins once enjoyed by print media companies have all but evaporated. In *Deciding What's News*, Gans presciently noted that the indifference to audience research that he observed among journalists might well change "should commercial considerations become more urgent" within news organizations.[20] This is, of course, precisely what has happened. The contemporary news business faces acute economic troubles, which make the past blasé attitude toward audience data and feedback much more difficult to sustain.

Journalism's present crisis emanates from several sources. First, the dawn of the digital era brought with it more competition to print news organizations. Networked digital media's lower barriers-to-entry for production and distribution led to a proliferation of news and news-like content, including by online aggregators that were free to the consumer, such as the *Huffington Post* and, later, *BuzzFeed*.[21] While a select number of marquee news brands, such as the *Wall Street Journal* and the *New York Times*, have been able to build a substantial base of paying digital subscribers, paywalls are not a viable solution for many lesser-known and smaller publications, and local news in particular has struggled.[22]

Second, large technology platform companies, with their enormous numbers of highly engaged users and the ability to target them with unprecedented precision, have proved irresistible to the very advertisers who previously relied on news organizations to disseminate their messages.[23] Large technology platforms such as Facebook and Google have also become crucial intermediaries between news and audiences, rendering media companies dependent on their mysterious algorithms for online distribution.[24] Even online-only media companies like BuzzFeed and Vox, which established themselves as digital-savvy upstarts who were more adept at social media distribution than their legacy media competitors, have struggled in the face of platform dominance over the media landscape.[25]

These economic difficulties are coupled with an atmosphere of growing public skepticism about the professional news media. Americans' trust in the mass media—defined as television, radio, and newspapers—has plummeted since the 1970s.[26] There are several reasons for this, but some have speculated that online and social technologies may be contributing factors: news consumers who have increasing control over their media diet may have less tolerance for a professional media model, in which editors make often opaque determinations about which stories will be covered, how they will be covered, and where they will be placed in a newspaper, broadcast, or website.[27]

Perhaps most importantly, each of these challenges has occurred in the context of a general trend toward what critical media scholar Robert McChesney calls "hyper-commercialism" in journalism.[28] Corporate consolidation was well underway in the media industry more than a decade before the spread of the internet and has continued largely unchecked by the Federal Communications Commission. The conglomerates resulting from large media mergers have tended to deemphasize long-term investments in quality journalism in favor of short-term profit accumulation, which they pursue via staff reductions and increased production pressures to compete in the relentless 24-hour news cycle.[29]

Where do metrics fit into this bleak picture? The newsroom analytics dashboard did not cause the financial and cultural calamities facing the news business. It is, however, both a powerful *symptom* and a vivid *symbol* of them. Put another way, newsroom metrics are a new patch of terrain upon which the long-standing tensions embedded in the very notion of journalistic autonomy are playing out. If, on the one hand, the audience primarily matters as a route to subscription and advertising revenue for news businesses, then metrics are an inappropriate incursion of market forces into the newsroom and best avoided. But if, on the other hand, the audience represents the democratic public (or at least an important slice of it), then metrics should factor heavily into journalistic practice, because the audience's size and engagement level speak to how effectively journalists are performing their sacred civic mission. The late *New York Times* media columnist David Carr succinctly summed up the conflict: "Just because something is popular does not make it worthy, but ignoring audience engagement is a sure route to irrelevance"—not to mention insolvency.[30] The chapters that follow will illustrate how this conflict suffuses journalists' approach to their work in the age of digital metrics.

The Journalism Labor Process: A Missing Piece of the Puzzle

Given the power of newsroom metrics as what sociologist Angèle Christin calls "contested symbolic objects," it's little wonder that they have become a focal point of journalism studies research in the digital age.[31] For journalism scholars, metrics have become an important lens through which to examine how contemporary journalists navigate digital technologies, the commercial aspects of their work, and their often fraught relationship to digital publics. Though it is varied in terms of methodology and normative perspective, the majority of this literature centers on what journalism scholar Rodrigo Zamith calls the "ABCDE of news production": attitudes, behaviors, content, discourses, and ethics.[32] Overall, this literature poses the following question: How have metrics changed journalists' norms, values, and practices—and how do these changes, in turn, affect the quality of news and the health of the public sphere?[33]

Many journalism scholars, especially during the initial rollout of newsroom analytics tools, saw the effect of metrics on journalism as primarily negative. To this group, metrics dashboards and "most viewed" lists serve as ever-present reminders of the audience's perennial preference for soft, frivolous news.[34] Metrics cultivate in journalists a dangerous tendency to equate audience popularity with newsworthiness, when in fact the two only sometimes (perhaps even rarely) overlap. Thus allowing metrics, instead of autonomous news judgment, to set the editorial agenda is an abdication of journalists' sacred professional commitment to serve the public interest.[35] Taken to an extreme, the thinking goes, metrics-driven journalism leads to a more homogeneous news landscape populated by "clickbait" headlines and a surfeit of stories about cute animals and celebrity drama—and, eventually, a weaker democracy.[36]

Other scholars have offered a more optimistic view. They argue that metrics, used thoughtfully, can have a salutary effect on journalists' values and practices.[37] Metrics help journalists move away from the condescending paternalism that has diminished public trust in the news media, this line of thinking goes, and become more in sync with the public they are supposed to be serving.[38] Media scholar Matthew Hindman expresses perhaps the strongest version of this view when he writes that "journalists *now have a positive obligation to use these new audience measurement tools*," just as a doctor should use the most accurate diagnostic test available and a lawyer must familiarize herself with relevant case law.[39]

In response to the question of whether newsroom metrics are—on balance—good or bad for journalism, a third group answers, "it depends." This scholarship emphasizes the importance of cultural, institutional, and situational factors in determining how metrics affect journalists' norms and practices. For example, in her comparative ethnographic study of newsrooms in the United States and France, Angèle Christin highlights the importance of national news cultures and institutional contexts in shaping how journalists make meaning from metrics.[40] This literature has valuably illuminated the complex ways metrics interact with journalists' norms, values, and everyday practices—what Folker Hanusch has called "journalistic culture."[41]

Yet to date, an important piece of the puzzle has been largely missing: the impact of metrics on journalists' working conditions. Although several scholars have addressed the use of analytics in newsroom performance evaluation, overall scant attention has been paid to the way metrics operate as a tool of labor discipline. While this gap may seem surprising, given how closely analytics dashboards resemble classic scientific management tools, it is consistent with a relative disinterest in working conditions that pervades the subfield of journalism studies.[42] As noted above, ethnographic and interview-based journalism research tends to focus on journalistic norms, values, and practices. Meanwhile, critical political economy media research, while deeply attentive to the material realities of news production, generally takes a more "macro" approach, attending to structural factors like the consolidation of media ownership or the role of advertising in the media field without examining how these factors shape editorial work in situ.[43]

In order to develop a holistic understanding of contemporary news production, we need a greater focus on journalists' *labor process*—the way material constraints and technological developments shape the everyday lived experience of journalism *as work*. In addition to the basic normative premise that all workers should be fairly compensated and treated with decency and dignity, a labor process lens is analytically important for several reasons. First, while newsrooms' working conditions and power relationships do not singlehandedly determine journalistic culture, it is reasonable to assume that managerial tactics and other aspects of the labor process affect how professional journalistic norms evolve and are put into practice.

Working conditions also have implications for the kind of news produced. We might reasonably surmise that bad working conditions in journalism—for example, "poor pay, hours and safety; powerlessness; boredom; isolation; self-doubt and shame; overwork; insecurity and risk"—are less likely to result in the kind of high-quality news *products* that contribute to the common good.[44] Some of the mechanisms underlying this connection are direct: as we will see in later chapters, journalists who are overworked and overwhelmed have difficulty creating news of high democratic value. Other mechanisms are indirect: poor compensation and working conditions limit who can afford to enter the journalism field, potentially rendering it more homogeneous and restricted to the already-privileged.

By extension, then, the journalistic labor process profoundly affects the state of the public sphere. While debates abound about the nature of the press's role in facilitating a self-governing democratic public, one is hard-pressed to imagine a conceptualization of the public sphere that would be *unaffected* by the journalistic labor process. For example, Mike Ananny argues that the press should function as a "listening structure"—both by listening on behalf of the public and directing its attention to new ideas and experiences and by "creating pauses for meaningful silences" that "give publics time to listen to what they hear."[45] But as we will see, real-time analytics dashboards extract increased productivity from journalists in a way that systematically disincentivizes silence, because the only guaranteed way to achieve higher traffic is to publish new content continually. In sum, research on the lived experience of *work* in newsrooms, taken alongside existing scholarship on journalistic culture and macro-level economic forces, facilitates a richer understanding of how the contemporary press fulfills its normative role (or fails to do so).

Another reason to adopt a labor process lens for understanding contemporary newsrooms is that digital journalists have increasingly begun to conceptualize *themselves* as workers.[46] Since 2015, a remarkable wave of unionization has swept through more than sixty online news outlets, often led by young journalists.[47] Accordingly, Nicole S. Cohen and Greig de Peuter point to the emergence of a "labor rights paradigm" in online newsrooms that departs from the prevailing discourses of entrepreneurialism and professionalism that had pervaded the field.[48] In the words of one of their interviewees, the labor rights paradigm gives digital journalists "a framework to talk honestly about our work and how it affects us."[49]

Of course, scholars need not always mirror the shifts in mindset of those we study. But the sheer breadth and intensity of the recent unionization wave in digital newsrooms should, at the very least, prompt more attention to the subjects of labor relations, power dynamics, and working conditions in digital newsrooms. By nearly any measure, journalistic work has become more precarious and unstable in the digital age, even for those who enjoy the relative stability of full-time employment.[50] Digital journalists increasingly face layoffs; they work long hours for low pay; and they perform a seemingly ever-expanding list of job duties as media platforms and formats proliferate. Furthermore—and most germane to this book—they do all of this while facing unending, technologically facilitated performance evaluation in the form of the real-time analytics dashboard. Given the circumstances, it seems that scholars, too, need a framework to analyze the conditions of contemporary journalistic work and how they affect journalists. Building such a framework is a primary goal of this book.

The Sites: Chartbeat, the *New York Times*, and Gawker Media

In the pages that follow, I draw on an ethnographic exploration of three illustrative cases: Chartbeat, a prominent news analytics company, and two news organizations that used its products, the *New York Times* and Gawker Media. This section sets the scene for the chapters to come by situating each of these research sites in its institutional context and organizational setting.

Chartbeat

CONTEXT

Chartbeat began in 2009 as a project within the NYC-based start-up incubator Betaworks. Chartbeat's founding CEO Tony Haile described the initial dashboard, which analyzed web traffic, as "almost like an art project."[51] That year,

Chartbeat founder Billy Chasen recruited Haile to turn this art project into a business in the competitive, fast-growing field of commercial data analytics. By then, Google Analytics was already entrenched as a primary tool for marketers; meanwhile, in news organizations, Omniture and comScore catered to advertising sales departments that used analytics to pitch their publications' online advertising space to potential buyers.

Chartbeat positioned itself very differently from these advertising-focused rivals. It promoted the Chartbeat dashboard as the first analytics tool designed for use *in newsrooms by journalists*, a stereotypically numbers-averse group that associated audience analytics with business-side, rather than editorial, operations. As we will see, the fact that journalists were the intended users of Chartbeat's product strongly influenced the design of the dashboard, the presentation of data, and the metrics that were included and omitted. In addition to being the first analytics company to cater specifically to newsrooms, Chartbeat set itself apart by emphasizing *real-time* data. Unlike other audience measurement services at the time, which gathered and displayed historical data on a site's traffic patterns at daily, weekly, and monthly intervals, Chartbeat's metrics rose and fell as readers arrived and left a site, with a delay of only a few seconds. (Chartbeat's name, a play on "heartbeat," was meant to evoke the real-time "pulse" of the audience.)

Since those early days, Chartbeat has become virtually ubiquitous in newsrooms: the company has more than 60,000 media-brand subscribers spread across more than 60 countries, and its clients include many of the highest-profile news publishers in the United States and around the world.[52] Chartbeat's approach to analytics has also been influential in the analytics field: numerous other analytics providers, from large firms like Google to small start-ups like Parse.ly, have mimicked aspects of Chartbeat's newsroom-focused, real-time analytics model. Chartbeat's reach has made it attractive to venture capital: since its founding, the company has raised a total of $38 million, after having closed its most recent funding round in July 2018 for $7 million.[53]

SETTING

In March 2015, the *Columbia Journalism Review* opened an in-depth, highly positive profile on Chartbeat by noting that the digital analytics company is "perched like a physical metaphor in an office six stories above the Strand [independent bookstore]—a century-old monument to paper."[54] It was easy to see the irony, especially given that in Chartbeat's office—located in a large, sunlit loft in the Union Square area of New York City—print of any kind was hard to come by. When I requested that my access agreement with Chartbeat be put on company letterhead to satisfy NYU's Institutional Review Board, I was told that there was no such thing. "We're a paperless company," explained Lana, an employee who was helping me coordinate the logistical aspects of my fieldwork.

Indeed, Chartbeat's culture, organizational vocabulary, and physical setting aimed to maintain the carefully calibrated balance between professionalism and informality for which digital technology start-ups are well known. Though Chartbeat shied away from using statistical or data analytics jargon in public materials and interactions with clients, the company's employees used the vernacular of the tech world with remarkable consistency. My first few weeks in the field amounted to a crash course in start-up lingo. Problems were "pain points." A piece of evidence that supported one of the company's views or claims was a "proof point." At the start of my fieldwork, I was told by multiple staffers on separate occasions that my entry into the company should be "frictionless," meaning they did not want my presence to create a distraction or disturbance. Terms or concepts that Chartbeat saw itself as having pioneered in the analytics world but had since been taken up by rival firms had been "hijacked."

During the time of my fieldwork, Chartbeat was in a period of rapid growth—the staff had nearly tripled in size in the year and a half before my fieldwork began. (On one of my early days in the office, a staffer asked me if I was a new employee; so many new people were joining the company at the time that he was having trouble keeping track.) There were about sixty full-time employees, spread across eight major staff teams.[55] The business side of the company included the executive team, which made big-picture strategic decisions; product, which decided what kinds of tools Chartbeat should offer and what features they should include; tech support, known as "Chartcorps," which fielded client questions, troubleshot, and conducted "on-boarding" trainings for new clients or existing clients learning new products; sales, which brought in new clients and re-upped with existing ones; and marketing, which produced Chartbeat's public-facing materials and conducted press outreach. The development side included engineering, which built Chartbeat's products; data science, which performed experiments and used Chartbeat's vast cache of data to study online news consumption behavior; and design/user experience, which conducted qualitative studies and interviews with clients— such as user testing for product prototypes—to ensure that Chartbeat's products were easy and fun to use. The company's teams collaborated frequently (e.g., design, product, and engineering often worked together, as did the sales, marketing, and executive teams).

Chartbeat's office was a pleasant, comfortable, and casual space, with a mini-shuffleboard table, a well-stocked fridge (complete with an ample supply of company-bought beer, replenished on a weekly basis), a record player, and an impressive collection of board games and remote-controlled cars. On my first day in the field, Molly, a business-side employee, proudly informed me that nearly every surface in the office was writeable—even many of the walls and tables—and, perhaps mindful of start-up clichés, added that this wasn't "just a gimmick." (My subsequent fieldwork confirmed that staffers did often use dry-erase markers to make notes or draw diagrams on the glass tables during meetings.)

Displays of the company's metrics were ubiquitous in the office. Most notably, there was an enormous projection on a prominent wall that showed a real-time count of the total number of "concurrent visitors" that were on all of Chartbeat's clients' sites combined and, beneath it, an automatically updating line that compared this "population" to that of a country (e.g., on a day when the count was hovering near 10 million, the display read, "Chartbeat's bigger than Belarus and 140 other countries!").

There were no individual offices or even cubicles at Chartbeat; rather, employees worked alongside members of their team in clusters of long tables (or sometimes on the office's numerous couches, armchairs, and oversize beanbag futons, with MacBooks perched on their laps or stomachs). To conduct calls or meetings, employees used the conference rooms that bordered the large open office space. Even the closed-door conference and meeting rooms were walled off by clear glass, so it was always possible to see who was meeting with whom.

Chartbeat's employees tended to be young—most were in their twenties or thirties—and mostly white and male.[56] Staffers seemed to enjoy a relaxed camaraderie; groups often gathered to chat over coffee or lunch at the large communal table in the office kitchen, and many participated in extracurricular group activities, such as a 30-day "paleo diet challenge." Several staffers had nicknames (e.g., "Bones," "DVD," "Lasers," "Brains," "Turbo") that were so consistently used in the office that I had to consult the website to learn their real names. The office also had several regularly observed traditions. For instance, on birthdays, staffers received a children's book signed by their coworkers instead of a card. When the company achieved a victory (such as a successful product launch or signing a big new client) employees gathered in the kitchen for speeches and celebratory champagne in plastic Solo cups. While such rituals were obviously intended by management to create a sense of belonging and attachment to the company, employees seemed genuinely to enjoy them. During my fieldwork, Lana once came in to work for an hour even though she was sick. When I asked her why she wasn't at home, she explained that the company had just landed a major new account and she didn't want to miss the celebratory toast.

The casual vibe of the physical space and promotional materials was echoed in Chartbeat's company policies. Like many technology firms, Chartbeat allowed employees "unlimited vacation time," meaning that employees were not allotted a particular number of days off as part of their contract but rather were instructed to "take vacation when they need it." The office also did not have set hours; as one employee put it, "as long as you get your work done, you can work whenever you want." (This policy particularly appealed to developers, some of whom preferred to work late into the night and come into the office midday.) In addition, there was no discernible dress code, and employees (especially the men) tended to dress quite informally; on several afternoons I noticed that employees had taken off their shoes and were padding around the office barefoot or sock-footed. Staffers were allowed to bring their dogs to work, and on any given day there were usually a few roaming around the office or snoozing at their owners' feet.

In sum, Chartbeat outfitted itself with many of the trappings of a paradigmatic digital technology start-up. Yet at the same time, the company needed to appeal to a client base—news organizations—that was generally rooted in a very different set of norms, organizational cultures, and traditions. As subsequent chapters will illustrate, Chartbeat's viability as a business depended in large part on its ability to straddle start-up culture and journalism culture.

The New York Times

CONTEXT

Founded in 1851 and purchased in 1896 by Adolph Simon Ochs, a member of the same family that still owns controlling stock in the company today, the *Times* has long been a towering institution in U.S. journalism. Under Ochs's leadership, the *Times* sought to compete with the sensationalist "penny papers" that then dominated New York news media, such as the *Sun* and the *New York Herald*, by targeting an elite readership and reporting the news cautiously, comprehensively, and accurately: "To Give the News Impartially, Without Fear or Favor." The paper thrived under this credo, increasing circulation from 9,000 at the time of Ochs's purchase to 465,000 when he died in 1935.[57]

It was largely due to Ochs's staid approach to journalism that the *Times* earned its reputation as the "paper of record" in the United States. In the words of one long-time editor, for much of the twentieth century the paper's editorial staffers felt an "obligation to print lots of things we knew no one much would read—the new members of the Peruvian cabinet, for example—just to get them on the record."[58] Looking back in 2004 at an issue from 1965, the *Times's* public editor found a "numbing collection of announcements, schedules, directories and transcripts."[59]

While the *Times* no longer aspires to be "the paper of record" in the same literal sense, a version of this lofty self-conception—that the *Times* is the worldwide apex of journalistic professionalism, offering the most comprehensive, most accurate, and highest-quality news coverage—still defines the organization today. This ethos posed major challenges as the paper initially struggled to adapt to the digital age—an endeavor which, especially in the early days of electronic media, required a willingness to experiment and take risks. During his 1998 fieldwork in the *Times* offices, media scholar Pablo Boczkowski overheard a comment that succinctly summed up the organization's dilemma: "We can't be the avant garde because we are the garde."[60] This tension between tradition and change persisted well into the twenty-first century. When journalism scholar Nikki Usher conducted fieldwork at the *Times* in 2010, she found that the paper's journalists were still struggling to reconcile the demands of online content production and a 24/7 news cycle with the work rhythms and organizational culture of a print newspaper.[61]

Financial troubles accompanied the cultural ones: the *Times's* print display and classified advertising, which had long accounted for the bulk of its revenue, dropped sharply in the 2000s. As an increasing number of consumers began to rely on social platforms (particularly Facebook) for news, the *Times's* storied brand wasn't translating into a large, loyal readership in the way it used to. Arguably the company's darkest period was 2009: its stock price plummeted 77 percent in just one year, the company famously took out a $250 million loan from billionaire Carlos Slim, and there were widespread rumors of an impending sale. To stabilize the situation, the *Times* implemented cost-cutting measures, including multiple rounds of buyouts and layoffs in the newsroom, and in 2011 it put its content behind a "metered paywall." It got to the point where David Carr, the *Times* media columnist, wondered aloud to a documentary filmmaker, "Could the *New York Times*, like, go out of business?"[62]

The *Times* did not, ultimately, go out of business. In fact, for now it seems to be thriving: although advertising revenue continued to flounder (and was expected to drop still further due to the Covid-19 pandemic), the *Times* has experienced massive growth in paid digital subscriptions: in 2020, digital revenue exceeded print revenue for the first time.[63] But my interviews there, conducted from 2011 to 2015, represent a pivotal period in the *Times*'s labored and at times awkward transition to being a "truly digital company."[64] As we will see in later chapters, the discomfort of the *Times*'s print-to-digital transition was reflected in the mix of ambivalence, anxiety, curiosity, and resentment staffers expressed toward metrics.

SETTING

The *New York Times*'s midtown Manhattan headquarters, which the company moved into in 2007, was designed by architect Renzo Piano to shepherd the organization into the future while also paying homage to its illustrious past.[65] The 52-story building, of which the *Times* occupied about half the floors, was almost entirely encased in clear glass, allowing for abundant natural light in the offices within—and even, in a nod to transparency, making some of the newspaper's goings-on visible from the street below. The tower's glass walls were partially covered by "horizontal ceramic rods" designed both to be "beautiful and to act as a sunshade." The floor-to-ceiling windows had blinds designed to automatically raise and lower themselves according to the weather. Sleek metal renditions of the *Times*'s logo hung above each of the building's entrances. The lobby boasted high ceilings, a lush interior garden walled off by glass and visible to those on the higher floors, and a multiscreen art installation called Moveable Type, which the *Times* described as an algorithmically generated "text collage" that provides "a fluid, ever-changing portrait of the *Times* by parsing its daily content and . . . archive."[66] Even the elevators had a slightly futuristic feel: rather than pressing a button once inside the elevator, riders selected their floor while waiting in the elevator bank and were directed to the correct elevator by high-resolution digital screens.

At the time of my research, the *Times*'s news division employed roughly 1,200 people (as of 2020 it had grown to 1,700) and was based on the second, third, and fourth floors of the *Times* headquarters.[67] With its rows of cubicles, the newsroom had a slightly more conventional office atmosphere than the building's lobby but was still visually impressive. In keeping with Piano's vision of lightness and transparency, a large area in the center of the second floor reached all the way up to a massive skylight well in the fourth-floor ceiling. This open area was flanked by open-air crosswalks and internal stairwells (painted bright red) that allowed for easy movement from one level of the newsroom to another and enabled people to see from the upper newsroom floors to the lower. It also served as the gathering place for the entire newsroom staff during major announcements, such as the annual "Pulitzer day" when the *Times* finds out how many of the prestigious prizes it has won that year. On more typical days, editors inhabited glass-walled offices that lined the newsroom's edges and corridors; reporters worked in the cubicles. Meeting and conference rooms were also transparent, walled off by large sliding glass doors.

The division of labor in the newsroom was formal and hierarchical, especially when compared to many online-only media organizations. The *Times* included sixteen different news sections (from business to politics to fashion and style to real estate), not including the weekly *Times* magazine or the opinion pages, both of which operated somewhat independently from the bulk of the newsroom. Some sections encompassed smaller subsections (for instance, business included subsections on media, the economy, and markets). Desks, as sections and subsections were known within the newsroom, were typically led by editors, with deputy editors and reporters who reported to them. Section editors and their deputies performed a number of roles, such as assigning reporters to cover breaking news and scheduled news events (e.g., the NBA finals or a White House press conference), generating and approving ideas for longer-term "enterprise" and feature stories (e.g., multipart series on childhood homelessness and the poor treatment of nail-salon workers in New York City), editing drafts of reporters' stories, and sometimes engaging in reporting and writing of their own.

In addition to editors assigned to specific desks, there were editors who oversaw content during a particular time of day (i.e., night news) or for the website (e.g., home-page editors). There was also a copy desk, which checked prose for factual and grammatical errors, prepared it for publication, and crafted headlines, as well as a standards editor, who enforced the *Times*'s detailed style guide and maintained a blog that called attention to stylistic issues such as "hyphens run amok" and "journalese," the editor's term for journalists' preferred clichés (e.g., "tome" rather than book, "teetering on the brink," and "afoot").[68] These editors and departments all reported to a small group of senior editors called the "masthead editors," who made the most significant editorial decisions, such as which stories would run on the newspaper's front page.

While all of these roles had either existed in the pre-internet era or, in the case of the home-page editor, corresponded to roles that existed then, there were also numerous newsroom positions that specifically pertained to online platforms. For instance, web producers prepared content for the website (and often engaged in reporting as well); social media editors wrote tweets, Facebook posts, and other content for social platforms; comment moderators ensured that every comment met the *Times*'s standards of decorum; and interactive news developers and designers created quizzes, ballots, polls, and other digital features to supplement news coverage.

The business operations of the *Times* occupied a cluster of higher floors; newsroom staffers often referred to the business side as "upstairs." Those who worked "upstairs" included advertising, marketing, research and development, a "consumer insight group" that conducted quantitative and qualitative studies on the behavior of current and potential *Times* subscribers, and a "business intelligence team" of developers, data scientists, and managers who parsed data to strategize and assess methods for revenue generation, like the *Times*'s metered paywall.

In many respects, the *Times* is not representative of other news organizations, even the legacy print newspapers it most closely resembles. There is arguably no other publication in the United States—possibly the world—with its symbolic significance and level of reputational capital.[69] Yet the very same features that set the *Times* apart also provide a particularly clear vantage point from which to see how metrics-driven rationalization manifests in a knowledge-work setting with abundant cultural capital.

Gawker Media

CONTEXT

Ever since its founding in 2002 by journalist and entrepreneur Nick Denton, Gawker Media positioned itself as a blogging company whose mission was, in part, to slaughter gleefully the stylistic and ethical sacred cows of legacy journalism. What started as one site blossomed into a highly popular and visible network of blogs that covered a range of topics, including consumer technology, politics, gaming, sports, automobiles, and women's issues. By the time of my fieldwork, all Gawker sites were housed on Kinja, the company's publishing platform, along with thousands of comments, discussions, and posts written by unpaid contributors. Gawker bloggers eschewed traditional media's tone of authoritative, view-from-nowhere objectivity in favor of tart and decidedly opinionated prose. While most traditional, non-tabloid news organizations shy away from publishing unsubstantiated gossip, Gawker's blogs published unconfirmed tips and rumors about powerful public figures (including—perhaps especially—items regarding their personal lives). Gawker also embraced the practice of paying for scoops and otherwise compensating sources, long considered taboo by most professional U.S. journalism outfits.

The most controversial way Gawker set itself apart from legacy journalism was through the company's aggressive use of metrics-driven performance assessments and incentives. Since its founding, Gawker had openly used metrics to evaluate staffers, stories, and sites. Metrics were not only influential at the company, but also highly visible. Walking into the company's then-headquarters in Manhattan, visitors were immediately greeted by three large screens that hung prominently above the main reception desk. The first screen displayed Gawker's famous Big Board, which showed a real-time ranked list (provided by Chartbeat) of the top posts by concurrent visitors across the Gawker network, along with green and red chevrons that indicated whether their traffic was accelerating or decelerating; the Big Board was also displayed on multiple screens on the office's editorial floor (Figs. 1.1a, 1.1b). The second screen displayed a large graph showing Gawker's "global uniques per month" since 2008—this visualization of Gawker's traffic over time showed that there had been peaks and dips, but the overall trend was a steady climb. The third screen showed the home page of Gawker's business site, which cycled through a series of large photos of attractive young people taken at company parties.

Gawker also made metrics publicly available online, along with graphs showing each staffer's daily, weekly, and monthly contribution to her site's count of unique visitors and pageviews. Tallies of pageviews and unique visitors were displayed alongside the byline of each post. In addition, while most of Chartbeat's clients kept their traffic figures strictly proprietary, Gawker allowed Chartbeat to use its data in training sessions and demos with new and prospective clients.

Taken together, these choices amounted to a powerful statement of organizational identity that both underscored and contributed to Gawker's reputation as a highly metrics-driven media company. As available and prominent as

FIGS. 1.1A, 1.1B. Big Board displays on the editorial floor of Gawker's former offices. Fig. 1.1a Michael Appleton/The New York Times/Redux; fig. 1.1b Scott Beale/ Laughing Squid, laughingsquid.com.

Gawker's metrics appeared to outsiders, they were even more so for the company's editorial staff. All writers and editors had access to Chartbeat, as well as Quantcast, which measured unique visitors. Shortly before the beginning of my fieldwork, the company had supplemented the Big Board with a leaderboard that ranked the top writers on Kinja by the number of unique visitors they had brought to the site in the previous thirty days. Red and green arrows appeared next to each writer, showing how many spots they had ascended or descended in the ranks over the previous thirty days.

Like many contemporary digital media companies, Gawker did not rely on traditional display advertising alone to support its business (though there was plenty of that on its sites). Rather, it drew revenue from several additional streams as well. A team called Studio@Gawker produced "branded content" for advertisers who not only wanted posts to appear on Gawker sites but also wanted them to be written in the signature Gawker voice. Some posts contained "affiliate links" to e-commerce sites, like Amazon, where readers could purchase the products being discussed in the post. Gawker also held branded promotional events, such as *Gizmodo*'s "Home of the Future," a weeklong installation of an "immersive, real-life vision of the urban home of tomorrow," which was sponsored by Verizon and Netflix and prominently featured products made by Dyson, Adidas, Patagonia, Breville, and many other companies.[70]

SETTING

Gawker's original headquarters occupied a nondescript brick loft building in lower Manhattan's trendy Nolita neighborhood. Unlike the *New York Times* building, which proudly announced itself, Gawker's office seemed to want to blend into its surroundings. There was no signage out front to alert visitors that they had come to the right place. Pushing open the unmarked and unlocked metal door at the street level, visitors were greeted by three long, narrow, and steep flights of rough-looking concrete stairs. Gawker's reception desk was located on the third floor, where most of the company's non-editorial staff, such as ad sales, tech, legal, and marketing, worked. The third floor had low ceilings, hardwood floors, and bright lighting. Each time I arrived at the office, I would be invited by the receptionist to sit in a small waiting area while she sent an instant message to whichever staffer I was scheduled to meet with, who would then come downstairs from the fourth floor, where editorial staff worked, to retrieve me. The waiting area had two faux leather club chairs separated by a glass coffee table strewn with magazines on a range of subjects

(*Sports Illustrated*, the *New Yorker*, *Variety*, etc.). It was located in an optimal spot to observe the foot traffic and central third-floor work area and to soak in the atmosphere of Gawker's business side. Because editorial staffers were often running late for interviews, I had ample opportunity to do so on several occasions. There tended to be a near-constant low murmur of conversation on the third floor, and music was often playing (sometimes Motown classics, other times more contemporary artists like Robyn). Employees sat at long communal tables, and it was not uncommon to see a staffer standing by—or even perched on top of—a colleague's work area, chatting. A large flat-screen television was mounted on one of the walls, and oftentimes a sports game would be playing on it. In sum, the feel of the third floor was slightly cramped, cluttered, and disheveled, but also informal and comfortable.

The editorial floor one story above had a starkly different atmosphere. Physically, it was a cleaner, more elegant space, with much higher ceilings, unobtrusive track lighting turned low, and sleeker architecture. Like Chartbeat's, the office was open-plan—staffers worked at rows of long tables with aisles in between, and each site's employees were clustered together. Meetings took place in two large, glass-walled conference rooms, and there were also tiny glass-walled rooms in which employees could conduct interviews or phone conversations, or otherwise obtain a modicum of privacy.

Architecture notwithstanding, the most striking difference between the business and editorial floors was auditory: the editorial floor was almost completely silent. There was no music playing, and although the office was arranged so that each site's staffers sat together, it was rare that colleagues exchanged spoken words at their desks. With its rows of mostly young, casually dressed people wearing headphones and typing on computer screens, Gawker's editorial floor often felt more like a university library during finals week than a bustling newsroom. While this could give the impression that editorial staffers at Gawker had little interaction with one another, in fact the opposite was true: writers and editors were interacting constantly on a variety of online communication platforms, including a collaborative work program called Campfire, Gmail's g-chat, Aol instant messenger, email, and Twitter.

Each Gawker site had a differently sized staff and editorial structures varied, but all sites had one site lead, a deputy site lead, and a team of writers. Site leads reported to the editorial director, who in turn reported to Denton, the founder and owner. Some sites had also editors dedicated to specific types of posts, like news or features, and some also had "editorial fellows" (Gawker's term for paid interns). Site leads had considerable discretion over the daily workflow of their staff. Some site leads followed a highly regimented posting schedule, while others took a looser approach. However they chose to arrange workflow, all site leads I interviewed felt pressure to maintain a constant stream of new content on their site. Producing the sheer volume of content required meant a heavy workload for writers—it was not uncommon for each to write six posts a day. It also meant that editors did not have time to do much to posts other than sign off on the concept, help with headlines when necessary, and decide when to post them. For feature or enterprise stories that were produced on a longer time frame, editors might work with a writer's copy and make suggestions for revision, but this kind of deeper involvement was the exception, not the rule.

Alison, a site lead, explained that she made sure there was a new post ready to go up every fifteen to twenty minutes during normal business hours (sites had part-time or junior staffers assigned to cover nights, weekends, and holidays, and posts were somewhat less frequent during those times). For Alison's staffers, the workday began at 8:30 a.m. Writers and editors signed into their group chat from home, greeted each other, and immediately began posting a flurry of links to stories from a range of other news sources that might make good fodder for posts on the site. (For instance, on one of the days I visited Alison's site's group chat, Lisa, an editor, posted five suggested topics for posts based on content from NPR, *HuffPost*, YouTube, *Glamour* magazine, and the *Guardian*.) Within a few minutes, Alison began assigning posts to writers, and by 10 a.m., writers began typing into the chat that their first posts were finished and queued up for publication, leaving it up to Alison to decide the order and timing of posts. Around midday, once enough posts were queued that the staff could be away from their computers for a spell, they began signing off the group chat and commuting to the office, where they signed back on and wrote more posts for the second half of the day. Staff began to trickle out of the group chat (and the office) around 6:30 p.m.

Once a post was published to a Gawker site, metrics almost immediately became available. The number of pageviews a post had garnered appeared on the same line as the author's byline; hovering a cursor over the pageview count revealed the post's unique visitor count (i.e., an approximate measure of the number of people who had not visited the site at any point in the thirty days prior to viewing the article). The unique visitor count was the one writers monitored most closely for their posts, as it was the one that factored into their bonuses (to be discussed further in chapter 2) and that Gawker's advertisers cared the most about.

Just as the *Times* has long been a trendsetter in the realm of legacy print journalism, Gawker's brand of editorial content was highly influential in the development of online media. Many stylistic features of digital journalism that are now considered commonplace, such as the use of informal language and an assertive authorial point of view, can be traced back to Gawker. The company's embrace of metrics, while often criticized as extreme, also left its mark on the broader digital journalism industry. Analyzing Gawker sheds light on dynamics and tensions that can arise in a metrics-saturated knowledge workplace.

Conclusion

This chapter has explored the specificities of journalism as a case of knowledge work—most notably journalists' unique normative role in shaping the public sphere and the contradictory nature of journalists' professional autonomy. Although the rationalization of audience understanding began in the 1930s with reader surveys and other rudimentary forms of audience data, journalists in the pre-digital age were not particularly interested in learning more about their audiences, nor did they face much managerial pressure to incorporate audience data into their workflow. Screening out audience information and feedback was a means for rank-and-file journalists to maintain their tenuous sense of professional status.

However, this state of affairs changed dramatically in the 2000s. As the news moved increasingly online, digital audience metrics proved to be far more granular than their analog predecessors. More importantly, as media companies contended with enormous losses in advertising and print subscription revenue, the growing dominance of large technology platforms in the media space, and increasingly concentrated corporate ownership, audience metrics came to be seen as an indispensable managerial tool. Metrics became both a symptom and a symbol of the potent economic pressures bearing down on the twenty-first-century news industry.

Journalism scholars took note: in the past fifteen years, scholarly research has proliferated—much of it ethnographic, some based on content analysis—examining the impact of metrics on journalists' norms, values, and practices. Yet, save for a few notable exceptions, very little of this research has explicitly conceptualized the analytics dashboard as a tool of labor discipline that profoundly shapes the working conditions and power relationships within contemporary newsrooms. I have argued that viewing audience metrics through a labor lens is useful for two reasons. First, working conditions not only affect journalists' ability to perform their normative social role, but also shape the development and expression of norms, values, and practices in ways both direct and indirect. Second, digital journalists *themselves* have increasingly understood their work as labor and have organized accordingly—a remarkable and significant shift.

In the second half of the chapter, I further set the stage for the remainder of the book by providing an overview of the institutional history and organizational context for each of the sites profiled in these pages: Chartbeat, the *New York Times,* and Gawker Media. The next chapters will take us deeper into the offices of these three companies in order to examine how metrics are created, interpreted, and put to use in the rationalization of journalistic labor.

PART I

Experiencing Metrics

2

The Traffic Game

Those numbers are always there and they're always staring you in the face. I am competitive by nature, and . . . that side of myself was kind of massaged into productivity through analytics.

—EDDIE, GAWKER MEDIA WRITER

Any work context involves an economic dimension (production of things), a political dimension (production of social relations), and an ideological dimension (production of an experience of those relations). These three dimensions are inseparable.

—MICHAEL BURAWOY, *THE POLITICS OF PRODUCTION*

AT AROUND 11 A.M. on a Monday in March, I sat in my apartment and used a guest log-in to sign in to a group chat program called Campfire. I had been invited to join the online chat of one of Gawker's sites for the day. Andrew, the site lead, had informed his staff in advance that I would be visiting Campfire and that I was studying the role of analytics at Gawker. Still, I was hoping to be able to enter the chat inconspicuously, so as not to distract the staff or disrupt the normal flow of group communication. I would have no such luck, however—as soon as I signed in, a banner appeared on the bottom of the group's chat window that announced, "Caitlin P. has joined." Nervous about how the staff would respond to my presence, I wrote, "hi everyone! Thanks for having me sit in today." Almost immediately after I posted my greeting, Colin, a writer, posted, "As I was saying, analytics are awesome." Joe, another writer, chimed in: "If I go a day without analytics, I get the shakes." I responded: "okay, I'll note that down :)" Colin then extended the joke by writing in quotation marks, as though he were me taking notes, "'Joe Faberman appears to have some kind of substance abuse problem.'"

Colin and Joe's riff had the immediate effect of making me feel more at ease in Campfire. By both lightly poking fun at the awkward nature of ethnography—being told to go about your business as usual while being observed in a decidedly unusual way—and satirizing Gawker's reputation as an insatiable traffic-hound, the writers acknowledged and then deftly defused the tension created by my entrance into their virtual workspace.

As I continued my research, however, it became clear that the exchange also spoke to a deeper truth: analytics tools—especially the real-time variety—have potent habit-forming properties. The user interface of the Chartbeat dashboard, in particular, made journalists feel as though they were playing something I call "the traffic game," in which they endlessly competed against their coworkers and themselves in an unpredictable race to achieve ever-higher metrics of audience attention.

My analysis of the traffic game builds on a body of research that has explored the role of workplace games in the labor process. In his ethnography of a factory shop floor, sociologist Michael Burawoy argued that the labor discipline cannot be accomplished through managerial coercion alone—it also requires workers' consent.[1] The shop-floor workers, including Burawoy himself, devised workplace games to pass the time and win each other's respect. In doing so, they ended up working harder than they otherwise would have—thereby inadvertently contributing to their own exploitation. If, as Burawoy contended, labor discipline relies upon workers' consent, a question arises: How is such consent achieved among a group of knowledge workers, like journalists, whose self-conception is based on a notion of professional autonomy?

Part 1 answers this question by examining Chartbeat's role in securing journalists' consent to the presence of metrics in their workflow. In Burawoy's case, consent was co-manufactured by both managers and the workers themselves. In the case of journalism, we will see that consent was technologically *engineered* by Chartbeat. In the first half of this chapter, I outline the specific ways Chartbeat's tools were designed to mimic key features of habit-forming games, such as immersive visual displays, instant-feedback mechanisms, ever-updating "scores" and rankings, and intermittent reinforcement. I then explain how these features—coupled with journalists' sense of job insecurity—led some Chartbeat users to consult the tool with a frequency and intensity bordering on the compulsive.

Crucially, unlike quantitative tools of labor discipline that are handled by managers—such as Frederick Taylor's famous stopwatch—Chartbeat's game-like features were designed to forge a powerful relationship *directly with the managed worker*. For example, at Gawker, most managers did not mediate interactions between writers and the Chartbeat dashboard: access to the tool was provided to all editorial staffers, but they were not mandated to use it. In the absence of explicit managerial coercion, many Gawker writers perceived their self-described "addiction" to Chartbeat as a personal failure of willpower rather than as a logical outcome of precarious work and managerial production pressure.

In sum, we will see that Chartbeat's analytics tool was designed to engineer journalists' consent to labor discipline while still leaving intact their cherished sense of professional autonomy. The chapter's second half outlines key consequences of the traffic game for the individual journalists who were "playing," for social relations within the newsroom, and for journalists' output.

Playing the Traffic Game

Psychologists are divided on the question of whether compulsive use of digital devices—and smartphones in particular—meets the clinical definition of addiction or should instead be described as merely maladaptive or problematic.[2] Whatever position one takes in this debate, it is nonetheless telling that many digital journalists *perceive* their orientation to analytics tools through the framework of addiction. When I asked Gawker writers and editors to describe their relationship to analytics in general and to Chartbeat in particular, often-times one of the first words I heard was "addicted." Eddie, a veteran online journalist and blogger who had done stints at several high-profile digital media companies before joining Gawker, put it memorably. He described himself as a "recovering Chartbeat addict" and explained that he had forced himself to remove the Chartbeat app from his phone at a previous job because of how often he was checking it. "At Gawker Media," he added ruefully, "it's like I'm a cocaine addict on vacation in Colombia."

While metrics were particularly prominent and ubiquitous at Gawker, the language of addiction is common in industry discussions of real-time newsroom metrics. A brief Chartbeat outage in 2011 prompted an article in *Adweek* titled "Stats-Addicted Editors Suffer from Chartbeat Withdrawal."[3] The story quoted several "jonesing editors" who became increasingly desperate to access their dashboards as the day wore on. "Waiting for #chartbeat to propagate their data to new DNS servers today makes me feel like a crack addict waiting on my next fix," tweeted a product manager at the About.com site ConsumerSearch. Chartbeat itself has acknowledged the habit-forming attributes of real-time analytics, albeit in more positive language. "Data is addicting," read a company blog post. "Like a 'runner's high,' it's a great feeling when you get that data moving in all the right directions."[4]

What, exactly, makes real-time analytics dashboards like Chartbeat feel so addictive to users? A few months into my fieldwork at Chartbeat I interviewed Daniel, an affable development-side staffer whose job included soliciting extensive feedback on Chartbeat's analytics dashboards and services from the company's clients. Midway through our conversation, I asked Daniel for his thoughts on why so many Chartbeat clients described themselves as addicted to the dashboard. He responded:

> One [reason] is just performance. It's such a fucking tough industry that you lose sleep, man. . . . It's so stressful that you are constantly worrying about whether you're getting enough traffic or not. So your eyes are glued to Chartbeat because your life depends on it.

In other words, Daniel surmised that at least part of the dashboard's addictive quality was due to its instrumental utility: journalists knew that the survival of their publication—and therefore their jobs—depended on traffic. Thus the dashboard was indispensable insofar as it provided a continual indication of traffic performance.

This assessment certainly resonated at Gawker, at least on an abstract level. While the company relied on a diverse array of strategies to generate revenue, from traditional display advertising on its blogs to internally produced "branded content" to promotional events, each of them depended on Gawker offering what advertisers would consider a large, demographically desirable audience. Metrics were the main vehicle to make writers and editors aware of the importance of audience size to Gawker's success—and to editorial staffers' continued employment.

Accordingly, in addition to the infamous Big Board and other prominent screen-displays of metrics adorning the office walls, Gawker had long experimented with an array of traffic-based pay-for-performance schemes. The ones that had been in place for several years at the time of my research centered on Monthly Unique Visitors, defined as inferred individuals who were visiting the site for the first time in the previous thirty days.[5] Each Gawker site had a monthly growth target of unique visitors, often referred to simply as "uniques," that was calculated based on an average of its traffic from the preceding months. Thus, the sites had different targets depending on their past audience size, but all were expected to have the same *rate* of growth. When a site exceeded its target, it received a collective bonus proportional to the amount by which the target had been surpassed (e.g., a site that brought in traffic 10 percent higher than its growth target would receive a bonus equivalent to 10 percent of the site's monthly total budget). Each site lead (Gawker's term for editor in chief) could dispense this bonus among writers as she saw fit.[6]

While monthly bonuses were based on site-level traffic, individual traffic numbers were also influential. The company calculated something called an eCPM (effective cost per mille) for all editorial staffers, which was the measure of how many dollars each employee earned in salary for every one thousand monthly unique visitors their posts brought to the site. Raises were also closely tied to individual traffic numbers: writers could strengthen their case for a raise by demonstrating sustained growth in unique visitors that was roughly proportionate to the raise they were requesting.

Given the connection Gawker management had drawn between traffic, remuneration, and continued employment, editorial staffers' fixation on metrics was hardly surprising. Still, the presence of metrics-based material incentives was not sufficient to explain Gawker staffers' self-professed addiction to Chartbeat in particular. Gawker's pay-for-performance system revolved entirely around monthly uniques, but, for reasons that will be discussed in depth in chapters 3 and 5, Chartbeat didn't measure these. (At Gawker, data on monthly uniques was supplied by Quantcast, another analytics vendor.) The Chartbeat dashboard allowed users to see how many "new" visitors were coming to a story or site, but it counted as "new" those inferred users that had not been to the site in the previous fourteen days, not the previous month. In addition, the Chartbeat dashboard's focus on real-time analytics meant that it showed users how many new visitors were arriving at the site or story *at that moment,* but was less useful for calculating how many new visitors had come over the past week, month, or year (Fig. 2.1).

Given this misalignment between Gawker's most emphasized metrics, on the one hand, and Chartbeat's, on the other, the sheer intensity of the feelings and behaviors that could develop around Chartbeat seemed perplexing, even—perhaps especially—to compulsive Chartbeat users. Andrew from Gawker noted that Chartbeat was "more addictive to look at" than Quantcast, even though he also found it "less meaningful" because "it has nothing to do

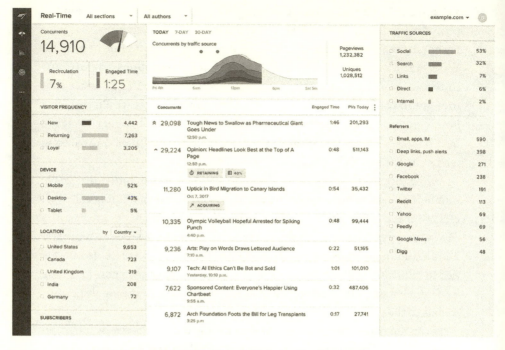

FIG. 2.1. A screenshot of Chartbeat Publishing, Chartbeat's real-time analytics
dashboard for newsrooms.

with how many [new] people [i.e., uniques] you're drawing in." Similarly, the
Adweek story mentioned above noted that the Chartbeat outage had "caused
a mild panic at many sites" despite the fact that the dashboard was "not
mission-critical." For the journalists quoted in the *Adweek* story, Chartbeat
addiction seemed disconnected from (or at least only obliquely connected to)
the measures of traffic on which, as Daniel from Chartbeat had put it, a journalist's "life depends."

The answer to what made Chartbeat so compulsively alluring, then, lay not
in its direct instrumental utility but rather in the dashboard's "UX" (the tech-
world abbreviation for "user experience"). Specifically, journalists experienced
their relationship to the Chartbeat dashboard as addictive due to several aesthetic and experiential qualities that made their labor process resemble a digital game.[7] Though Chartbeat did not invoke the language of games to describe
the draw of its analytics tools, the company's dashboards and leaderboards had
an unmistakably game-like look and feel, largely due to the presence of three
design features: a dynamic visual display, the possibility for endless play, and
an inscrutable mixture of chance and skill.

Dynamic Visual Display

The Chartbeat dashboard's bright colors and fluctuating numbers made for an immersive visual display whose constant movement demanded a high level of attention from users. The concurrents count, an approximate measure of the number of visitors currently on a particular site that was located prominently in the upper left-hand corner of the dashboard, rose and fell every few seconds as visitors landed on and left a site; the needle on the accompanying dial quivered accordingly.[8] Meanwhile, the list of "top pages" in the center of the dashboard continually shuffled and reshuffled itself.

The allure of the display was inextricably linked to its ephemeral quality. A story might rise to the number one spot on the top-pages list only to be displaced moments later; an exceptionally high concurrents count, though thrilling, often proved maddeningly fleeting. These qualities could induce in users a kind of metrics-related fear-of-missing-out, or FOMO: one gets the feeling that looking away from the Chartbeat dashboard, even for a moment, might cause you to miss something exciting or important. As Aaron, a development-side Chartbeat staffer, explained, the dashboard "wants you to watch it." Speaking about the dynamism of the concurrents count, Aaron said, "when people talk about it being addictive, I can only imagine that it's because of that. Because you're like, 'I don't want to turn away because there's a guy [who just landed on the page] and I don't want to miss *him*.'"[9] Other Chartbeat users reported similar experiences of continually watching the dashboard. Andrew told me that he found Chartbeat more addictive than Quantcast because "you're watching in real time the needle move and the stories move."

I myself experienced the hypnotic effect of this perpetual motion during my fieldwork. On one slow afternoon in the Chartbeat offices, I was seated at an empty desk that was positioned opposite an office wall onto which was projected an enormous continuously updating count of the number of concurrent visitors across all of Chartbeat's client sites. For the duration of the time I spent watching (tellingly, I lost track of how long it was), the number fell from just over 6 million concurrent visitors to just over 5 million. Later, I wrote in my field notes: "watching the numbers fall, updating every few seconds so I barely had time to register the number currently on the screen before it changed again, was strangely mesmerizing."

The dashboard's attention-seeking quality was central to the broader user experience Chartbeat was trying to cultivate. This became especially clear a few months into my fieldwork, when Molly, a senior business-side staffer, led a "competition lunch" in the employee lounge. The purpose of the meeting was to give staffers an opportunity to compare notes on Chartbeat's primary rivals and have an informal discussion about how Chartbeat could improve its position in the analytics market. Though the meeting was optional, around fifteen staffers participated—mostly those who worked on client- and public-facing teams like sales, Chartcorps (Chartbeat's tech support team), and branding and marketing. Employees who spoke most regularly with clients, such as salespeople and members of Chartcorps, relayed what they had heard clients say about competing firms, while Molly took notes on a large white-board. Though Chartbeat had cornered a large share of the editorial analytics market, having been the first company to specialize in real-time metrics for newsrooms, the company was facing an ever-growing onslaught of competition. This presented Chartbeat with a dilemma: its dashboard had to be sufficiently distinct from its rivals for the company to distinguish itself, yet clients often asked Chartbeat to incorporate metrics or features that they had seen in competitors' tools.

Midway through the competition lunch, one such feature came up: email reports. One of Chartbeat's competitors made it possible for users to receive reports, automatically generated and emailed to them at customizable intervals, that provided information on the previous day's or week's traffic, compared with that of the preceding period. John, one of the business-side staffers present, said a client had described the competitor's email reports as being "configurable, concise, easy to digest." As a snapshot of traffic patterns that arrived ready-made in the client's inbox, the email report demanded less of her engagement and attention than Chartbeat's real-time analytics dashboard, and she liked this. At the time, Chartbeat did not offer an email-report feature, and Ella, another staffer present at the meeting, asked the group if there were thoughts about adding one. Molly responded that "audience perspectives," a new feature in Chartbeat's dashboard that provided historical data about metrics over the past week or day, could serve a similar purpose. She added that the question of whether or not to add email reports was ultimately "another discussion" and moved on to a different topic.

Chartbeat did eventually release an email-report feature. But the fact that the company did so years after their primary competitors illustrates the degree to which the experiential quality of the real-time dashboard was thought to be as central to Chartbeat's appeal as the metrics themselves. The very qualities

John's client had praised about the competitor's email reports—their concision and their ability to be quickly and easily digested—were nearly diametrically opposed to the absorbing, even "mesmerizing" aspect of the Chartbeat dashboard. Email reports threatened to pull users away from, in Aaron's words, "the whole thing that makes [Chartbeat] work as a product."

Endlessness

As with many addictive games, where there is always another level to beat or another round to play, Chartbeat's dashboard possessed a quality of endlessness.[10] Before Chartbeat introduced real-time analytics to newsrooms, analytics were delivered primarily via periodic reports, whose static, historical format lent a sense of finality to the day's, week's, or month's traffic. By contrast, the Chartbeat dashboard discouraged the user from experiencing time in discrete increments; one moment simply flowed into the next, indefinitely. Eddie described Chartbeat as "relentless": "There's never gonna be a time when you can close your MacBook and be like, Chartbeat's all set, our traffic's good, we're ready to go."

As with many of the most popular technology platforms, Chartbeat's endlessness promised eternal novelty. Just as the infinite scroll feature on platforms like Facebook and Twitter ensures that users will always be stimulated by novel content, in Chartbeat there was always something new to see: concurrent visitors arriving at the site or leaving, a newly published story ascending the top-pages list, a spike or dip in readers' average "engaged time," and so on.

At a company like Gawker, the effect of this apparent endlessness was intensified. Because Gawker sites' growth targets were based on their past growth, any traffic success merely upped the ante for the *next* success. In an instant-message exchange, Alison told me that as her site's audience grew over time, she held herself to ever-higher standards. This, in turn, led to a feeling of perpetual dissatisfaction with her site's traffic, despite the fact that it was among the biggest sites at Gawker. "It's just that once you have a taste of a major [traffic] blow up, everything else after that feels underwhelming or, in my messed-up head, like a failure," she explained.

Eddie's explanation of his addiction to analytics—and particularly Chartbeat—is instructive. He had asked to conduct our interview after work at a bar near the Gawker headquarters, assuring me over email that he'd be "much more talkative" over drinks. Due to a miscommunication, Eddie showed up at the bar two days earlier than we'd planned; I raced to meet him but was still fifteen minutes late. After I showed up and apologized, Eddie assured me that he hadn't minded waiting at all. He had been playing 2048, a numeric-puzzle game, on his phone and was currently enjoying a winning streak. When I joked that I was sorry for interrupting the game to conduct our interview, Eddie replied it was actually good that he'd been interrupted, because "if you play too long without taking a break, you mess up." Later in our conversation, I asked Eddie why he had called Chartbeat "insanely addictive." He responded,

> That's like asking me what's so addictive about 2048. [Chartbeat is] a game. It's a big game, and it's one that you want to win. But it's also one that has no clear end or conclusion. . . . Once you hit your [concurrent visitors] cap, [then you say] let's raise the cap and let's hit that! What's our 30-day max [the maximum number of concurrent visitors the site had in the past 30 days]? Let's beat it, and let's come up with a new 30-day max! It's endless. And it is a big video game, full of high scores, and master players, and hopefully only a few Game Overs.

If achieving a large amount of traffic produced a "high" that users like Eddie compared to drug use, it is unsurprising that over time one would need to achieve larger and larger amounts of traffic to achieve the same euphoric feeling. Researchers have hypothesized that a similar pattern exists on social media sites, whereby people come to feel dependent on the boost of dopamine that gets triggered by interaction or affirmation (such as someone liking a Facebook post or sharing your tweet) and thus engage in increasingly heavy use of the platforms.

The Balance of Chance and Skill

A third game-like quality that made Chartbeat feel addictive was the dashboard's tantalizing suggestion—though crucially, not its guarantee—that writers and editors could *change* the way the numbers moved by taking the correct actions. Anthropological analyses of games and play have argued that entering the "play state" or "play element" requires games that balance contingency with control. If there is too much random chance, players become anxious; if there is too little, the game is boring.[11] Compelling games often provide what behavioral psychologists call "variable rewards": players win some rounds and lose others at intervals that feel unpredictable—even when, as in the case of video poker, they are in fact governed by a computer program.[12]

The quest to draw traffic to news sites is often portrayed as a Faustian bargain that a journalist purposefully decides to enter into (or not): if she writes about sexy, sensational, outrageous, or heartwarming topics, the clicks and unique visitors will come; if she refuses to do so, they won't—or at least, not in nearly as high numbers. In other words, it is usually assumed that digital journalists know what it takes to achieve high traffic. If that is the case, the most important question is not *how* to boost traffic but whether the actions required to do so are prohibitively damaging to journalists' reputation and the integrity of the profession.

Yet the reality was rarely so straightforward. To excel at the traffic game, journalists needed a mixture of luck and skill that was elusive and difficult to reliably reproduce. Journalists spoke regularly of being surprised by traffic. Pieces they expected to be "hits" often drew a smaller-than-anticipated audience, while articles that seemed "niche" could unexpectedly become popular. Even at Gawker, a company known for its unabashed pursuit of clicks and uniques, staffers vacillated on the question of whether there existed a dependable editorial formula for achieving high traffic. On the day I visited Andrew's site's group chat, there was a debate about which angle the site should take in covering a new software feature released by a big technology company. A writer had originally composed a "newsy" post; Andrew instructed him to write an additional post that was more "service-oriented" (as in, helping readers figure out how to use the feature rather than simply reporting on its existence). In email to me afterward, Andrew explained that he had been pushing the writer to find the angle with "the largest possible audience." Comparing the eventual traffic earned by the two pieces, his service-oriented angle proved to be the more successful one. Yet while Andrew took pride in his ability to identify the angle that had drawn more traffic in that particular instance, he also spoke of a strong element of uncertainty with regard to metrics more generally: "It is kind of mysterious: how *do* you actually get that many people to come to the site?"

Of course, the uncertainty and mystery of the traffic game is not solely because of Chartbeat. As subsequent chapters will explore further, it is also due to the outsize power and opacity of the social media platforms whose algorithms govern the distribution of contemporary news, as well as the inherent interpretive ambiguity of metrics in fields of cultural production.

Consequences of the Traffic Game

The instantaneous and endless feedback of the Chartbeat dashboard, coupled with the uncertainty and variable "reward" structure of web journalism, pulled users into a powerful behavioral loop that had consequences for the Gawker newsroom's working conditions, social relations, and outputs. This section will illustrate how the traffic game extracted increased productivity from writers and editors, obscured the power imbalance between writers and the company's upper management, and redirected journalists' competitive tendencies away from rival publications and toward themselves and their own colleagues.

Extraction of Increased Productivity

The traffic game is a powerful tool for extracting increased productivity. At Gawker, writers and editors developed strategies to try to boost their numbers in the face of relentless, addictive forms of measurement and mysterious traffic patterns; these strategies usually involved harder work. For instance, one of the few dependable actions to boost both individual and site traffic was simple (if not easy): post more.[13] To increase their post count, Gawker writers produced what Alison called "filler"—short pieces that drew heavily from aggregated material. They also engaged in a practice called "pub and fill": when a story broke that was expected to generate high audience interest but about which details were not yet available, Gawker writers would race to publish a bare-bones post to capitalize on the initial wave of audience attention and then fill in details later. Because Gawker sites tended to have large baseline audiences, even filler and pub-and-fill posts could be counted on to draw at least a few thousand readers, and some of these would inevitably be monthly uniques, the most highly valued metric at Gawker.[14]

Posting more was an especially sound strategy to drive down writers' eCPM numbers; as noted above, eCPM was Gawker's metric for the number of dollars a writer earned in salary for every thousand monthly uniques her posts garnered. At the end of every month, Gawker site leads received a color-coded chart from management showing the eCPM figures for everyone on their editorial staff. Each site was expected to maintain an average eCPM of $20, meaning that writers' posts pulled in an average of 1,000 unique visitors for every $20 they got paid in salary. Liam, a site lead, explained that writers with an eCPM of $2 were coded bright green on the chart because of how much traffic their posts attracted relative to their salary. By contrast, writers with an eCPM of $98 would be coded in "bright red" and he would be "pressured to fire them." To avoid having to do so, Liam simply encouraged those writers to post more:

> [I tell them,] "Unfortunately you need to post more this month. . . . Any numbers at all are gonna help." . . . People respond to that relatively well

because I'm not saying, "You have to post bikini photos" or something like that. But I'm saying, like, "You literally just have to post more. Like, write another post tomorrow." You know what I mean? You just have to get *something* on the website, it doesn't even matter what it is. It's like, if you post *anything*, you're gonna get several thousand people.

The practice of posting frequently to gain incremental traffic bears resemblance to what is known in the field of game design as "grinding," that is, "any activity that a player can do repeatedly with minimal or no risk that results in an in-game reward." Some well-known games, such as Farmville, consist almost entirely of grinding: "The game tells you, 'click on this thing for 300 points.' There's no reason not to click on it, so it's just a chore the game makes you do."[15] Almost by definition, grinding is boring: it requires the player to perform the same rote actions over and over. But players put up with it—to a point—because games that incorporate grinding "dangle a reward that will come to [players] in the future in exchange for [grinding] action in the present." Although grinding is often maligned by the game design community, it persists because it is a reliable way to lengthen players' engagement with a game.[16] However, excessively relying on grinding carries its own risks for game designers: "Instead of lengthening the time players will play the game, they may become frustrated, quit, and never come back."[17]

The strategy of writing a large number of posts that are each guaranteed to attract at least a modicum of traffic is the blogging equivalent of grinding—and it was similarly effective at extracting increased productivity from "players." Indeed, incentivizing grinding is a less risky strategy for newsroom managers than it is for game designers: although some staffers may have found high-volume posting tedious, the threat of losing their jobs generally prevented them from giving up on grinding as a recreational game player might.

Grinding in the blogging world had an additional element of intrigue: there was always the tantalizing possibility that any ground-out post could become a surprise viral hit. As Eddie put it, "The more blog posts you put out there, the more chance it'll get picked up by [the political blog the] Drudge [Report], or something will go viral." He drew a comparison to gambling to elaborate on this point: "[Going viral is] more or less like playing the lottery. You pick your numbers and you're diligent about it, and the more lottery tickets you buy, the more likely you are to hit it big." Jackie, a senior writer, shared with me an example of this kind of unexpected virality: "We posted this thing about a Russian ice skater doing a performance to Ginuwine's 'My Pony.'

Totally big, totally huge [traffic]. We had no idea that that was going to be so huge. And then we have other things that we think are going to be home runs and will sort of do decent traffic." The unpredictability of these variable rewards was a powerful incentive for writers to continually increase their post volume.

Gawker writers' practice of posting frequently in hopes of getting a viral hit illustrates how the traffic game has reshaped the operating logic of journalism in the digital age. In key respects, traffic pressures have rendered online news outlets more similar to other fields of cultural production than to their print newspaper and magazine counterparts. Drawing on the work of media theorist Bernard Miège, it is useful to distinguish between two modes of cultural production. In fields that operate according to a "written press" logic, a bundled cultural commodity is produced at regular intervals and meant to be consumed by a loyal audience. By contrast, in an "editorial" or "publishing" logic, media companies mitigate the risky and unpredictable nature of cultural markets by building a catalog of media products, such that the "inevitable failures are balanced out by hits or successes."[18] The editorial logic is typical in the book publishing, music, and film industries. By contrast, print journalism long abided by the written press logic, according to which newspapers and magazines were produced and sold as bundled media products, largely to loyal paying subscribers. Although several print news outlets, such as the *New York Times*, experimented with a more editorial logic in the early days of their transition to digital formats, those that are able have since reverted to the written press logic, implementing metered paywalls that rely on paying digital subscribers.[19]

However, online-only media companies (e.g., Gawker, BuzzFeed Inc., and Vox Media) have largely taken a different path, in which they make most content free to audiences and rely on high traffic—gained largely through social media distribution—to attract advertising revenue.[20] This model hews closer to an editorial logic: each article exists as an unbundled, stand-alone cultural commodity under the umbrella of a broader media brand. This mode of journalistic production relies on the occasional traffic "hit" to offset low-traffic posts. Alison's description of her editorial thought process exemplifies how the editorial logic manifested at Gawker: "Sometimes there are . . . really long beautiful pieces that are very thought out and only do 10,000 uniques over 24 hours, and that kinda sucks. But I wouldn't change it. It's just the pressure to be like, OK, what are we gonna do now to make up for that?"

Since individual Gawker posts succeed or fail as discrete media commodities, each one needs its own promotional strategy. This promotional labor, which Angèle Christin calls the "invisible work of visibility," is another way in which the traffic game extracts productivity.[21] In interviews, Gawker writers and editors reported taking numerous actions after a post was published to try to boost its numbers, such as tweaking the headline, swapping out the accompanying image, crafting a Facebook post, or sharing it multiple times on Twitter. In an essay titled "When Silicon Valley Took Over Journalism," Franklin Foer, former editor of the *New Republic* magazine, vividly described this dynamic: in a newsroom that uses Chartbeat, Foer wrote, "no piece has sufficient traffic—it can always be improved with a better headline, a better approach to social media, a better subject, a better argument."[22] To Eddie, there was a seemingly unlimited number of actions one could take to try to boost a story's traffic, though no guarantee that any would work: "You can always do something else, or post something else to Facebook to see if it sticks, or try tweeting a story again to see if maybe it'll get pickup now instead of this morning." By providing limitless opportunities to improve one's "score," the traffic game created strong incentives for writers to work continuously—and engendered feelings of anxiety when they stopped.

As with grinding in recreational games, the continual grinding required by the traffic game is relatively low-risk for its journalist-players: as we have seen, ground-out posts guarantee at least *some* monetizable traffic, and there is always the possibility that one will turn out to be a surprise hit. In the fierce competition for online attention, *not* grinding seems like the far more risky option.

However, grinding in the traffic game had substantial non-monetary costs. Although the writers I spoke to at Gawker enjoyed the thrill of the occasional viral hit, in general many of them found grinding tedious and demoralizing (chapter 3 addresses these feelings in more detail). In addition, there are opportunity costs to consider: all the time Gawker writers spent grinding was time they couldn't use to pursue stories they found more fulfilling to work on and that might have had greater civic value. As Eddie put it: "[Traffic] compels me to produce more. However, producing more, blogging more, keeping the post count up, necessarily means that I don't take time to work on the longer, slower, reported-out features." Finally, the ceaseless pressure to grind out posts results in ever more public speech. Yet, as Mike Ananny has argued, a healthy, self-governing public requires journalists to provide not only speech but also space—and sometimes silence—so that people can listen, absorb, and reflect. By incentivizing online journalists to publish and promote content at a relentless pace, the traffic game in effect punishes the very silences that could enrich civic life.[23]

Obfuscation of Managerial Pressure

We have seen how the dashboard's instantaneous feedback and intermittent reinforcement made it a powerful tool for extracting increased productivity for writers, who increased the pace and volume of their blogging in an attempt to be successful in the traffic game. In this respect, Chartbeat is one in a long line of managerial techniques that induce a work speed-up. As discussed in the introduction, some scholars and journalists have characterized real-time analytics tools as the digital-era instantiation of the "scientific management" style popularized by Frederick Taylor.[24] Taylor's treatise, *The Principles of Scientific Management*, instructed industrial managers to subdivide productive tasks into the smallest possible component parts and meticulously monitor and time workers as they performed them to discover the most efficient method of execution. In his essay on newsroom metrics, Foer saw in Chartbeat strong echoes of Taylor's approach: "Like a manager standing over the assembly line with a stopwatch, Chartbeat and its ilk now hover over the newsroom."[25] In many ways, the comparison is apt: the emphasis on quantitative measurement and relentless optimization of the labor process is common to both Taylorist managerial techniques and Chartbeat.

Yet there is a crucial difference. In classic Taylorism, the surveilling and evaluating actions of management are made explicit to the worker via the presence of the stopwatch-wielding manager. By contrast, because rank-and-file journalists used Chartbeat themselves, the analytics tool did not *feel* to them like a form of managerial coercion. Instead, writers perceived the practice of repeatedly checking Chartbeat as something they chose to do as individuals (or, perhaps more to the point, were unable to stop themselves from doing).

Kevin, a Gawker writer, noted that his fixation on traffic had bled into his personal life: he had a habit of checking the Chartbeat Big Board on his phone when he was out socializing with friends, in the same way that he would periodically and absentmindedly check Instagram. Andrea, another writer, felt she had become "obsessive" with metrics "in a way that feels a little unhealthy." She elaborated: "Chartbeat is always perpetually open, even if I'm not working."[26]

Kevin's likening of his behaviors with Chartbeat to his behaviors with his personal Instagram account underscores the blurring of work and leisure that real-time metrics facilitated both offline and on the screen.[27] Importantly, it also highlights how writers could come to feel that their compulsive behaviors around Chartbeat were the result of a lapse in personal willpower, as opposed to a combination of habit-forming user experience design and managerial pressure. Earlier in our interview, when I asked Kevin if he checked Chartbeat on his phone, he sighed and replied sheepishly:

KEVIN: Yes. I'm not supposed to.
CP: You're not supposed to?
KEVIN: No, no, we don't have to look at traffic that much.

Similarly, when I asked Andrea to what extent her "obsessive" behaviors with Chartbeat were an attempt to satisfy her bosses' expectations, she replied, "None. I mean, they've never told me to look at it . . . and I think from the times I've talked to them they seemed surprised that I'm always looking at it."[28]

Some individuals in editorial management positions shared this perception. Andrew told me that he wished his site's writers would look at metrics far less than they did, but he felt powerless to stop them:

This company believes in transparency so they make a whole lot of stuff available . . . I kind of wish [my writers] could be at peace with the fact that while it's available, they shouldn't look at it, because ultimately just please do a good job and let me stress about it. . . . But I can't say [to my writers], "Forget that password that you found out." . . . How would I tell them not to [look at metrics]?[29]

Andrew acknowledged that the universal availability of data was the result of a decision made by "this company," by which he meant Gawker's leadership. Yet it is telling that his (well-meaning) frustration is directed not at the company's executives for making data widely available and influential but rather at the writers on his staff, who "shouldn't look at it." Andrew's placement of responsibility on writers, rather than the company's upper management, echoes Kevin's and Andrea's tendency to blame themselves for their "obsessive" and "unhealthy" fixation on metrics.

In this way, the Chartbeat dashboard not only mediated managerial production pressures at Gawker; it also *obscured* those pressures. If the Chartbeat dashboard was, in essence, a souped-up Taylorist stopwatch, then writers like Kevin perceived themselves to be both the monitored worker *and* the watchful manager. Chartbeat's ability to generate this feeling of individual accountability likely helped facilitate its acceptance in newsrooms—especially considering that journalists, like many knowledge workers, expect to maintain some autonomy over their labor process.[30] Yet, as the next chapter will illustrate, the feelings of self-recrimination Chartbeat engendered in journalists could be highly demoralizing and disenchanting, forcing Chartbeat to take steps to alleviate them.

Competition Turned Inward

In addition to extracting increased productivity from writers, the game-like user experience of real-time analytics tools like Chartbeat can restructure "lateral relations" in the workplace—making coworkers less cooperative and more competitive.[31] News production has long been a fiercely competitive enterprise, especially in heavily commercialized media markets such as the United States. However, historically this competition has been mainly externally oriented. In *Deciding What's News*, his classic 1979 ethnographic study of U.S. newswork, sociologist Herbert Gans documented the extreme lengths to which rival magazines and news networks would go trying to outpace each other in scoops, and the ways in which such rivalries influenced story and cover selection. *Newsweek* would, for instance, abandon a story-in-progress if *Time* ran a similar story first, and vice versa. Beating one's primary competitor to a story was considered evidence of superior news judgment and efficiency.

While Gans acknowledged the presence of competitive dynamics within news organizations, the most intense rivalries existed *between* similar magazines, newspapers, and news broadcasts. At the *New York Times*, where, as later chapters will illustrate, access to analytics was tightly limited, this type of externally focused competition for the most current and relevant stories remained quite salient. Randall, a *Times* editor, explained that the newspaper was in a constant "battle with the *Wall Street Journal* and the *Washington Post* . . . and some other papers, like the *Guardian* in London," to be the first to publish stories and demonstrate the most astute news judgment.

At Gawker, however, competition took an altogether different form. Writers and editors at Gawker tended to describe themselves as intensely competitive individuals. When asked what kind of person was likely to thrive at Gawker, Eddie said, "I think people with—this sounds weird but—a competitive athletic background do well with the metrics-driven model." Eddie had rowed on his high school and university crew teams and hypothesized that athletes in sports like crew or track, where each person's talent is boiled down to a single time or score, were particularly well suited to Gawker's metrics-infused workplace. Angie, a writer, echoed this point: "For the most part everyone that works here is competitive. Competition is very much in the fabric, in the DNA of this company."

Thus competition played as much—if not more—of a role in the work lives of Gawker writers and editors as it did for *Times* journalists. However, the competitive drive took a very different shape in Gawker's metrics-saturated context. Unlike their counterparts at the *Times*, in their daily work Gawker staffers were far more focused on *intra*-company competition than they were on beating rival companies such as BuzzFeed Inc., Vice Media, and Vox Media. Alison explained that, out of Gawker Media's eight main blogs, she always wanted her site to be in the top four in terms of traffic. "I don't ever want to be in the bottom four. Like I was looking yesterday and I was like, argh, *Deadspin*'s pulled away, I gotta get caught up." Andrew, who edited a site that focused on a relatively niche subject, told me he didn't care about traffic levels of external sites that covered the same topic as his own. Instead, he preferred to compare his site's rate of traffic growth to that of other Gawker sites: "If sites about all these other topics can grow to the extent that they're growing, then why can't my site?"

Why would editors like Alison and Andrew compare their site's traffic to others that covered entirely different subjects, just because they were owned by the same company? The reason soon became clear: analytics tools had shaped the nature of competition at Gawker by making intra-organizational comparisons constantly available and intensely habit-forming. Indeed, the centrality of metrics in Gawker's physical office environment, as manifested by the presence of the Big Board, not only encouraged such comparisons but also rendered them quite literally hard to avoid.

In contrast, Gawker staffers had relatively little information about rival media companies' traffic. When I asked Alison, "Do you compare [your site's] traffic to other kinds of similar blogs?" Alison responded, "No. . . . Well, a lot of the information is unavailable." A staffer at *Kotaku*, Gawker's gaming site, echoed this point: "I don't even know what other gaming sites are doing [in terms of traffic]." By making intra-company comparisons so readily available, visible, and influential, Gawker's executive leadership had channeled employees' formidable competitive tendencies toward each other and away from more topically similar sites for which they did not have access to traffic figures.

If, as I have argued, the competition for traffic has game-like elements, then ignorance of other teams' scores makes it difficult to play against them. Gawker staffers could, of course, compare their sites to external rivals using the same criteria that Gans's subjects had—such as the "timeliness of [rivals'] news judgment and the speed with which that judgment was implemented"— simply by reading those sites.[32] But the strong emphasis on traffic, both at Gawker in particular and in online media in general, has made these print-era criteria less compelling fodder for competition.

Commensuration—that is, applying a single numerical standard to two or more qualitatively different entities in order to render them comparable—can powerfully shape cognition.[33] Once a numerical ranking exists and becomes visible, more nuanced and context-sensitive forms of evaluation tend to get drowned out. When I mentioned to Alison over instant message that I was surprised she compared her site's traffic to that of *Deadspin*, given how substantively distinct the two sites seemed, she initially agreed: "Yeah, totally! I realize a lot of what I'm saying here is crazy." Yet a moment later, she added: "But also, bigger is bigger." Indeed, simply by rendering seemingly dissimilar sites commensurable, or comparable according to the same metric, the Big Board effectively papered over the substantive differences between them.[34]

Conclusion

This chapter has argued that real-time analytics tools like Chartbeat have strong habit-forming properties built into their user experience design. Through features like immersive visual displays, the potential (and pressure) to continually beat one's traffic records, and a finely calibrated balance of chance and skill, Chartbeat ensnared journalists in what I have called the traffic game: an ongoing competition against their coworkers and themselves to boost their metrics-driven "scores." In this way, analytics dashboards are not dissimilar to other digital tools and services, such as social media sites, that are designed to be maximally absorbing to compete in an ever-intensifying arms race for our attention. Yet unlike digital gaming and the recreational use of social networking sites, journalists' exposure to audience metrics is something that takes place in—indeed, is increasingly required by—the workplace and within the context of a highly unstable profession. In sum, journalists find analytics dashboards addictive precisely because the tools combine game-like qualities with the sky-high stakes of professional precarity.

If a confluence of design decisions and economic circumstances encourages journalists to consult metrics compulsively, the second half of the chapter considered the implications of this state of affairs for the working conditions and social relations of the contemporary newsroom. In the context of Gawker, the ubiquity and dynamism of real-time metrics pushed editorial staffers to work harder and produce more. This is common to other historical forms of workplace assessment, but Chartbeat manifested a crucial difference: the dashboard's addictive properties obscured the role of management in implementing metrics-based systems of surveillance and evaluation, because writers interpreted their compulsive behaviors around metrics as a failure of personal willpower rather than as managerial subordination. Furthermore, writers' compulsion to continually check the dashboard further blurred the line— already barely discernible—between the bloggers' work and leisure time, and between their personal and professional selves. In other words, real-time metrics prompted staffers to write more, engage with work-related matters during their leisure time, and continually try to optimize headlines, share images, and social media strategies—all while making this harder work feel like a personal choice. Management simply had to make Chartbeat's tools widely available; the product's habit-forming design did the rest. These findings suggest that game-like metrics tools may take hold as a method for managing knowledge workers who, because of their expectation of greater workplace autonomy, are likely to chafe at more explicit managerial methods of intensifying work.[35]

While the media field has always been intensely competitive, the traffic game has also altered the character of media competition. Previous generations of newsroom ethnographers found that journalists focused their competitive energies on similarly themed publications owned by rival companies. By contrast, the availability and prominence of metrics within Gawker Media directed staffers' competitive impulses inward, toward themselves and their colleagues under the Gawker umbrella. The result was that, in daily work, staffers were far more focused on surpassing Gawker sites other than their own in uniques and placement on the Big Board than they were on besting the news judgment of external competitors.

Taken together, the findings presented in this chapter suggest that, when seeking to understand the role of digital technologies in managing knowledge workers, we would do well to pay more attention to the field of user experience design. What kinds of thoughts, feelings, and experiences do companies like Chartbeat seek to create in and for their users, and why? By taking user experience seriously as an object of analytical attention, we begin to understand why journalists develop such strong emotional attachments to metrics-driven performance-evaluation products like Chartbeat. We also see how these attachments can have deleterious consequences for their relationship to their work and to each other.

The analytics dashboard's addictive properties had obvious benefits for Gawker management, in the form of increased worker productivity, and for Chartbeat, in the sense that selling a habit-forming product tends to be good for business. Yet this approach to user experience design also carried risks. The very same features that made the Chartbeat dashboard so habit-forming could also make it feel to writers like a relentless, demoralizing grind—which, in turn, threatened to alienate them from the product altogether. The next chapter will examine how Chartbeat sought to limit these negative reactions by imbuing metrics with a sense of existential and professional meaning.

3

Enchanted Metrics

It's not the identity of the number [that matters]. It's the *feeling* that the number produces. That's the thing that's important.

—AARON, CHARTBEAT EMPLOYEE

TWO WEEKS AFTER my initial interview with Alison, the Gawker Media site lead we met in chapter 2, she and I had a follow-up conversation over Aol Instant Message. During this exchange, Alison patiently answered my detailed questions about her editorial workflow, and specifically about how she decided which of the site's posts would be cross-posted to its social media pages. "Facebook makes or breaks a post" in terms of traffic, she messaged me. She explained that while "big headlines"—those she deemed to be her site's most newsworthy posts— "automatically get sent to FB [Facebook], I can send a small one and it might do just as well. . . . Let's do a real-time example!" Referencing a post that had been published on her site a few minutes prior, Alison wrote she had decided to cross-post it on the site's Facebook page in an attempt to boost its traffic, because "right now [it] only has 21 views—horrible."

After posting the story to Facebook at 1:07 p.m., Alison typed to me: "Let's see what happens. Maybe nothing. I still can't predict this stuff." I wrote that I was refreshing the post on her site to see if the view count had gone up, but Alison explained that it was still too soon to tell: "If anything happens it'll take a few minutes," she wrote. "It's been a slow stretch for us so I'm not optimistic." A minute ticked by, then another. While we waited, I opened a new line of questioning, asking Alison about her process for optimizing headlines for social media. But Alison didn't answer right away. Instead, she typed: "these are the days when I'm feeling bad, we've not had anything blow up." Alison's site's traffic was indeed significantly lower on this day than it had been on the day of our first interview, when she had jubilantly told me that her site "broke 9,000" concurrent visitors on Chartbeat due to a particularly highly trafficked post.

At 1:12 p.m., five minutes after Alison had posted the low-traffic post to Facebook, it still hadn't appeared on the Big Board, Chartbeat's real-time ranking of Gawker Media stories with the highest numbers of concurrent visitors. "So it won't blow up, I already know," she wrote. I asked if there were any other stories lined up in her site's publication queue that she thought had potential to "blow up"; Alison listed a few upcoming posts that "could do okay." But, she added, "we're in a bit of a slump right now so I'm pessimistic, ha." Then she continued, unprompted: "And then you get in this really worried, desperate place—like, crap, where is the viral post, when will it fall in our laps . . . and that is a really unpleasant feeling. It definitely affects my mood."

A few minutes later, Alison remembered that one of her writers was preparing a post ranking 30 candy bars that was set to be published in the coming days. This realization reassured her: "That's going to do well, whenever we get it up. (Just knowing that's imminent makes me feel a bit better.)" However, the candy bar post was still too far in the future to provide Alison with much consolation in the moment: "as of right now, looking at today, I feel like crap," she wrote. "Like I've been failing for 5 hours now and I'm not sure I will stop failing. Tomorrow hits a reset button."

The following afternoon I instant-messaged Alison to see how the "reset" had gone. She wrote that her emotional state had improved dramatically since our last exchange, due to an increase in her site's traffic, and seemed to feel a bit sheepish about her negative outlook the day before. "I'm in a much better mood today, so sorry about being bleak," she wrote. "Today's much better: we had a blowup item at the eod [end of day] yesterday that carried us overnight and is still doing well today, and we've had some other stuff today that's done well."

Reflecting later on my exchanges with Alison, I was struck by the sheer intensity of the negative emotions she described experiencing as a result of low site traffic—evident in her use of words like "worried," "desperate," "really unpleasant," and "failing"—and how dramatically they contrasted with her more chipper attitude the following day once her site's traffic had climbed. Indeed, many Gawker Media staffers told me their moods rose and fell with the traffic numbers reported in the dashboard, sometimes to a degree that alarmed them. As Eddie, a writer, put it: "I'm actually concerned by the extent to which my emotional well-being is dictated by the number of hits on my posts. I talk to my therapist about it!"[1]

Of course, it is hardly unheard of to have one's emotional state be influenced by feelings of professional success or failure. These feelings of self-blame may be exacerbated by the "enterprise" discourse that has become widespread in knowledge work, wherein individual workers are cast as quasi-entrepreneurs who are at fault when businesses falter.[2] Still, the degree to which "professional success/failure" and "metrics" seemed to have become conflated in the minds of many Gawker writers was noteworthy, especially because racking up high numbers of uniques and concurrent visitors is not the reason staffers had pursued a career in blogging to begin with, even at a media company with a reputation for being as metrics-driven as Gawker.

The emotional volatility that staffers like Alison and Eddie experienced as a result of their traffic suggested that sustained exposure to real-time analytics tools could, over time, make attracting high traffic start to feel like an end in itself, divorced from any particular instrumental or editorial goal. Chapter 2 illustrated that this was in large part due to the dashboard's game-like features—such as continually updating "scores" and rankings, intermittent reinforcement, and instant feedback mechanisms—and that these features made Chartbeat an effective tool at extracting greater productivity from editorial workers. However, as this chapter will demonstrate, Chartbeat's approach to user experience design had a potential pitfall: the dashboard's game-like features, while strongly habit-forming, could also make the quest for traffic feel demoralizing, tedious, and meaningless. Chartbeat could, in other words, induce a profound sense of *disenchantment* in its journalist-users—which, in turn, might turn them off from the tool.

This chapter examines the relationship between quantification and disenchantment, and shows that Chartbeat sought to break this long-standing association by pursuing three strategies intended to make metrics feel *meaningful* to users. First, Chartbeat staffers took a cheery, lighthearted tone in branding materials and interactions with users in order to alleviate any negative feelings about low traffic. Second, Chartbeat sought to "reenchant" the dashboard through design elements and discursive framing that tapped into ideas of magic, mystery, and transcendence. Finally, Chartbeat discursively positioned itself as being deferent to journalists' editorial judgment and seamlessly aligned with their professional values and norms.

Metrics-Driven Disenchantment in Journalism

The fact that Chartbeat could engender feelings of disenchantment is not altogether surprising: sociological work examining the role of quantitative measurement in modern life has long warned that it can provoke a deep sense of unease, meaninglessness, and existential dread. Max Weber famously argued that modern science and capitalism delegitimized non-rational sources of value and meaning but provided nothing with which to replace them. Contrasted with art, Weber claimed, the incrementalism of scientific practice renders it necessarily lacking in inherent meaning. While one beautiful work of art does not invalidate or devalue another, new scientific discoveries necessarily displace their predecessors. As Weber put it:

> Every scientific "fulfilment" raises new "questions"; it asks to be "surpassed" and outdated. . . . In principle, this progress goes on ad infinitum. And with this we come to inquire into the meaning of science. . . . Why does one engage in doing something that in reality never comes, and never can come, to an end?[3]

Traditional measures of journalistic excellence—or, to use Weber's term, fulfillment—resemble art more than science: one year's Pulitzer Prize–winning story does not outstrip another's; today's front-page investigative article does not diminish yesterday's. The quest for traffic, by contrast, demands something quite similar to the steady, unending march of incremental scientific progress that Weber describes. Indeed, the passage from Weber quoted above is strikingly similar to Eddie's statement, quoted in chapter 2, comparing Chartbeat to a game that "has no clear end or conclusion. . . . Once you hit your [concurrent visitors] cap, [then you say] let's raise the cap and let's hit that! What's our 30-day max? Let's beat it, and let's come up with a new 30-day max! It's endless."

As metrics become ever more influential in news organizations, they can crowd out traditional sources of journalistic fulfillment—yet they do not offer an alternative form of substantive meaning. Each "high score" in the traffic game is ultimately bested by an even *better*-performing article; each viral "hit" quickly becomes a new traffic target that must be exceeded.

Chapter 2 illustrated that this endless quality was a powerful habit-forming property that paid short-term productivity dividends for newsrooms that used Chartbeat. However, the feelings of demoralization and exhaustion reported by Eddie, Alison, and others raised the possibility that the habit-forming power of the dashboard would diminish over time—or even eventually provoke a backlash among users. Indeed, many journalists have regarded Chartbeat and other real-time analytics tools with suspicion, viewing them as a potent symbol of declining editorial standards, deteriorating working conditions, the inappropriate incursion of commercial concerns into the newsroom, and the managerially enforced obsolescence of editorial judgment.[4] For example, in March 2014, the *Times* warned that "risks abound when reporters play in [web] traffic";[5] the same year, a series of feature stories in the *American Journalism Review* asked, "Is chasing viral traffic hurting journalism?"[6]

At times, this cautious skepticism has intensified into outright hostility. A writer for the *Gothamist* blog memorably described Chartbeat as "a giant, coal-and-kitten-blood-powered factory located somewhere in the middle of Death Valley that counts up every single precious little click on websites like *Gawker* in order to calculate each blogger's exact worth as an employee."[7] When the *Columbia Journalism Review* published a positive feature story about Chartbeat in 2015,[8] a data and technology reporter at *ProPublica* posted a series of mocking tweets in which she imagined what would have transpired had Bob Woodward and Carl Bernstein used Chartbeat when investigating President Nixon's Watergate break-in: "'Carl—CARL! We've got a source to meet!' 'In a minute, Bob. We're spiking! And—look! Someone's reading our story in Omaha!' . . . 'Bob. We're down to 23 readers. I don't know if I can do this anymore.' 'Here's a bright idea, Carl. Let's publish ANOTHER F-ING STORY.'" The reporter ended the series by writing sarcastically, "In conclusion, Chartbeat is the future of journalism☺☺."

Although journalists' antipathy toward metrics has diminished somewhat in recent years, these attitudes presented a challenge for Chartbeat, especially in the relatively early iterations of the product when the company was still trying to get "buy-in" from newsroom users.[9] The remainder of the chapter will discuss the rhetorical and design strategies the company employed to manage this challenge.

Affective Labor to Manage Users' Negative Emotions

Digital analytics tools have a reputation for laying bare uncomfortable but necessary truths about news audiences—especially in comparison to the analog audience research methods that preceded them.[10] An accurate, holistic, and unsparingly detailed picture of the audience was a key aspect of what Chartbeat was selling. The company's website claimed that its dashboard allowed clients to "see what interests visitors and adapt your site instantly," "equip your team with decision-driving data," and "know what content sparks and holds readers' attention." This discursive positioning aimed to attract the high-ranking business- and editorial-side staff (such as top editors, business development managers, and members of news organizations' product teams) who had the authority to purchase a Chartbeat subscription. In positioning itself this way, Chartbeat tapped into a conventional narrative of Big Data—that it provided a systematic, unbiased way of making decisions that in turn would lead to more accurate predictions and greater economic returns.[11] If the proliferation of Chartbeat in newsrooms around the world is any indication, it was an effective sales pitch.[12]

However, appealing it may have been for news executives and managers, this kind of unvarnished truth-telling was often demoralizing for the rank-and-file newsroom staffers who regularly interacted with the dashboard. It was common for users to be disappointed with the concurrents count, scroll depth, or engaged time for their stories: in meetings and calls with Chartbeat staffers, I observed journalists describe various data points on the dashboard as "sad" and "super pride-crushing." Many journalists have written publicly about the negative or ambivalent feelings aroused in them by Chartbeat data. The technology writer Farhad Manjoo used Chartbeat data about his readers as fodder for a disgruntled piece in *Slate* titled "You Won't Finish This Article." "Ugh," wrote Manjoo in response to Chartbeat data indicating that many of his readers shared social media links to his stories without having actually read them. "As a writer all this data annoys me. It may not be obvious—especially to you guys who've already left to watch *Arrested Development*—but I spend a lot of time and energy writing these stories."[13]

Journalists' negative feelings about their performance data could lead to disillusionment with Chartbeat itself, which would in turn be problematic for the company's business model. Like all subscription-based businesses, a perennial concern for Chartbeat was client "churn"—that is, clients who opt to discontinue their subscription. Although journalists did not control their employers' purse strings, their acceptance of Chartbeat mattered nonetheless: Chartbeat had found that one of the biggest predictors of churn was a decline in the frequency and breadth of Chartbeat usage in the client's newsroom. Negative feelings about Chartbeat could also impact the acquisition of new clients: Amanda, a Chartbeat employee who worked with smaller, lower-trafficked publishers, acknowledged that the experience of looking at the dashboard could be "harsh" for these small news organizations, adding that some elected to stop using Chartbeat even before finishing their free trial.

Thus Chartbeat faced a strategic dilemma (especially in its early years, before metrics had become a more taken-for-granted presence in newsrooms). On the one hand, the company's reputation for providing pull-no-punches, "decision-driving" audience data was a key selling point for news organizations.

On the other, this reputation also put Chartbeat in the unenviable position of being the bearer of bad news—and in the news industry in the early 2010s, there was a lot of bad news.

Chartbeat staffers navigated this conundrum by performing various types of *affective labor* in an attempt to manage users' feelings about their data—and, by extension, about Chartbeat. Melissa Gregg defines affective labor as "work with an emotional, communicative, or symbolic dimension."[14] Following this definition, we can conceptualize Chartbeat employees' efforts to create and maintain a particular "brand identity" as a form of affective labor. This work was carried out with the aim of counteracting feelings of discouragement and self-doubt that could be brought on by low metrics and instead cultivating positive associations with Chartbeat's products.

For example, Chartbeat's marketing and branding team consistently strove to project a tone of lightheartedness, accessibility, and gentle irreverence. Simon, a business-side employee, explained in our interview that the company aimed to be "really casual and friendly and conversational" in its written materials. On the company website, employees didn't have formal titles listed; their headshots were accompanied by labels like "wordslinger," "account wrangler," "salesologist," "operating thetan," "figure outer." (One employee cheekily winked at this tradition, writing "quirky title TBD.") Dogs also enjoyed pride of place on Chartbeat's website; each canine had a headshot, title (e.g., "Princess and Chief Ignorer"), and bio ("pooping, wagging, leash-pulling, being cute") listed right alongside those of the company's human employees.

The optimistic, cheerful tone also permeated Chartbeat's staffers' interactions with clients. On a bright afternoon in late October, I accompanied Tyler, an employee on Chartbeat's business side, to a client meeting with the online team of a popular radio show. The purpose of the meeting was to train the team to use the new version of Chartbeat's signature newsroom analytics product, Chartbeat Publishing. Tyler conducted many product trainings for prospective and current clients at Chartbeat, and on our subway ride to the radio show's office, I asked what this was like. How did journalists react when they saw their own performance data (instead of a generic demo) in the Chartbeat onscreen dashboard for the first time? Did they get excited? Tyler responded that they did but that sometimes clients had the opposite reaction—they became upset because their numbers weren't as high as they expected. "And when they say that," Tyler explained, "the card I play—and what I really believe—is that facing the low numbers is the first step towards boosting them."

He became animated as he went on: "If you're sick, wouldn't you rather go to the doctor and find out, rather than just be sick and not know?"

While Tyler adamantly defended the value of clients "facing the low numbers" in our conversation, his tone changed once we were in the room with the clients. During the meeting Tyler performed affective labor to buffer the clients against any feelings of concern or discouragement their analytics might engender. This labor mainly took the form of providing reassurance that several of the client's metrics were not actually low compared to those of Chartbeat's other clients. Early in the training, Tyler displayed on his laptop a bar graph that broke down frequent visitors to the client's site by the number of times they visited per week. The vast majority visited once: the bar for one visit appeared to be more than two-thirds bigger than the bar for two visits. The bars for three, four, and more visits dropped down nearly to zero. Still, Tyler told the clients that their number of two-time visitors was good, comparing it favorably to that of other clients: "sometimes we see visits per person per week drop off so much after one."

Tyler then pulled up another bar graph, this one illustrating the number of people who visit additional pages on the client's site (going up in increments of pages—two, three, four, and so on) after arriving at the home page. He acknowledged that the number dropped off substantially after the first page but suggested this was because the client's landing page had a lot of content on it—"people stay on your landing page." Similarly, Josh Schwartz, the Chartbeat data scientist who provided the graphs Manjoo used in his piece for *Slate*, assured Manjoo he should be "very pleased" with *Slate*'s scroll-depth figures, which were "notably good" compared to those of the average Chartbeat client. (This momentarily cheered up Manjoo, until he realized *Slate*'s superior scroll depth was probably attributable to the site's layout rather than to content that persuaded audiences to read further down its pages.)

A tone of cheerfulness and approachability was also baked into the dashboard itself. Leading up to the launch of the revamped Chartbeat dashboard, debates in meetings often revolved around the question of whether particular terms (e.g., "recirculation") were too technical or "jargony" and thus might lead clients to feel intimidated, or alienated from the dashboard. One day, as Simon was walking me through the latest prototype of the new dashboard prior to the launch, he voiced dissatisfaction with the phrasing of a "tool tip" that was programmed to appear beside an underperforming metric: "doing a lot worse than usual." Chartbeat engineers had written the tool tip, and Simon was dismayed by its blunt negativity; he took care to see that the language was softened in the final product.

In sum, Chartbeat's public-facing presentation was carefully cultivated to project an aura of almost relentless positivity and to counter the idea that metrics were cold, dry, and demoralizing. At times, the company's steadfastly cheery tone stood in stark contrast to the gallows humor favored by many journalists. After a public event at which Chartbeat staffers had spoken on a panel, an online journalist joked to me that he wondered what was in the water at the Chartbeat office because "they always seem so *happy*." In addition to taking an optimistic tone whenever possible, Chartbeat also sought to instill in the dashboard a beguiling sense of mystery.

The Reenchanted Dashboard

To Weber, quintessentially modern institutions such as capitalism, bureau-cracy, and the administrative state required "technology and calculation" to develop and rationalize their operations. Weber considered rationalization to be incompatible with enchantment: the former sought to explain worldly phe-nomena as a means to better predict and control them; essential to the latter was the belief that some phenomena are irreducibly mysterious and thus un-able to be tamed by human activity. Yet there is a paradoxical aspect to Weber's argument: the "disenchantment of the world" that results from rationalization can feel confining, nihilistic, and dehumanizing. These very feelings can, if unchecked, impede the achievement of "rational" ends—especially the end of higher profits.

It is sometimes necessary, then, for highly rationalized settings to be "reen-chanted," particularly if they must attract and retain customers. As sociologist George Ritzer writes, "continuing to attract, control, and exploit consumers" can be a challenge in rationalized environments: "Rationalization is needed to accomplish these objectives on a large scale, but the resultant disenchant-ment can have the opposite effect. It is this that leads to the necessity for reen-chantment."[15] Following cultural theorist Guy Debord, Ritzer argues that re-enchantment happens partly through the creation of spectacles that obscure and distract from the rationalized machinery of the underlying system.

At first glance, it seems unlikely that Chartbeat's tools would incorporate spectacles to produce reenchantment. After all, unlike casinos, Disneyworld, or other highly rationalized consumer experiences, Chartbeat does not primarily promise its clients fun: its dashboards are intended to be used not for recreation but for work. Furthermore, we have seen that many of the company's promotional materials emphasize Chartbeat's utility as an aid for instrumental decision making. That is, the dashboard is presented as a tool that demystifies the online news audience by rendering it calculable, manipulatable, and (in theory at least) monetizable.

Yet my fieldwork revealed that the dashboard also contained concerted efforts at reenchantment—and that reenchantment was, in fact, central to the tool's appeal. Several of Chartbeat's trademark "real-time" analytics served up a brew of mystery and existential reassurance. The concurrents count and its accompanying ever-moving dial, which were placed in the dashboard's most visually prominent spot (the upper left-hand corner), proved particularly enchanting for users. Cynthia, a *New York Times* reporter who was generally anxious about the potential effects of metrics on her own work and on the journalistic field in general, nonetheless found herself drawn in by the dashboard's concurrents count:

> When I saw Chartbeat for the first time I was like, Oh my god. I was like, it's amazing. . . . When you make something—like when I saw the analytics for [an in-depth series Cynthia reported]—it's like, wow, this is how people are consuming what I spent all this time doing. . . . Because you just send it out into the void and you don't know. I mean, you'll get emails [from readers] and whatever, but [with Chartbeat] it's like you can say, wow, 20,000 people are reading this *right now* or whatever. You know, that's *powerful.*

Even Chartbeat staffers who were intimately familiar with the inner mechanics of the technology were susceptible to the power of the concurrents count and its accompanying dial. As Aaron, a Chartbeat employee who sometimes wrote posts for the company's blog, explained:

> The whole real-time thing, like to me that's the whole thing that makes [Chartbeat] work as a product. You know, I write blog posts and I watch it. Those are the moments when you realize why it's a successful product, because I watch it, and *nobody* reads my stuff [on the blog], right? . . . If you look at it, you're like, "There are three people reading this [right now]." . . . And then somebody else comes in and you're like, "Oh, shit, there's a fourth! Who's *that* guy?!" And that's the magic.

In her in-depth ethnographic study of the world of machine gambling, anthropologist Natasha Dow Schüll explores the powerful pull that electronic gambling technologies can have—indeed, are *designed* to have—on players.

The gambling addicts profiled in Schüll's book describe falling into a trance-like state while playing on the digital machines; they become increasingly oblivious to the external world and even to their own bodily functions. Even the machines' creators could not resist falling into "the zone":

> When designing, they operate within the domain of calculative rationality—they pick a machine's colors and sounds, formulate its sophisticated mathematical algorithms, calculate its payout rates and risk probabilities, and scrutinize its performance. . . . When playing, however, calculative rationality falls away.[16]

Like Schüll's game designers, Aaron was extremely knowledgeable about the technology behind the Chartbeat dashboard and had an extensive background in data science and statistics. But when he was watching the concurrents number and dial needle rise for a blog post *he* had written, his specialized expertise and intellectual knowledge of the dashboard's inner workings did not prevent him from becoming enthralled by the tool.

Aaron's use of the term "magic" to describe the dashboard's appeal was also not unusual: the company frequently used language that was inflected with religious, spiritual, or magical connotations to describe Chartbeat and its effect on newsrooms.[17] A tool tip in the dashboard that would appear next to a high-performing story read, "There's magic happening here." On Chartbeat's website, the title of one of the company's sales associates was "Making Chart-believers"; other employees had titles like "Office Wizard" and "Website Whisperer."

This sort of mystical language leavened the otherwise rationalist tenor of many of Chartbeat's promotional materials. It sought to signal that Chartbeat wasn't "a giant, coal-and-kitten-blood-powered factory" out to ruthlessly quantify and systematize every element of journalistic work. When a tool tip said about a high-performing story, "There's magic happening here," it left room for mystery. The tip didn't attempt to explain or account for the high traffic performance; indeed, the use of the term "magic" implicitly *forestalled* attempts to discover rationally the cause of the story's success.

The reenchanted nature of the dashboard became even more apparent in instances when clients drew exceptionally high traffic to their news sites, such that they achieved what Chartbeat called the "broken dial." Chartbeat was priced so that each client site had a maximum number of concurrent visitors that it had paid Chartbeat to track. If the number of visitors on the client's site exceeded that numerical cap, the dial "broke": users would see that the dial and the number of concurrents had hit the cap, but the dashboard would not show *by how much* the cap had been exceeded. (For instance, if a client's cap was 5,000 concurrent visitors, the dashboard's dial would "break" when the site reached 4,999.) Molly, a business-side Chartbeat staffer, explained to me that the broken dial occasionally resulted in an upsell, as clients who repeatedly hit their cap could pay to raise it. However, even when the broken dial didn't directly lead to greater revenue for Chartbeat, it had a valuable emotional impact on clients. When the concurrents cap was exceeded, Aaron explained, "the dial looks incorrect. . . . The product is broken, but in a fun way. If you didn't have that sort of excitement, it wouldn't work."

Midway through my fieldwork at Chartbeat, I listened in on a product testing session that made clear just how exhilarating the broken dial could be and how central it was to Chartbeat's appeal. In the session, which was conducted over the phone, a pair of Chartbeat staffers demonstrated the new dashboard to a client using a screen-share and solicited her feedback on the design and functionality. The client, who was the editor of a midsize website focused on environmental news, said that her company had briefly considered discontinuing its account with Chartbeat in favor of a rival analytics service but within a few days had "crawled [their] way back" to Chartbeat. Daniel, one of the development-side employees facilitating the conversation, asked, "What is it, do you think, that was the most compelling aspect of Chartbeat?" The client answered:

> First of all, if you're into traffic as most sites are, seeing that big number [she then recited the number of concurrents on her site at that moment—750], that's a really good number. And we're capped at 2,000 concurrent users, so we always think—if we're at 1,999—we always *imagine* we're at 2,450 or 5,150, but we probably [just] can't see it 'cause we're capped. So we always have that kind of illusion, like that optimism going on.[18]

For this client, the broken dial did exactly the opposite of what we might expect a tool of rationalization to do: rather than providing technical information about her audience, it allowed her and her team to imagine an audience size that was more than twice the size of their cap, regardless of whether or not the imagined number had any basis in reality. In this instance, Chartbeat's role as a facilitator of (potentially deluded) optimism had taken precedence over its self-described mission to provide clients with an unflinchingly accurate picture of their traffic. Importantly, this was not an oversight on the company's part but a strategic choice that, in this case, had prevented the client from discontinuing

FIG. 3.1. Chartbeat's "Go for broke" promotional T-shirt, which
celebrated the broken dial.

their subscription. The broken dial eventually became a part of Chartbeat's
marketing strategy, as the promotional T-shirt in Figure 3.1 attests.

Just as negative feelings about low traffic could translate into negative feelings about Chartbeat, the thrill of breaking the dial could endear Chartbeat
to users. As Daniel put it:

> When [a client] does hit a home run, and you see the Chartbeat dial go up,
> and you see the red line go up, then that euphoria—Chartbeat gets to be
> part of that experience. So as long as we're in the room, like high-fiving you,
> then we get a lot of positive association with that moment.

Daniel's use of the term "home run" is significant because it taps into what
made the broken dial such a powerful facilitator of euphoria. Legal scholar
Arthur Leff's analysis of the game-like elements of the legal system in the
United States (or the "Usa tribe," as Leff winkingly referred to it) is instructive
here. In a passage worth quoting at length, Leff noted that in "Usa" games,

> the rules are formulated such that a certain amount of something is defined
> within the game as the "right" amount. More is not better, nor (most of the
> time) is it worse; it is, strictly speaking, in terms of the game, *irrelevant*. This
> aspect of Usa ludic rules is perhaps clearest when one considers games that
> define achievement against spatial constraints. For example, the home run

in baseball is a ball hit into the stands, on the fly, in fair territory (all as defined). For purposes of the game it makes not a whit of difference how close to the stands a fly ball is hit so long as it falls short, nor how far a home run is hit so long as it clears the fence. In football, there are no additional points for a football kicked far over the crossbar, nor is there more of a victory in chess for blocking a King's move with two threatening pieces for each possible square. In Usa games, enough is enough.[19]

As the preceding pages have illustrated, the Chartbeat dashboard provides precious few moments akin to what Leff describes here. Recall, for instance, Alison's feelings of worry and desperation during a fallow traffic period, or Eddie's comment that Chartbeat was "relentless." The broken dial was a welcome—if fleeting—respite from this feeling of relentlessness because it exited the realm of quantification altogether. In doing so, it provided users with a moment, exceptionally rare in the traffic game, when "more was not better." Once a journalist's story broke the dial, it became unnecessary to know, nor did the product *allow* her to know, by how much she broke it. In the moment the dial breaks, as when a baseball flies over the outfield wall or a football clears the goal posts, "enough is enough."

In this respect, the broken dial bears a striking resemblance to two expressions that have become popular in the social media age: to "win the internet" and to "break the internet." Both expressions are loosely defined as publishing something—whether an article, a tweet, a photograph, or some other type of content—that is both widely shared on social networks and picked up by professional news outlets (e.g., the famous dress, first written about by *BuzzFeed*, that appeared to be different colors to different people). As with the broken dial, a piece of content must garner exceptionally high metrics to be thought to have "broken" or "won" the internet in the first place. But once something is categorized as having broken the internet, the particularities of the metrics themselves become secondary, even irrelevant. What started as a difference in quantity becomes a difference in kind. As such, to break the dial—or, relatedly, the internet—feels powerfully thrilling and even, as a *New York Times* staffer put it (Fig. 3.2), beautiful.

Notably, Chartbeat Publishing for Ad Sales, Chartbeat's (now defunct) dashboard that was specifically designed for advertising-side employees of news organizations, did not have a breakable dial. One Chartbeat staffer who had worked with both journalists and advertising-side users told me that the latter group did not expect—nor even seem to desire—the same kind of emotional stimulation from the dashboard that reporters and editors did. Rather,

Tyson Evans ✔
@tysone

The beauty of breaking Chartbeat's
odometer on a big news day.

10:26 AM • June 26, 2015

💬   ↻ 8   ♡ 30   ↥

FIG. 3.2. A member of the *New York Times* strategy team (and a former editor) tweeted a screenshot of the broken dial the day the U.S. Supreme Court issued its major marriage equality ruling.

they simply wanted clear, reliable figures that they could incorporate into a sales pitch or share with advertisers to demonstrate the outcomes of a campaign. As such, Chartbeat Publishing for Ad Sales was far more in line with how we typically envision a rationalist measurement tool.

The contrast prompts a question: Why were journalists, as a group, so drawn to the "magical" aspects of the Chartbeat Publishing dashboard? As my fieldwork progressed, I came to see powerful elective affinities between the re-enchanted components of the dashboard and the very concept of news judgment. As journalism studies scholars have noted, news judgment is often perceived (even, or perhaps especially, by those who possess it) as mysterious and fundamentally unable to be rationalized. As Stuart Hall put it, "'News values' are one of the most opaque structures of meaning in modern society. All 'true journalists' are supposed to possess it: few can or are willing to identify and define it. . . . We appear to be dealing, then, with a 'deep structure' whose function as a selective device is un-transparent even to those who professionally most know how to operate it."[20] In my interview with Amy, an experienced *New York Times* reporter, she struggled to articulate exactly what her news judgment consists of:

> CP: What is journalistic value to you? How do you sort of think about that concept in your own work, and making determinations about what kind of stories you want to pursue and things like that?
>
> AMY: That's a very good question and I don't think I have an answer that I can stand behind. Because it's complicated for me to—it deserves a better answer than whatever I could say off the top of my head. But yeah, I don't know how to answer that. I think I would need about a month to come up with a good answer.

When journalists *do* venture a description of news judgment, they often portray it as something that is not cerebral or rational but rather embodied, experiential, and visceral. When I asked Randall, an editor at the *New York Times*, how he made determinations about which events were newsworthy, he responded: "Well, I mean I've been doing—I grew up with the Associated Press, that's where I started my career, so I kind of know just from brutal experience what has the smell of an important story." In her analysis of the "journalistic gut feeling," Ida Schultz spoke to a Danish editor who explained that the criteria for selecting stories are

> somehow part of your spinal cord, part of how you assess and form an opinion about news stories. But it's not as if it's a checklist you pull out, asking yourself, "Okay, how many criteria does this story apply to?" No. . . . For me, it has something to do with feeling.[21]

Not only does this editor portray news judgment as visceral and residing within his body, but also he explicitly sets it *against* the rational and standardizable process of systematically crossing items off a checklist. As sociologist Gaye Tuchman put it in her examination of the ritualistic elements of news production: "It would appear that news judgment is the sacred knowledge, the secret ability of the newsman which differentiates him from other people."[22]

Thus, for Chartbeat's dashboard to display the broken dial or say about a highly trafficked article that "There's magic happening here" not only incorporated an element of enchantment into a tool that is typically associated with precisely the opposite. These reenchanted elements also served as a way to demonstrate deference to the sacred, unexplainable quality of journalistic judgment, as this is the implied source of "magic" of which the numbers are a mere reflection. As the next section will illustrate, this was but one way that Chartbeat enacted a performance of deference to journalists' "sacred" judgment and their professional authority.

Performing Deference to "News Judgment"

Although "news judgment" is mysterious and difficult to pin down, it is nonetheless central to journalists' professional identity. This is especially true because, as we saw in chapter 1, journalism lacks several of the other classic markers of a profession, such as a licensing requirement or a system of abstract knowledge.[23] Given the profession's fuzzy boundaries and atypical qualities, journalists are particularly vulnerable to—and anxious about—being displaced and delegitimized by new technologies. In the internet's earlier days, these anxieties manifested as an ongoing debate about whether bloggers should "count" as journalists or not.[24] More recently, metrics have come to be regarded as potential threats to journalists' professional judgment and authority, insofar as they offer alternative (and often cheaper) means to determine a subject's newsworthiness and produce news.[25]

This presented third-party analytics companies like Chartbeat with a dilemma that is by now familiar to us. If journalists rejected Chartbeat as an existential threat to editorial judgment, that could be, in turn, an existential threat to Chartbeat, whose business model depends on retaining long-term clients. Therefore, Chartbeat staffers enacted a *performance of deference* to journalists' sense of editorial judgment. During the meeting I attended with Tyler, he showed the clients a feature of the dashboard that displayed a list of "top referrers": websites that referred the highest numbers of visitors to the client's site. After suggesting the journalists consult this list, Tyler hastened to add, "you already know it intrinsically, but the data confirms it." Statements like these were notable for the extent that they contradicted the typical narrative of analytics—that is, that the value of metrics resides in their ability to show established experts things they *wouldn't* otherwise know. By contrast, here Tyler cast Chartbeat as a corroborator of existing journalistic knowledge, rather than as a source of enlightenment.

The dashboard itself was also designed to perform deference to users' interpretive abilities and decision-making skills. During the development of the revamped dashboard, it was decided that the tool would not include algorithmically derived recommendations about which stories to cover, where to place them on home pages, and when to publish them—even though the incorporation of such features might have helped client sites boost their traffic.[26] When asked about Chartbeat's rationale for omitting algorithmic recommendations, Daniel, a development-side staffer who helped design the new version of the dashboard, explained:

> We had a competitor who made a tool that made suggestions to editors. . . . Like, "Put this here, promote this story." And editors were like, "I'm not using this damn thing. . . . You're telling me to put stuff in the lead spot I would never put there." So we said, "Listen, we're not taking away your job; we're enhancing your ability to make those decisions."

In a similar vein, Rudy, a business-side staffer at Chartbeat, invoked his own youth as a way of performing deference to clients' judgment:

> It's not like we're automatically putting that Miley Cyrus [story] at the top [of your home page]. We'll tell you, "it's generating . . . engagement and . . .

concurrent visitors." But does that mean you want to do it? Yeah, maybe, but that's up to you . . . I'm not going to tell you how to do [your job]. I'm . . . twenty-five [years old], what do I know about how to publish a two-hundred-year-old paper?

These quotes illustrate that performing deference to editorial judgment became a way for Chartbeat to distinguish itself from competitors that *did* provide algorithmic recommendations to news organizations about story placement and assignment. An anecdote about a Chartbeat competitor that exemplified this dynamic was invoked so frequently in internal meetings and interviews that I began to consider it part of the company folklore. At the *Guardian's* Changing Media Summit in 2013, the digital editor of the British tabloid *The Sun* appeared on a panel with Dennis Mortensen, founder and CEO of Visual Revenue, an analytics company that, unlike Chartbeat, provided algorithmic recommendations to news organizations about story placement and assignment. In speaking about his experiences using the product, the *Sun* editor said:

> It's a really valuable tool, but the one thing I've always said to Dennis . . . is that you kind of have to ignore it sometimes. Great example: last week, [the] new pope [was elected, and] Visual Revenue is telling us, screaming at us, "Nobody is interested in this story! They're far more interested in the Katy Perry story. Put that above the pope. Put the pope way down at the bottom of your home page. Nobody really wants to read it on your website." And of course, at that point—and there's lots of examples of that every day of the week— the human being has to intervene and say, "Okay, they may be more interested in Katy Perry in a bikini today. However, the pope is a far more important story."[27]

That even an editor at a tabloid like the *Sun* so frequently found Visual Revenue's recommendations inappropriate is indicative of the precarious relationship that journalists of all stripes can have with analytics companies. At Chartbeat, "Katy Perry versus the pope" (the shorthand with which Chartbeat staffers referred to this incident in internal conversations) became a powerful symbol. This was in part because, as Molly put it, "we don't feel that's how data should be used." But the story also served as a cautionary tale of the feelings of alienation or irritation that could result in users when an analytics company was seen as clumsily and arrogantly overstepping its mandate.

These examples illustrate that Chartbeat's success depended on the company's ability to strike a delicate balance: Chartbeat needed to show that its metrics had something to contribute to editorial decision making, *without* making journalists feel that their expertise was undermined and their professional status under threat. Reaching this equilibrium was especially fraught because of the range of news organizations that subscribed to Chartbeat's services: while larger publications may have bristled at the idea of editorial recommendations, some smaller ones ("on the lower end of the market," as Eli, a business-side staffer, put it) wanted explicit advice. Eli acknowledged that this was "a tension," which Chartbeat had coped with by "surfacing opportunities" for clients rather than "making recommendations." Mark, another business-side staffer, was more blunt in his analysis. In our interview, he explained that Chartbeat's color-coded "Heads Up Display" (HUD) features, which overlaid a client's home page with balloon-shaped "pins" showing whether a story's traffic is high (green), low (red), or average (yellow) compared to other stories that have occupied the same spot in the past, were effectively recommendations without announcing themselves as such. "We're never going to say, 'Move this [story] to there,'" Mark explained. "But we're going to say, 'Hey . . . this [story] is doing really well there so, you know, use your own judgment.'" Mark's comment illustrates the way in which some Chartbeat staffers conceptualized their deference to clients' editorial judgment as explicitly performative.

Professing Allegiance to Journalism's Norms and Values

In addition to performing deference to editorial judgment, Chartbeat professed allegiance to journalistic norms and values. Studies have shown that new metrics must be seen not only as practically useful but also as *morally legitimate* if they are to become taken for granted in media industries.[28] The surest way for new measurement methods to achieve moral legitimacy is to ground themselves within the field's already-established norms and ethical guidelines. In journalism's case, Daniel Hallin and Paolo Mancini have argued that journalistic professionalism in the West is defined by three primary norms: autonomy, a public service orientation, and a low degree of instrumentalization by state and business actors.[29] This list, though not comprehensive, provides a solid framework with which to understand the ethics policies at many U.S. news organizations (e.g., that there must be a "wall" separating the editorial side of a publication from the business side, that journalists should not accept large gifts from sources, that sources' claims should be corroborated independently whenever possible, and so on).

If Chartbeat was going to be perceived as morally legitimate by would-be users, communicating alignment with journalism's fundamental norms was crucial. Yet it was also a struggle, because metrics were often seen as incentivizing the production of vapid, "empty-calorie" content that, while popular, might in fact do the public a *dis*service.[30] Chartbeat sought to surmount this challenge and build the dashboard's moral legitimacy in two ways.

First, Chartbeat took great pains to argue that there was in fact no tension between the stories that journalists consider most important and those that are popular with audiences—*provided that one's analytics tool measures the right things*. While rival newsroom analytics tools displayed metrics such as pageviews and unique visitors, Chartbeat deliberately omitted these metrics from its dashboards. This was in part because, as chapter 5 will discuss in greater detail, such metrics were too strongly associated with the profane world of online advertising. Instead of pageviews and uniques, Chartbeat centered its dashboard around what the company called "engagement metrics"—analytics that it claimed were designed to reward not just a quick "hit" or click that could be monetized by advertisers but rather the audience's deeper, more substantive interaction with a story.[31] These included engaged time, an average measure of how long visitors spend engaged with a site's content; recirculation, the percentage of people who visited at least one additional page on a site after the one at which they arrive; and visitor frequency, which divided readers into three categories—new, returning, and loyal—based on how often they visited a site.

Chartbeat claimed that, in contrast to metrics likes uniques and pageviews that incentivized the production of superficial clickbait, its engagement metrics rewarded the kind of meaty, meaningful stories that resulted from in-depth reporting. In an internal meeting about how to "message" the new dashboard in conversations with current and prospective clients, Pete, a high-ranking business-side staffer who interacted frequently with Chartbeat's biggest clients, explained how staffers should frame the dashboard's focus on engagement metrics: "When you [the news organization] make that the center of what you're going for—can I make this person come back [to my site]?—all your calculations change, and they change in a way that aligns wonderfully with good journalism." This kind of messaging highlights Chartbeat's attempts to distance itself from the broader news analytics industry (in which it was in fact a leader) and instead assert its allegiance to the editorial values and professional self-conceptions of its intended users.[32]

Chartbeat's efforts to reinforce this positioning are continual and ongoing. Every year the company publishes a list of the "100 most engaging stories," which it defines as the stories across its network of client sites that audiences spent the most cumulative minutes looking at. The company blog post introducing the 2016 list invited readers to "see the stories that defined the breadth, the depth, and the power of journalism in 2016" and emphasized the popularity of politics coverage, breaking news, and stories about "justice and rights," including "major investigative pieces rooted in undercover work." While politics and breaking news are indeed heavily represented on the list (perhaps unsurprising given the presidential election of that year), Chartbeat's write-up did not mention other stories that ranked highly: an alligator attack at Disney World, a list of ten Pokemon Go tips, and a woman "crashing" her own funeral to the surprise of her husband, who had paid to have her killed.[33] That these types of more sensationalist stories show up on most-popular lists even when Engaged Time is the metric (as opposed to non–"engagement metrics" like pageviews) suggests there may an insurmountable gap between stories that are rewarded by metrics and stories considered most prestigious by journalists.[34] That Chartbeat omitted any mention of them in the company's blog post about the list is illustrative of the kind of image the company sought to present.

As the most-engaging stories list makes clear, Chartbeat was not always able to convincingly insist on a seamless alignment between "popular" and "good" stories. The company also pursued a second discursive strategy to bolster the moral legitimacy of its dashboard. Even though it was at times unavoidably obvious that analytics were designed to help news organizations make more money, Chartbeat staffers framed these efforts not as pursuing profit for profit's (or shareholders') sake but as a *subsidy* for the kind of reporting that journalists considered serious and important.[35] That is, in instances when Chartbeat could not persuasively claim that its metrics directly supported the production of serious journalism, the company portrayed itself as indirectly supporting it, by helping to create the material conditions of possibility for such work to continue. In a 2015 interview with the *Columbia Journalism Review*, Chartbeat's then-CEO Tony Haile said that the company's "singular purpose" was to ensure that "twenty years from now, the journalist that wants to investigate the corrupt politician actually has the means to do so. As in: There is enough money to invest in that person to do that job."[36] Haile's remark rests on the premise that news organizations would inevitably use the higher revenue that resulted from increased web traffic to augment their "watchdog" reporting capabilities—a dubious assumption, considering that as of 2015, newsrooms at daily newspapers were half the size they were in 1990, even as some of their financial fortunes had improved.[37] Yet Haile's comment is notable for how it draws a discursive link between the use of analytics and the kind of journalistic practice that carries the greatest prestige in the field. By positioning metrics as a subsidy for high-quality journalism, Haile establishes Chartbeat as not merely unthreatening to editorial values but indispensable to their very survival.

Chartbeat also explicitly distanced itself from business considerations. In the pre-digital age, journalists distrusted audience research in large part because it was "under the auspices of nonjournalists"—specifically, the business departments of news organizations.[38] This association between analytics and business persisted into the early era of digital newsroom analytics, especially because the first newsroom analytics providers, such as Google Analytics, had been originally designed for the domains of e-commerce or online advertising. Chartbeat sought to overcome the prevailing perception of analytics as business-focused by discursively emphasizing the concerns of the newsroom.

For example, Chartbeat named its spinoff advertising-focused analytics tool Chartbeat Publishing for Ad Sales in an attempt to reassure journalists that a tool initially developed for *editorial* use was being repurposed for *business* use, as opposed to the more typical reverse scenario. Molly emphasized this point at the "competition lunch" meeting where employees discussed Chartbeat's various rivals. She explained to her assembled colleagues how to position Chartbeat rhetorically against a small competitor that was gaining ground:

> What makes us different is that because we come at it from both sides, we have this power of understanding how to bridge that gap [between editorial and advertising]. We don't do something that cuts legs off of editors and says, "Screw you guys, you don't have any money, we're going after ads." [Instead, we say,] "Everything we do on the ad side is to support great work you're doing on the editorial side."

Of course, the connection between analytics, audience size, and revenue was not lost on journalists, nor did Chartbeat staffers expect it to be. But the lengths to which the company went to play down and reframe the association between metrics and money is further illustration of Chartbeat's performance of affective labor to appeal to journalists' professional self-conceptions— particularly, in this case, a notion of journalistic autonomy that rests on journalists' ability to do "serious" work with the smallest possible degree of direct interference from state or business actors. In sum, Chartbeat sought to imbue metrics with meaning by demonstrating alignment with journalists' familiar normative frameworks.

Conclusion

Taken together, the two chapters that comprise part 1 of this book have illustrated something that often gets lost in professional and scholarly debates over whether metrics are good or bad for journalism: analytics tools are not exogenous forces that descend, fully formed, upon newsrooms and produce effects on journalists' labor process and values. Instead, we have seen how journalists and analytics tools engage in the "mutual shaping" of each other.[39] Journalists' long-standing skepticism of and anxiety about analytics prompted Chartbeat to design a habit-forming user interface that could overcome journalistic hesitance. These design decisions resulted in the "traffic game" described in chapter 2, which in turn got journalists fixated on analytics and extracted increased productivity from them, without being perceived as managerial coercion.

However, chapter 3 has shown that some of the very features that made the traffic game habit-forming (e.g., its endlessness) could also make it feel demoralizing and alienating to journalists—raising anew the prospect of a backlash among rank-and-file users and a risk to Chartbeat's business model. Chartbeat thus pursued additional design and discursive strategies to ward off these feelings, such as the eschewal of algorithmic recommendations and the incorporation of the broken dial.

Moving beyond the case of journalism, this back-and-forth between Chartbeat and its journalist-users lends itself to two takeaways about how the rationalization of knowledge work unfolds. First, because knowledge workers have a relatively high degree of cultural capital and an expectation of professional or aesthetic autonomy, successful tools of labor discipline in knowledge-work fields are likely to be designed (and redesigned) with the aim of achieving worker consent *without* being perceived as a form of managerial coercion.

Second, gaining knowledge workers' consent to the rationalization of their labor process involves building some decidedly nonrational elements into analytics tools. Chartbeat was able to establish itself as an effective engine of labor rationalization in news organizations because it (1) incorporated unrationalized moments of mystery, excitement, and even enchantment into its tool; (2) performed deference to journalists' editorial judgment; and (3) professed allegiance to the profession's fundamental norms and values. We might expect to see similar strategies deployed by analytics companies designing tools for other knowledge-work fields.

Part 1 has shown how and why journalists become committed users of analytics tools and what this means for the way they carry out and relate to their work. Yet while analytics are habit-forming, they can also be confusing: journalists are continually negotiating between multiple mandates, and, as we have seen, Chartbeat refrained from providing too much in the way of interpretation and directives as a way of performing deference to journalist-users. The result is that even as journalists compulsively consulted metrics, the meaning of the data was often ambiguous or even entirely opaque. It is to this subject— how journalists make sense of what analytics tools are telling them and act on these interpretations—that part 2 will now turn.

PART II
Making Sense of Metrics

4

The Interpretive Ambiguity of Metrics

If one story gets 425,000 hits and another one gets 372,000, is that meaningful, that difference? Where does it become important and where doesn't it?

— SAM, *NEW YORK TIMES* REPORTER

Anyone that tells you that they've uncovered the secret to virality is probably a bullshitter.

— ANDREA, GAWKER MEDIA WRITER

IN 2004, journalist Michael Lewis published *Moneyball*, a bestselling book about how baseball general manager Billy Beane was able to turn around the flailing and cash-poor Oakland Athletics with a clever use of statistics. To do so, Beane had to ignore the conventional wisdom of traditional scouts, who chose players based on intuitive—and sometimes downright bizarre—assessments of ability (e.g., a player with an "ugly girlfriend" lacks confidence and therefore shouldn't be drafted). Beane enlisted the help of a Harvard-trained statistician named Paul DePodesta to draft and trade players using an analytics-driven approach called sabermetrics. Among DePodesta's data-generated insights: batters who regularly draw walks may be boring to watch, but they are a highly valuable asset because they manage to get on base; attempting to steal a base—though exciting for players and fans—is almost never worth the risk, statistically speaking. Relying on numbers rather than gut instinct to gauge potential, the story goes, Beane and DePodesta built a roster with players who had been systematically overlooked by scouts and were thus inexpensive. They also avoided wasting the A's meager payroll budget on players who were superficially appealing but overrated. The result was a 2002 season record that surpassed those of far wealthier teams and included a record-breaking 20-game winning streak.

With its cast of beleaguered-underdogs-turned-triumphant-visionaries, *Moneyball* makes for a compelling story. But just as striking as the events themselves is what a powerful and widespread cultural narrative *Moneyball* has become (especially in the years since Lewis's book was adapted into a hit movie in 2011). *Moneyball* turned out to be a tale perfectly suited to the dawning of the so-called "Big Data" era. In the years since its publication, *Moneyball* has taken on the status of legend, allegory, and how-to guide in contexts far beyond baseball. In one widely quoted passage, John Henry, a billionaire investment manager and major-league team owner, explains the parallels he sees between professional baseball and the financial markets in which he had built his career and fortune: "People in both fields operate with beliefs and biases. To the extent you can eliminate both and replace them with data, you gain a clear advantage."[1]

Henry's quote exemplifies what we might call the "Moneyball mindset." While the Moneyball mindset's applications and manifestations vary somewhat, it is a way of thinking that is generally comprised of four core tenets: (1) data is unencumbered by human "beliefs and biases"; (2) data is superior to intuitive and experiential forms of knowledge; (3) data and intuitive forms of knowledge are usually in tension with one another; and (4) data, if used wisely, provides strategic advantages that can overcome an organization's deficits and challenges.

The reach of the Moneyball mindset is vast. Cursory Google searches unearth pages of popular press articles gushing about the potential of Moneyball-style thinking for transforming political campaigning, book publishing, medicine, urban planning, and so on. Scholarly and popular books evangelizing the promise of "Big Data" have argued that the Moneyball mindset can be applied universally.[2]

It was, then, perhaps inevitable that the Moneyball mindset would be applied to the journalism field, especially as metrics became more granular and accessible.[3] The parallels were clear enough: it was easy to paint anti-metrics diehards, who claimed that they had an ineffable sense of "news judgment" that allowed them to divine what would resonate with readers better than data ever could, as the newsroom equivalent of the out-of-touch baseball scouts who tried to stop Beane from implementing his revolutionary approach. To publishers facing intensifying revenue pressure, there was also powerful appeal in the notion that metrics would allow news organizations to tap into hidden pockets of value that would enable them to stay afloat—or even thrive, as the A's had under Beane's leadership.[4] If data could help the Oakland A's pull off a dramatic and unexpected winning streak, why couldn't it help a news website struggling to bring in readers and revenue?

But, as this chapter will illustrate, applying the Moneyball mindset to the actual *work* of journalism presents particular challenges. This is not only because, as previous chapters have shown, journalists were wary of analytics as a potential force of displacement and usurpation. It is also due to the fact that the news industry differs in significant ways from professional baseball. A baseball team has a single, definable goal: to maximize wins. Furthermore, it is possible to know definitively if a team is making progress toward achieving that goal by looking at its record compared to those of other teams. Finally and perhaps most significant, all participants in the field agree unanimously about whether the goal has or has not been attained. Players and coaches of rival teams may disagree about whether an umpire made the correct decision to call someone safe at home plate, but no one disputes that the team with more runs at the end of nine innings is the winner. Not coincidentally, other fields that have become high-profile examples of the Moneyball mindset at work, such as political campaigning and retail, share aspects of these characteristics.

By contrast, journalism does not possess these traits. Unlike baseball teams, commercial news organizations in democratic societies have multiple goals that are often in tension and difficult, if not impossible, to commensurate. In the introduction, I argued that just as artists must contend with the "art-commerce relation," journalists continually navigate the "democracy-commerce relation"—that is, the long-standing tension between journalism's civic and commercial aims.[5] As an "axis point in the political struggle" between democracy and commerce, it's no surprise that journalists are often embroiled in heated debates about what—and whom—journalism is for.[6] In this chapter, I show how journalism's conflicting mandates, coupled with Chartbeat's reticence to offer rationalized explanations for traffic patterns or make editorial recommendations, complicated the process of interpreting traffic metrics.

In particular, I highlight three types of interpretive ambiguity that accompany news analytics. First, there is *meaning uncertainty*, which is a simple and self-explanatory term: journalists did not know what metrics meant and were unsure how to make sense of them. Part of this meaning uncertainty stemmed from debates about what metrics broadly symbolized: as Angèle Christin has shown, journalists are conflicted about whether metrics represent market pressures or "the mood and opinions of a broad, civic, and unitary algorithmic public."[7] In addition to metrics' contested symbolic significance, the process of interpreting metrics for individual stories was also beset by commensuration problems. It was intuitively obvious to most journalists I interviewed that different stories, sections, writers, or publications were qualitatively distinct from each other. Yet it was unclear to them *how* those differences should be best expressed or accounted for numerically.

The second type of interpretive ambiguity is *causal uncertainty*. When a piece disappointed or exceeded traffic expectations, journalists were often unsure why it had done so. This causal uncertainty, in turn, led to a third type of interpretive ambiguity, which I call *action uncertainty*. Since it was often unclear why one article had attracted high traffic while another had not, journalists were often flummoxed about how, if at all, to adjust their editorial practices.

Because journalism does not have a sole outcome that can be easily prioritized and optimized for, interpretive labor is required to make sense of analytics. This chapter will show that journalists relied on a range of strategies and heuristics to assign meaning to ambiguous metrics. These interpretive strategies are consequential because of the influence that metrics now wield in many contemporary news organizations, despite the fact that their meaning is so often unclear. In other words, the interpretive ambiguity of news metrics was not merely frustrating for journalists—it also had direct implications for their working conditions. An article whose traffic is interpreted as disappointing will be placed and promoted differently than an article that is seen as a traffic hit;[8] a journalist who is seen as drawing reliably high traffic might have a different career trajectory (e.g., in terms of pay, promotion, and job security) than one who is seen as struggling to attract a sufficient audience. Given these high stakes, the question of who gets to make sense of metrics—and have their interpretations be considered authoritative in a news organization—is hotly contested. Subsequent chapters will show that struggles over who performs interpretive labor to assign meaning to metrics, how, and with what consequences are central to understanding the role of metrics in contemporary journalistic work.

Negotiating Journalism's Multiple Mandates

In the United States and other democratic countries where the press is highly commercialized, there is a conflict between most journalists' status as employees of (or freelancers for) corporate, profit-seeking entities and their status as autonomous professionals seeking to perform a vital civic mission.[9] Critical journalism scholars have long been concerned with this conflict; some have argued that mainstream journalists are essentially stenographers for the rich and powerful, or that much of journalism exists so there will be something to run advertising against.[10] These concerns have only intensified in recent years, as advertising revenue has plummeted and the traditional "wall" between the business and editorial departments of news organizations (already of dubious structural integrity) has been increasingly destabilized by alternative revenue-generation strategies.[11]

Pronounced and urgent as it may be in the present moment, the tension between boosting profits and serving a democratic public is not the only way in which journalism's aims are multiple and complex. One need look no further than the fourteen categories for Pulitzer Prizes to see that journalistic excellence, as defined by those internal to the field, can itself take many forms.[12] Pulitzers are awarded for "distinguished examples" of investigative reporting, breaking news reporting, explanatory reporting, public service reporting, feature writing, commentary, and several other types of journalism. Crucially, while stories are ranked within each of these categories based on judges' assessments of their relative excellence, the categories *themselves* are not ranked against or even compared to one another. For instance, explanatory reporting is not considered better or more important than breaking news reporting; the Pulitzer Prize committee treats them as qualitatively distinct and deserving of equal recognition.

In addition to the multiplicity of goals that exists at the field level, individual news organizations differ from each other in terms of their structure, intended audience, revenue model, and mission. The *Washington Post*, *People* magazine, and *Adweek* are all considered media organizations that employ journalists, but they arguably have far less in common than do, say, the Oakland A's and the New York Yankees. Given the heterogeneity of the journalism field and its aims, it is not hard to see why metrics—which by definition evaluate stories, people, and organizations according to a set of uniform numerical standards—would pose particular interpretive challenges. The following sections will examine these in greater depth.

Meaning Uncertainty

The first type of interpretive ambiguity was uncertainty about how to interpret metrics at a basic level. As discussed in chapters 2 and 3, Chartbeat went to great lengths to make the analytics tools that journalists found habit-forming and nonthreatening. An important part of these efforts was an attempt to make the tools easy to understand, even for the relatively numbers-phobic. Even a metrics novice could look at the Chartbeat dashboard and see a clear visual representation of whether, for instance, concurrent visitors were increasing or decreasing.

Still, it is one thing to see a number rising or falling and quite another to understand what that information means. Parker, a long-time *New York Times* staffer who worked in newsroom operations and had extensive access to and experience with analytics, told me that the most common question reporters asked him upon seeing metrics for a particular story was, "Is this good?" Betsy, a *Times* editor who was known around the newsroom for her digital savvy, lamented the fact that most journalists at the paper lacked a "baseline" of average performance for a story: "They don't know if 100,000 pageviews is good or bad." Felix, a writer at Gawker, made a similar point: "We're looking at these numbers all the time, but thinking about them completely irrationally." When I asked him to elaborate, Felix responded, "Like, looking at Chartbeat, what the fuck does that *mean*?"

Meaning uncertainty often stemmed from the substantial qualitative differences between articles. Though most anything published on a Gawker site was considered a "post" (or, at the *Times*, a "story") and its traffic ranked against others thus categorized, particular posts and stories differed from each other in ways that staffers saw as substantial and important to account for. Articles tackled vastly different types of subject matter, were authored by different writers, were published on different days of the week and at different times of day, and received different placement on the home page (and, in the case of the *Times*, in the print edition and the mobile app) and different levels of visibility via promotional actions like mobile push alerts and social media posts. Further complicating matters, each story, once published, entered into a broader information environment that was ever-changing, unique, and largely outside the newsroom's control. Another news organization might publish a high-profile scoop that monopolized the spotlight; Facebook might suddenly change its algorithm to disfavor a particular type of news content or publication; an unanticipated world event might occur and require wall-to-wall coverage. (Linda, a *Times* editor, told me ruefully about a devastating exposé on the tilapia industry that had the misfortune of being published the same day as the raid that killed Osama bin Laden.)

This complex mix of internal and external factors presented obstacles for quantitatively evaluating news stories against each other in a way that would be considered fair and legitimate. Social scientists who study quantification argue that the more dissimilar two entities are—or rather, the more dissimilar they are perceived to be by actors on the ground—the more fraught the process of commensuration. Sociologists Wendy Espeland and Michael Sauder write that "commensuration is most jarring and seems less like measurement and more like artifice when it encompasses things that do not already seem alike."[13] Indeed, some journalists reported experiencing frustration and perplexity when they tried to interpret metrics-driven rankings of stories that seemed qualitatively dissimilar. As Ben, interactive news editor at the *Times*, put it: "It's almost like, you rarely have an apples-to-apples comparison."

At both the *Times* and Gawker, journalists attempted to compensate for the lack of an apples-to-apples comparison by adjusting their traffic expectations for stories in a way that took some of these mitigating factors into account. Yet doing so proved difficult in practice. It was intuitively obvious to many journalists I interviewed that, say, a 3,000-word feature story about the civil war in Syria published on a Friday afternoon would have fewer views than a recap of the Superbowl Halftime Show published the morning after the game. But *how many fewer*? How should the stark qualitative differences between these two stories—to say nothing of various contextual factors—be accounted for numerically? As Ben explained, "We don't have a great sense of context for whether something is more or less than we would expect. When you're looking at a raw number, it's hard to know how that fits into what you would expect." Chartbeat was not especially helpful at providing the sense of context that Ben was hoping for. With its ever-shifting list of "top stories" displayed prominently at the center of the dashboard, Chartbeat announced itself as fundamentally a form of commensuration. And, as Wendy Espeland and Michael Sauder put it, commensuration is "notable for how rigorously it simplifies information and for how thoroughly it *decontextualizes* knowledge."[14]

In the absence of a ready-made interpretive schema with which to understand analytics, staffers relied on quantitative heuristics that were intuitively familiar. James Robinson, the erstwhile director of newsroom analytics at the *Times*, described reporters' search for an intuitive framework with which to understand metrics:

They often don't know how to interpret [traffic numbers]. . . . They search for things to compare that number to . . . Our numbers line up so it's almost like a salary scale. So you can say, "Your story got 20,000 visits" and they're like "Oh, 20,000, I couldn't live on 20,000 a year." But then [if] you say, like,

150,000, they're like, "Oh, that's pretty comfortable, that's good." And if you say a million visits, it's like, "Oh, I'm a millionaire!"[15]

Sports analogies were also common—perhaps unsurprisingly, given the game-like user experience of analytics dashboards. Betsy used baseball metaphors to help reporters understand metrics, referring to stories' traffic performance as a "solid single," a double, a grand slam—and, for exceptional successes, winning the World Series "because we only have one of those a year."

Journalists' tendency to draw on familiar quantitative heuristics to interpret metrics aligns with research showing that people make sense of new or unfamiliar technologies by developing "shared cognitive structures" or "frames." "To interact with technology, people have to make sense of it," write organizational scholars Wanda J. Orlikowski and Debra C. Gash. "And in this sense-making process, they develop particular assumptions, expectations, and knowledge of the technology, which then serve to shape subsequent actions toward it."[16] Often, such frames take the form of analogies, especially when the operational mechanisms that make a technology work are invisible or otherwise inscrutable to the user. For instance, an interview-based study found that people unfamiliar with the inner workings of Radio Frequency Identification (RFID) tags often considered them to be analogous to Global Positioning Systems (GPS) like those embedded in smartphones.[17] In another study examining laypeople's "mental models" of electricity, researchers found that people tend to compare it to either "flowing water" or "teeming crowds."[18] Similarly, a study exploring people's theories about home heat control found that some users believed that a thermostat operated as a valve (like a burner on a gas stove), while others thought that it operated according to feedback from a temperature sensor (like an oven).[19]

Sometimes a technology's creators, designers, and marketers make a concerted effort to encourage prospective users to see it in a particular way. For instance, as Tarleton Gillespie has pointed out, the tendency of large technology companies such as Google, Facebook, and Twitter to refer to their products as "platforms" is part of an attempt to discursively frame them as objects that neutrally and unobtrusively amplify others' voices.[20]

As the "platform" example makes clear, such analogies are not merely doing descriptive work; they also play an active role in structuring our understandings of technology. Whether we devise them on our own or they are provided to us, analogies can be generative of thought and action, sometimes with powerful consequences. Consider how our expectations of companies like Google and

Facebook would differ if they discursively framed themselves as "editors," "curators," or "publishers"—all of which are arguably more apt analogues for their products than "platforms."[21] Similarly, those who perceived RFID as analogous to GPS grew wary of the former, because they saw it as enabling a more intensive and continual form of surveillance than it actually did.[22]

We must note that many classic studies on laypeople's technological frames share an important feature in common that sets them apart from our case. Because phenomena like electricity and technologies like RFID and home thermostats are well understood by scientists, it is possible to adjudicate between conflicting analogies and identify some as more apt than others. In the study examining conflicting mental models of electricity, the authors explain that they chose to focus on the case of electricity for their research in part because "it is tractable: We can define ideal correct understanding."[23]

Journalism, by contrast, affords no such tractability: it is ever-changing, has multiple aims, and is socially constructed in the most literal sense. There is almost never a definitive, objectively correct answer to the question of whether a certain number of pageviews for an article is "good": it depends on the subject of the story, the day and time of publication, the news cycle, the amount of promotion it receives, the normative and instrumental goals of the author, editor, and news organization that published it, the opaque social media platform algorithms that play a large role in distributing it, and many other factors. Metrics that measure the performance of news articles—and the performance of the journalists who produce them—present interpretive challenges that have no clear or easy answers.

In addition to their complexity, these interpretive challenges also have high stakes. It is not lost on journalists that the frames used to interpret traffic—that is, to decide if a particular story's pageview count is "good" or "bad," a "home run" or a "double"—are highly influential in shaping managerial perceptions of how effective they are at their jobs. When the management of the *Washington Post* and the Washington-Baltimore Newspaper Guild, which represents *Post* reporters, reached an agreement over a two-year contract in June 2015, one of the union's key demands was that reporters would gain greater access to metrics. Why? According to the Guild, "Metrics are already showing up in performance reviews," despite the fact that, as the Guild co-chair Fredrick Kunkle explained, it was "not clear how to fairly gauge people's performance relative to others when their missions are so variable. That is, how do you judge traffic performance between someone covering Hillary Clinton and someone covering Scott Walker—let alone someone covering county government in

Washington's suburbs? And yet it seems likely that these sorts of evaluations will appear in performance reviews soon."[24]

Kunkle's comments illustrate how the metrics cart was put before the interpretive horse. In other words, the ubiquity and influence of metrics have outstripped the development of shared cognitive frameworks with which to make sense of them. As will be discussed in greater depth later, the result is that the ability to interpret metrics—and have one's interpretations be considered dependable and authoritative—has become a coveted and contested currency of power in contemporary newsrooms.[25]

Causal Uncertainty

We have seen that journalists often struggled to form expectations of a story's traffic performance and evaluate it after the fact. However, even in extreme cases where meaning uncertainty was negligible—when, for instance, a story's traffic was so exceptionally high as to be unanimously considered a success— interpretive ambiguity sometimes persisted. In these instances, it usually took the form of *causal uncertainty*: it was unclear *why* a specific story was performing the way it was on the dashboard. Many writers I interviewed recounted instances where they had been baffled by a story's anomalously high or low traffic. Josh, a *Times* business reporter, told me about one such case that continued to mystify both him and the web producer who showed him the traffic data: "There's this one article I wrote [several months ago]. I wrote it on the subway. It took six minutes to write. It is about a [personnel change at a high-profile company]. It still gets tens of thousands of views a month." While Josh was happy to have such unusually high sustained traffic to a months-old piece, he was unsure why this particular article was getting so much attention, when he had written so many other seemingly similar pieces (many of which he had put far more work into).

In his famous 2008 essay "The End of Theory," Chris Anderson (then the editor in chief of *WIRED* magazine) wrote that big data had rendered obsolete models of the world that were based on an understanding of causal mechanisms. "Google's founding philosophy is that we don't know why this page is better than that one: If the statistics of incoming links say it is, that's good enough," Anderson argued. "Who knows why people do what they do? The point is they do it, and we can track and measure it with unprecedented fidelity."[26] Other big data enthusiasts have since echoed this theme, claiming that with a large enough *n*, one need not know *why* X and Y are related; correlations are sufficient to provide valuable and actionable knowledge.[27] In a critical take on the manifestation of this way of thinking in education, legal scholar Frank Pasquale writes that in algorithmically driven systems "the mind and body can be treated as 'black boxes.'" Proponents of such systems see no need to understand why particular teaching methods result in better or worse student outcomes: "The critical issue was simply figuring out what was the optimal pattern of stimulus to guarantee the right results in the future, to ensure proper functioning of one part (the student) in the whole (the labor market)."[28] Pasquale sounds a warning about this development: he argues that a lack of interest in unearthing causal mechanisms can lead to an impoverished understanding of the social world, with results that can be downright harmful.

Indeed, seeming indifference to causal mechanisms has gotten the large technology platform companies into some trouble in recent years, as the limits and risks of relying on what Anderson called "agnostic statistics" have come into full view. Algorithms' tendency to make "decisions" based on correlations alone has led to racist and otherwise discriminatory search results,[29] manipulation by bad-faith political actors, and sometimes astonishing callousness. One highly publicized case involved Facebook's "year in review" feature, which automatically compiles users' highest-engagement photos into a slideshow. Upon opening the app on Christmas Eve 2014, Facebook user Eric Meyer was immediately confronted with a large photo of his late six-year-old daughter, who had passed away that summer; the picture was bordered by clipart of dancing cartoon people and party balloons, and was captioned "Eric, here's what your year looked like!" While just about any human would immediately understand the extreme insensitivity of putting a celebratory border and caption around that photo, the algorithm's lack of causal reasoning prevented it from doing so. The automated system that compiled Facebook's year-in-review slideshows didn't know *why* that particular photo of Meyer's daughter had generated so much engagement, only that it had. As Meyer put it in an essay he wrote about the incident: "Algorithms are essentially thoughtless."[30] His choice of adjective is apt, both in the sense that algorithms literally lack the higher-level cognitive processes that we typically consider "thought" and in the more colloquial sense that algorithms can be inconsiderate, discriminatory, or even cruel.

In addition to these kinds of insidious effects, the lack of causal explanation in analytics tools could be maddeningly frustrating for users, like *Times* reporter Josh, who wanted to develop an understanding of what drove traffic to news content. As chapter 3 illustrated, Chartbeat's tool tended to be agnostic about causal factors, often opting instead for more mystical language—for example, "there's magic happening here"—in the pop-up "tool tips" that accompanied exceptionally high-performing stories in the dashboard.

As I've argued, this agnosticism was partly the result of the company's strategic attempt to "reenchant" the dashboard. If, as Weber contended, the scientific method's emphasis on uncovering the causal reasons behind earthly phenomena was a major source of disenchantment with the modern worldview, then it follows that companies like Chartbeat might eschew attempts at causal explanation as a way to forestall journalist-users' feelings of disenchantment and alienation.

Yet even if Chartbeat had *wanted* to provide causal explanations as to why a particular story had performed "well" or "poorly," it would have proven difficult to do so, because of the sheer number of factors—many of them entirely outside a newsroom's control—that could conceivably affect traffic performance. As Eddie, a Gawker writer, put it, "Everything clicks for a different reason." A/B testing tools (including one debuted by Chartbeat after the conclusion of my fieldwork) allow journalists to perform a trial run of multiple headlines for a single story simultaneously and identify the one attracting the most traffic. But such tests can be cumbersome to run for every story, are less reliable for sites with smaller audiences, and only allow newsrooms to isolate the effect of headlines and images. Other potentially significant factors influencing a story's traffic, such as its subject matter and the "news mix" at the time of its publication, are difficult to measure. And as news distribution has become increasingly reliant on the inscrutable and frequently changing algorithms of large technology platforms, journalists contend with ever more of what Angèle Christin has called "radical uncertainty about the determinants of online popularity."[31]

Because there were no generalizable causal laws that could explain a story's traffic performance, journalists at the *Times* and Gawker developed "folk theories" to help them fill the interpretive gap. A folk theory is a collectively shared, non-expert explanation of how something works.[32] Journalists in both newsrooms, but especially Gawker, formulated such theories to try to explain why some stories were traffic "hits" while others were flops. When a story underperformed relative to expectations (which were often themselves a product of folk theorizing), Gawker editors and writers performed a sort of informal postmortem in an effort to determine what had caused the low traffic. The headline was often singled out as a likely culprit. As Felix put it, "bad traffic is almost always a bad headline"—and, inversely, the headline is "usually a big part" of high traffic.

Writers also considered some topics to be of inherently greater interest to audiences than others (though as we saw earlier, the question of how much greater was continually up for debate). In the instances where Felix didn't think low traffic could be attributed to a bad headline, he felt it was usually because the story was "just lame"—that is, about a topic that readers did not find particularly compelling or worthy of their attention. Similarly, Eddie told me that "people click what they click. And people are gonna click on a story about sex or weed more than they'll click on a story about, I don't know, drones or 3-D printing, any day of the week." Lisa, an editor for a different Gawker site, rattled off a list of topics that she felt could reliably produce high traffic: "People love unhinged letters. . . . Unhinged sorority girl! Unhinged bride! [Or], 'Look at what this douchebag wrote me.' . . . And people like cute things that kids did. People like heartwarming videos with interspecies friendships."

Such lists were not based on any systematic review of traffic data but rather on a general and intuitive *feel* for traffic patterns that writers had gleaned in part from observing metrics over time and in part from long-held collective notions about what kinds of content interested news audiences (such as the age-old journalism adage, "if it bleeds, it leads").[33] According to Felix, while a select few writers at Gawker took a more methodical approach to devising causal models to explain traffic patterns—people who, as he put it, "spreadsheet their shit"—these writers were the exception. Rather, he explained, metrics were "just kinda something you absorb over time so you kind of have this sense for how data works, you know?" For all the comparisons to *Moneyball* we have become accustomed to seeing in discussions of data analytics, writers' use of metrics arguably had more in common with the method of the traditional baseball scouts, who drew on their years of experience to make gut-level assessments of players, than it did with the data-driven sabermetrics method employed by Billy Beane and Paul DePodesta.

Folk theories are often conceptualized as a way people alleviate their anxiety about new, intimidating, or complex technologies by demystifying what is unfamiliar. Indeed, we've seen that Gawker journalists crafted folk theories to explain traffic patterns that might otherwise seem mysterious and inscrutable. Interestingly, however, at times Gawker writers and editors explicitly *declined* to folk-theorize about metrics, instead embracing the unknowability of the causal mechanisms that were driving traffic to their sites and stories. As Felix put it: "Sometimes you just gotta let it go . . . sometimes shit hits and you have no idea why." As we saw in the instant-message exchanges that opened chapter 3, Alison, a Gawker site lead, was extremely hard on herself when her site's traffic was below where she believed it should be. Alison explained that it "feels horrible" when a story gets significantly worse traffic than she had predicted, a testament to the emotional power and influence of real-time newsroom analytics for the journalists who encounter them in the workplace every day. However, Alison also told me that, while she sometimes wondered if an underperforming post could have had a better headline, at times she also stopped herself from proceeding with that line of thinking: "Sometimes I'm just like, you know what? The internet wasn't in the mood for this today. I think that's totally a thing."

Alison's characterization of "the internet" as an autonomous, cohesive entity whose motivations and tastes were shifting and mysterious is an example of what media researcher Taina Bucher has called the algorithmic imaginary: "the way in which people imagine, perceive and experience algorithms and what these imaginations make possible."[34] We have seen that Alison was often quite unforgiving toward herself about her site's traffic. But occasionally setting limits on causal speculation, as she did here, functioned as a form of psychological self-care that helped her cope with the intense time and traffic pressures of the job. Telling herself that "the internet just wasn't in the mood" for a particular post was Alison's way of absolving herself from personal responsibility for low traffic, just as Felix did in moments when he decided to "just let it go." There are striking echoes in these statements of the type of reenchantment that was discussed in chapter 3. To say "the internet wasn't in the mood for this today" is, somewhat paradoxically, both a type of causal explanation and an acknowledgment that there can never *be* a causal explanation—or at least not a knowable, mechanistic one.

However, to say Alison's internet imaginary functioned as a source of reenchantment and psychological reassurance is not to suggest that it was delusional. Thinking of "the internet" as a singular, omnipotent being with unpredictable mood swings, as Alison did, may seem bizarre or even silly at first blush. Yet Alison's formulation wasn't actually that far off. As noted above, digital news sites—especially those, like Gawker, that are free to access and do not have paying subscribers—rely on a handful of large technology platforms such as Facebook, Google, and Twitter to refer much of their traffic. These platforms, in turn, use proprietary and dynamic algorithms to make some content more visible to users than other content. Given the circumstances, it is understandable that journalists like Alison would become resigned to the lack of control that accompanies such a dramatic imbalance of power between platforms and publishers.

By eschewing casual speculation about how algorithms work, writers like Alison and Felix mirrored the rhetoric of big data proponents who have disdained the importance of causal explanation in the digital age. Yet there is a key difference. As we have seen, big data enthusiasts dismiss the need for causal explanation on the grounds that if a data set is sufficiently large, then one can take strategic action based *solely* on correlation. For instance, when Walmart discovered that strawberry PopTarts sold at seven times the usual rate in the days leading up to a hurricane, the chain began stocking extra PopTarts and positioning them prominently in its stores whenever the forecast predicted one.[35] Walmart executives needn't know why shoppers craved that particular toaster pastry when faced with turbulent weather; the company could take goal-directed action based on the correlative finding alone.

This kind of action based on strong correlation is difficult to replicate in journalism for two reasons. First, as we have seen, there is no single goal in journalism but rather a multiplicity of aims that often seem incommensurable and, at times, mutually exclusive. Second, any patterns of correlation journalists may observe between a particular aspect of a story and traffic are subject to change based on shifts in platform algorithms that journalists are powerless to control or even fully grasp.

Thus, when journalists reject mechanistic explanations of traffic, they do so not because an understanding of causal mechanisms is unnecessary for taking action, but rather as a way to give themselves permission *not* to take incessant action. After all, if the internet simply isn't in the mood for a certain story, the journalist is powerless to influence the traffic outcome: there is no sense in continuing to tweak the headline, or promoting the post on a new social platform, or switching out the main image to try to boost the numbers. In sum, the periodic refusal to engage in mechanistic causal speculation allowed Gawker journalists to take a break from the otherwise relentless hunt for higher traffic.

Such a respite was only temporary, however. Generally speaking, Gawker journalists *did* feel pressure to take editorial action in response to traffic data—but they were often unsure of precisely what kind of action to take.

Action Uncertainty

A key aspect of the Moneyball mindset is that analytics data is not merely interesting but also useful. To some authors, the instrumental utility of analytics is so central that it becomes part of the very definition of the data: for instance, Viktor Mayer-Schönberger and Kenneth Cukier define big data as "the ability of society to harness information in novel ways to produce useful insights or goods and services of significant value."[36] News analytics companies frame their products in a way that emphasizes their usefulness. The "about" page on Chartbeat's website described the company as a "content intelligence platform for publishers" that "empowers media companies to build loyal audiences with real-time and historical editorial analytics." A company blog post announcing a new feature promised insights into subscribers that were "robust and action-able for publishers." Parse.ly, one of Chartbeat's main competitors, employed similar language on its website: "Parse.ly empowers companies to understand, own and improve digital audience engagement through data, so they can en-sure the work they do makes the impact it deserves." For both companies, the usefulness of analytics was central to the sales pitch.

And yet, in large part because of the meaning uncertainty and causal uncer-tainty that often accompany metrics, journalists were often unsure precisely what, if any, action to take in response to what they saw on the dashboard. If it is unclear whether or not a story is succeeding or failing (because it is unclear what the expectations are or should be for each story), then it is also unclear how to capital-ize on traffic success or buffer against failure. Even in cases where a story's success was clear but the *reason* for the success was not, there were still no easy answers about what one should do next. Josh, the *Times* reporter who was befuddled by continually high traffic to the story he had written in six minutes, explained that he didn't know how to put the knowledge to use. Paraphrasing conversations he'd had with a *Times* web producer who showed him metrics for his six-minute story, Josh said: "We talk about, 'well, what do we do with it?' And we haven't ever fig-ured it out. We don't know what the value of that [information] is, you know? And we don't know what we should do differently as a result."

Josh's dilemma was not new: in Herbert Gans's 1979 newsroom ethnography, an editor explained that, according to his magazine's market research depart-ment, the bestselling cover image was an attractive woman on a red back-ground. The editor complained that this information was of limited utility: "how often can I run such a cover on a newsmagazine?"[37] Still, Josh's sense of paralysis in the face of metrics was striking because it stood in such stark con-trast to the prevailing cultural narrative about big data: that it not only is ac-tionable but also will uncover hidden pockets of value to anyone smart enough to leverage it.

Josh explained that even if he put aside thorny normative questions about how much metrics *should* guide his editorial agenda (which are the subject of the next chapter), practical challenges would remain. Without knowing pre-cisely what it was about his six-minute story that was generating so much traf-fic, there was no surefire way to reproduce the success in his future work.

Even at Gawker, which had a strong reputation for taking editorial action based on traffic numbers (or, in the parlance of the field, producing "clickbait"), staffers were often unsure of which actions to take. For instance, while Eddie confidently asserted that posts about "sex or weed" would always outperform posts about "drones or 3-D printing," he also chafed at the notion that there was a particular editorial strategy that would always boost traffic. Eddie had worked at another digital publication before coming to Gawker, where he told me that his editor's bosses "would always tell him to bring them more viral hits. When we'd get [one of our articles picked up] on [the] Drudge [Report] or on Reddit that would go wild [i.e., drive a large amount of referral traffic to the site], they'd be like, 'oh, do this more often!' And we'd be like, 'you guys don't get it, this isn't a switch, there's not a formula.'"

Alison also had been frustrated by failed attempts to replicate a particular post's surprisingly high traffic. She related an instance in which, after being shocked by the high traffic for a short post about the upcoming series finale of a popular television show, she had instructed the writer to produce a follow-up post immediately after the final episode aired. "I said, 'I need you to cover this first thing in the morning. I don't care what you write, but you need to cover it.'" But the second post hadn't performed nearly as well as the first, for reasons that remained unclear to Alison. Felix struck a similar note in our interview, explaining that while he consulted metrics constantly, he wasn't interpreting it "in any kind of rational way." "I have this number," he told me, "but I don't really think about how I could get to whatever other number I want to get to."

Alison, Eddie, and Felix had found through experience that the mystery of the traffic game could be mitigated somewhat with vigilance and harder work, but it could not be eliminated. There was always an element of the game that resisted rationalization and systematization.

Conclusion

As *Moneyball* became a powerful cultural allegory about the promise of big data to pay dividends for beleaguered organizations and industries, some in the media field hoped that audience metrics could help news organizations in the same way that sabermetrics had boosted the Oakland A's. Yet this chapter has shown that the Moneyball mindset was a preposterously poor fit for journalism. Metrics in journalism are characterized by interpretive ambiguity in a way that baseball statistics are not. There are several reasons for this: the journalism profession's multiple competing mandates, news organizations' dependence on technology platforms' inscrutable and ever-changing algo-rithms for distribution, and Chartbeat's strategic reluctance—discussed in chapter 3—to interpret metrics for clients or make overt recommendations based on them. Taken together, these factors meant that it was often unclear to journalists what metrics *meant*, *why* some stories performed better than others in terms of traffic, and what, if any, editorial *actions* they should take in response to traffic data. Yet the ambiguity of metrics has not stopped the data from becoming powerfully influential—over time, metrics can mean the dif-ference between a journalist getting a bonus or getting laid off, between cover-age of a topic being expanded or scaled back.[38]

These findings suggest that similar interpretive ambiguities might arise in other knowledge-work fields that are perennially trying to balance the dictates of the market with non-market aesthetic, civic, ethical, or profes-sional priorities. Cultural workers are one such case, as analytics such as song streams, Goodreads rankings, and video plays threaten to disrupt artists' understandings of how to navigate the art-commerce relation.[39] We can imagine metrics creating profound uncertainty in other cases as well, even—perhaps especially—in paradigmatic professions such as medicine, law, and academia, that are finding themselves increasingly marketized.

Returning to the case of journalism, all of the metrics-related uncertainty documented in this chapter left journalists with a gaping interpretive void: they had lots of data but struggled to devise frameworks with which to make sense of it. Chapter 6 will illustrate that the ability to interpret metrics, and have one's interpretation be considered authoritative, became an important currency of power in news organizations—and one that was highly contested.

Of course, the questions raised by metrics were not only the logistical ones taken up in this chapter (e.g., what does this number mean and what should I do with it?). In determining the appropriate role of metrics in a newsroom, there were also *normative* questions at stake: What is the nature of editorial integrity, and what kind of working conditions threaten—or, conversely, support—it? Where should audience feedback fit into the news production process? Can the profit imperatives of commercial news production coexist with the profession's civic mandate, and if so, how? Here, too, ambiguities abounded. The following chapter will show how, in the absence of clear, profession-wide normative standards around handling metrics, journalists drew their own symbolic moral boundaries between acceptable and unaccept-able uses of the data.

5

Clean and Dirty Data

Ideas about separating, purifying, demarcating and punishing transgressions have as their main function to impose system on an inherently untidy experience. It is only by exaggerating the difference between within and without ... that a semblance of order is created.

—MARY DOUGLAS, *PURITY AND DANGER*

Data without context is dirt.

—OM MALIK

IN LATE JANUARY 2012, A. J. Daulerio, then the editor in chief of *Gawker*, Gawker Media's flagship site, published a post on the site announcing an experiment. Every day for the next two weeks, he explained, a different *Gawker* editorial staffer would be assigned to "traffic-whoring duty," and their sole task would be to publish whatever posts they thought would earn the most unique visitors. Daulerio laid out a few ground rules for "traffic-whoring days": photo galleries were prohibited, as were pornographic and racist posts. Other than these basic parameters, the writer assigned to traffic-whoring was "free to add things to the site they presume will make the little Chartbeat meter freak out." Daulerio proffered a few suggestions of such topics, the tamer of which included "dancing cat videos," "Burger King bathroom fights," and "sexy celeb beach bods."[1]

Daulerio's post made plain his enthusiasm about the experiment. First, he wrote, it would be fun to see what each day's designated "traffic whore" came up with—"like seeing each writer's id on the page." Second and more importantly, delegating the unabashed pursuit of traffic to one person would free up other staffers to "spend time on more substantive stories they may have ne-glected due to the rigors of scouring the internet each day to hit some imagi-nary quota." Based on the size of *Gawker*'s staff at the time, doing a single day of "traffic-whoring" would buy each staffer nine days during which the pres-sures of the traffic game were supposedly greatly alleviated.

Daulerio's choice of the term "traffic-whoring" reflects the brash, intention-ally provocative sensibility for which he was known. (In its coverage of *Gawk-er*'s experiment, the journalism trade publication *Nieman Lab* opted instead to refer to the practice as "page-view duty.")[2] But the nature of Daulerio's ex-periment, as well as the precise language he used to describe it, illustrates the symbolic boundaries journalists constructed as they tried to preserve their professional self-conception and retain control over their work in the face of intensifying metrics-driven pressures. This chapter will show that these boundaries often existed within a particular conceptual schema, according to which some forms and uses of metrics were categorized as clean—meaning that they were seen as harnessing analytics while mitigating the threat to jour-nalists' status, autonomy, and integrity—while others were categorized as dirty or contaminating.

To understand why this is so, it is useful to draw on social scientific ideas about how we classify dirt and cleanliness. For example, social anthropologist Mary Douglas famously argued that dirt is not an absolute category but rather one that is culturally and contextually defined in ritualistic ways that seek to minimize ambiguity. To Douglas, objects and practices get *labeled as dirty* not because they possess any particular inherent attributes but because they vio-late norms or collective systems of classification:

> Dirt is never a unique, isolated event. . . . It is a relative idea. Shoes are not dirty in themselves, but it is dirty to place them on the dining-table; food is not dirty in itself, but it is dirty to leave cooking utensils in the bedroom, or food bespattered on clothing; similarly, bathroom equipment in the drawing room; clothing lying on chairs; outdoor things indoors; upstairs things downstairs; under-clothing appearing where over-clothing should be, and so on.[3]

A social group's collective boundaries delineating cleanliness and dirt might seem bizarre or even random to the uninitiated. But Douglas argues these boundaries (and the dutiful work of maintaining them) serve an important purpose: they make an environment seem more sensible and under control to those inhabiting it.

For journalists confronting a precarious labor market and a work environment characterized by rapid, destabilizing forms of technological change, clean/dirty boundaries have particular appeal. At first glance, Daulerio's decision to designate a daily staffer whose sole job was to seek traffic might seem to have little in common with, say, a prohibition on leaving cooking utensils in the bedroom. Yet it is telling that Daulerio's choice of the term "whoring," while obviously tongue-in-cheek, explicitly links the practice of chasing traffic to a stigmatized form of sex work.[4] Sociologists have long been interested in "dirty work"—that is, types of labor that are widely considered disgusting, degrading, or morally condemnable. Research on dirty work has explored not only who performs this kind of work and why, but also the cognitive justifications of those who *don't* perform such work themselves but nevertheless want it to be done, or believe it must be done, by someone else.[5] When dirty work takes place within organizations, where possible it is separated from the organization's primary operations and high-status members. *Gawker's* "traffic-whoring" experiment was born of a similar impulse: to recognize the material necessity of traffic-chasing while also wanting to clearly label it and cordon it off, thus protecting more pristine areas of the editorial operation from its polluting influence.

This chapter details journalists' efforts to draw clean/dirty boundaries with regard to metrics.[6] We will examine four types of such boundaries. First, journalists drew boundaries between specific types of data, such that certain metrics (e.g., pageviews) were thought to incentivize the production of clickbait and were thus labeled as dirty, while others (e.g., time spent reading) became associated, partly through the branding work of Chartbeat, with the kinds of "serious" stories with which journalists prefer to align themselves and thus were considered clean. Second, within particular newsrooms certain types of roles and editorial responsibilities were coded as clean or dirty based on their orientation to analytics, as with Daulerio's decision to designate a daily "traffic whore." Third, journalists tried to draw boundaries between clean and dirty uses of analytics in editorial work, though these proved difficult to maintain in practice.

These boundaries, while clearly discernible at the organizations I studied, were fraught and continually shifting in nature. While there is no formal body governing journalism ethics as in professions like medicine or law, the field has nonetheless coalesced around a set of normative guidelines, according to which some actions are near-universally considered to be beyond the pale of legitimate journalistic practice (e.g., fabricating stories), while others (such as giving sources the opportunity to approve their quotes in advance of publication) are fodder for ongoing intra-industry debate.[7] Metrics fall decisively into the latter category: the nature of metrics-related boundaries varies from outlet to outlet and there is no profession-wide consensus on what constitutes appropriate data points, uses of data, or organizational configurations where metrics are concerned. These field-level inconsistencies resulted in a fourth type of clean/dirty boundary: journalists tended to perceive the organization at which they were employed as being on the "clean" side of metrics use, while the practices of rival organizations were often characterized as dirty.

The actual content of the boundaries discussed in this chapter may seem odd, at times even arbitrary. But what matters about metrics-related boundaries is not necessarily *where* they are drawn but rather the fact that they exist and are collectively upheld within a given newsroom. This chapter argues that clean/dirty boundaries reflect journalists' ongoing efforts to mitigate the threat that metrics pose to both their professional status and their control over the labor process.

Boundaries in Journalism—and Why
Metrics Threaten to Breach Them

When faced with a status threat, professionals draw boundaries between themselves and other groups in order to protect their authority, shore up social status, and secure material resources.[8] Journalists are no exception.[9] For example, as blogging gained popularity as a news-distribution medium in the 2000s, journalists highlighted errors made by bloggers in election reporting in an attempt to preserve their own authority as a more trustworthy and reliable source of political news.[10]

News organizations have also historically drawn boundaries between their editorial and business operations. During the twentieth century, when news organizations generally enjoyed high profit margins, journalists were to some extent structurally insulated from commercial pressures. Business considerations were seen as having their place in the news *organization*, but not in the news*room*. As communication scholar Daniel Hallin explains, "Prosperity meant that the 'profane,' commercial side of the news organization didn't have to conflict with its 'sacred,' public service side . . . journalists could think of themselves more as public servants or as keepers of the sacred flame of journalism itself than as employees of a profit-making enterprise."[11]

Of course, the so-called "wall" protecting the editorial side from the business side was hardly impermeable: commercial pressures found their way into newsrooms through direct means, such as advertiser boycotts, and indirect ones, such as journalist self-censorship. Yet if the existence of the wall was always only a partial truth, it was nonetheless an important one, which guided journalistic practice and self-understanding for many decades.

In the twenty-first century, however, the wall between advertising and editorial has come to seem to many in the industry like an unsustainable luxury in the fiercely competitive digital "attention economy." A number of novel digital revenue-generation strategies have blurred the boundary between advertising and editorial. One such strategy is "native advertising" (sometimes known as branded content), in which in-house teams at media companies create bespoke ad campaigns that mimic the publication's tone and format for corporate clients.[12]

Although many journalists harbored misgivings about tactics like native advertising, metrics became a—if not *the*—key object of their collective professional anxieties. There is a reason for this: metrics directly and explicitly penetrate editorial operations in a way that other new revenue-generation strategies have not. Unlike, say, native advertising, efforts to maximize traffic cannot be relegated to the business side.[13] After all, *editorial* content is what attracts the pageviews and unique visitors that ad sales are based on. It follows that most attempts to optimize such content's traffic (e.g., headline-crafting, image selection, and story assignment) necessarily fall under the purview of the editorial side. In addition, we have seen that metrics generate considerable fascination and powerful habits among journalists, and that Chartbeat sought to portray analytics tools as a window into the audience's wants and needs that could facilitate, rather than impede, the profession's ability to perform its public-oriented mission. In sum, analytics are ambiguous in that they don't fall decisively on one side or the other of the "wall" between editorial and advertising.

As *Gawker*'s "traffic whoring" experiment illustrates, journalists coped with the disorienting ambiguity of metrics by classifying traffic-chasing as dirty work: something that must be done but is easier to countenance if it is separated from the pristine core of the editorial operation. It has become something of a cliché in business and consulting circles to say that "data is the new oil"—a supposedly "raw" material that has great monetary value if processed and refined in the right way. But my fieldwork revealed that journalists often thought of audience data less like crude oil and more like the mercury in a compact-fluorescent lightbulb: useful for performing a circumscribed set of functions but also highly toxic should it escape its confines, and thus requiring extremely careful handling. The remainder of this chapter will examine *how* this careful handling of metrics was carried out within Chartbeat, Gawker, and the *New York Times*, via boundaries delineating clean versus dirty metrics, newsroom roles, uses of metrics, and news organizations.

Dirty & (Relatively) Clean Metrics

The first audience metric to gain prominence in newsrooms was the pageview. Pageviews, also known as hits or clicks, are a measure of how many times a particular URL has been loaded. Pageviews date back to the early 1990s when the main source of web analytics was server logs, which could capture time stamps and IP addresses but little else. On their own, pageviews do not communicate any information about the person (or bot) doing the clicking, nor about what actions they take once the page loads (e.g., it is not known from pageviews whether a reader perused every word of the story, got bored halfway through, or closed the window immediately because they had navigated to it by mistake). The advent of cookies in the mid-1990s enabled sites to track users and capture more details about their behavior as they navigated to and from the site.[14]

Still, the pageview has had considerable staying power, partly because it became an important currency in the online advertising market. For websites selling advertising on the basis of cost per thousand impressions (CPMs), pageviews are a useful metric to communicate to prospective sponsors. In this sense, pageviews are similar to subscription and sales numbers that characterized twentieth-century print media but with one important difference: pageviews measure performance at the story level rather than the publication level, allowing news organizations to calculate the precise amount of advertising revenue earned by each story published. This characteristic, coupled with the difficult economic circumstances in which many newsrooms found themselves in the late aughts, contributed to fears that knowledge of pageview counts would contaminate editorial judgment by incentivizing journalists to produce the type of content that came to be widely known as clickbait.

The malleable meaning of the term "clickbait" has become something of a running joke in online media circles, prompting a *Nieman Lab* writer to wryly define it as: "noun: things I don't like on the internet."[15] There do, however, seem to be two prevailing definitions—one broad and one considerably more narrow. The former focuses on the "click" aspect of clickbait. For example, the *Oxford English Dictionary*, which officially added the term in 2016, defines clickbait as "content whose main purpose is to attract attention and encourage visitors to click on a link to a particular web page."[16]

The second, narrower, definition emphasizes the concept of "bait," characterizing clickbait as content that "tricks" readers into clicking on a headline by overpromising and then fails to deliver. For instance, the "curiosity gap" headline styles popularized by sites like *Upworthy*, which deliberately omits crucial information in order to entice the reader to click (e.g., "A boy makes anti-Muslim comments in front of an American soldier. The soldier's reply: priceless"),[17] were memorably called a "particularly virulent strain of hyper-optimized clickbait" by erstwhile *BuzzFeed News* editor in chief Ben Smith.[18] Smith is hardly the only journalist to invoke the language of disease, dirt, and contamination when speaking about varieties of reader-baiting content. For example, in describing "sharebait," a term that refers to content that "panders" to audiences' already-held beliefs or aspects of their identity (e.g., courtesy of *BuzzFeed*, "42 problems only cat owners will understand"), *Atlantic* editor James Hamblin called it "just as dirty as clickbait, if not more."[19]

Both the broad and narrow definitions of clickbait implicate metrics. Pageviews in particular were thought to encourage the production of clickbait because all clicks are counted equally, regardless of whether the person was disgusted, enthralled, bored, or disappointed by the story they clicked on. An article in *WIRED* drew a direct causal link between pageviews and clickbait: "The page view notoriously spawned that most reviled of Internet aggravations: clickbait. Quality became less important than provocation; the curiosity gap supplanted craft."[20] If clickbait was dirty and pageviews encouraged clickbait, then pageviews were dirty by association. *WIRED*'s framing is emblematic of a tendency common in media coverage of newsroom metrics to construct a normative opposition between metrics, on one side, and professional craft and quality, on the other.

Chartbeat sought to challenge this dichotomy and cleanse the reputation of metrics in two ways. First, rather than attempt to redeem the pageview, Chartbeat simply distanced itself from that particular metric. As we saw in chapter 3, Chartbeat's analytics dashboards did not measure pageviews at all, and the company's messaging, particularly in its early days, co-opted journalists' criticisms of them. In promotional materials, Chartbeat suggested that journalistic skepticism about newsroom analytics was actually due to a misguided tendency to conflate "metrics" with "pageviews": "Many journalists are understandably conflicted about data in the newsroom. For many publishers, 'data' and 'metrics' are simply jargon for 'pageviews' and too often used to justify a great many journalistic sins in pursuit of numbers and quotas."[21] The use of the term "journalistic sin," with its strong religious inflection, underscores the centrality of clean and dirty language to industry discussions of metrics and editorial judgment.

If pageviews represented the path to journalistic perdition, "engagement metrics"—Chartbeat's specialty—were positioned as the road to redemption. The company referred to its two favored measures of engagement, engaged time and recirculation, as "the golden metrics." "Like time, attention is finite," explained a Chartbeat white paper on the "battle for attention." "As a metric, [attention] correlates directly with quality and consumption, not clicks and pageviews."

Chartbeat's promise that its "golden metrics" would usher in "a web where quality content makes good business sense" had strong appeal to news organizations facing unprecedented financial trials. It is not difficult to see why Chartbeat's insistence that *its* metrics, unlike pageviews, were wholly compatible with "pure" editorial judgment was such a soothing notion—and a winning marketing strategy for Chartbeat in the early days of newsroom metrics.

As discussed in chapter 3, Chartbeat's second strategy for assuaging journalists' anxieties about a metrics-driven takeover of their craft was to perform deference to editorial judgment. Rather than purport to provide knowledge and tools that would equip journalists to radically retool their approach, Chartbeat staffers often emphasized how the company's metrics corroborated what, as Tyler put it, journalists already "know intrinsically." We have seen that, in an attempt to reassure journalists who were anxious about metrics, Chartbeat largely refrained from giving explicitly prescriptive advice about how to maximize traffic. For example, the dashboard did not make recommendations about where to place particular stories on clients' sites, when articles should be published, or which topics merited follow-up coverage.

However, this approach presented a reputational challenge of its own—one that was also often spoken about using the language of pollution and contamination. If the dashboard was thought *not* to reshape journalistic practice, it was then vulnerable to being cast as a vacuous distraction: something that piqued journalists' interest and stoked their egos without providing tangible benefits. In the early 2010s, high-profile technology and business journalists began to complain about "analytics porn," by which they meant metrics that are exciting and fun to look at but ultimately empty and a bit seamy.[22] Other writers drew a rhetorical connection between metrics and sinfulness, calling pageviews in particular a "vanity metric"—a term coined by Eric Ries, a tech entrepreneur and the author of a business book called *The Lean Startup* (a copy of which sat on the bookshelves in the Chartbeat office), who defined it as "numbers which look good on paper but aren't action oriented."[23] In a 2012 post, technology blogger Om Malik analogized analytics to pollution: "Data, I believe is like plastic. You can use it to make wonderful things. However, like plastic, it can be a great polluter and create havoc on the environment."[24]

In this context, Chartbeat faced the task of navigating two distinct clean/dirty boundaries: if its dashboard proved *too* influential in reshaping journalistic work, it risked being seen as a contaminator of journalists' sacred editorial judgment. If, by contrast, it was seen as insufficiently actionable, it might be viewed as unsavory and sensationalist "data porn." Thus Chartbeat's marketing attempted to walk a fine line between performing deference, on the one hand, and emphasizing the practical usefulness of its metrics, on the other. Judging from the high take-up of Chartbeat in a wide range of news organizations, the combination of messages seemed to accomplish that goal: establishing Chartbeat firmly enough on the "clean" side of the clean/dirty divide that its tools could be adopted without journalists feeling as though their core professional identity was contaminated or compromised.

Clean and Dirty Newsroom Roles

Daulerio's "traffic-whoring" system was just one of the ways Gawker Media experimented with delineating editorial work aimed solely at generating traffic. *Gawker* and *Gizmodo*, two of the company's biggest and best-known sites, employed full-time writers to cover what was sometimes referred to as the "viral beat"—aggregating material from other sites and social platforms that they deemed likely to be shared on social media and thus bring in a large number of uniques. Those on the viral beat often occupied the top spots on the leaderboard that ranked editorial staffers by traffic, and their posts—on topics ranging from celebrity gossip to interspecies animal friendships to a video of a man lighting a birthday cake with 72,000 candles on it—often drew the biggest audiences across Gawker sites. Though I never heard the term "traffic whore" used to describe them, in interviews their colleagues nonetheless discursively set them apart from the rest of the newsroom. As Will, a writer, explained

The top three guys [on the writers' traffic rankings] are always Anthony, Seth, and, like, Rob or Todd. But I mean, that's because their jobs are specifically finding viral traffic stuff. So they're always going to be in the top three and everybody knows that. And they subsidize the rest of the company to an extent.

Will distinguished this select group of staffers, whose singular goal is "finding viral traffic stuff," from the rest of the company's editorial staff. This discursive boundary implicitly elevated the journalistic integrity of everyone else in the Gawker newsroom (because they have aims other than simply drawing traffic), while also justifying their comparatively lower traffic. Traffic rankings commensurated all editorial staffers according to a single numerical standard. But Will's comment is an example of *de*-commensuration: "the deconstruction of a metric to reveal qualitative differences in objects being evaluated."[25] In noting that those on the viral beat "subsidize the rest of the company," Will also acknowledged the necessity of viral-beat work to the viability of Gawker's ad-based business model. Like Daulerio's rotating traffic-whoring duties, Will portrayed the viral beat as separate from the newsroom's core journalistic mission, but as strengthening the newsroom's practical ability to perform that mission.[26]

Notably, not all staffers agreed with this characterization. My conversation with Liam, a site lead who was relatively new to the company at the time of our interview, illustrated the ways in which boundaries between clean and dirty newsroom roles can be contested internally. When I asked Liam about the notion that having designated staffers on the viral beat eases traffic pressure for everyone else, he was skeptical:

I think that it sounds good to tell the public that that's what it does. Internally, though, I don't think that's what it does. . . . I mean it *should*, but I feel like instead it kind of . . . ups the ante—like it makes people feel like they are not performing where they could be.

To Liam, efforts by Will and others to de-commensurate the viral-beat staffers by discursively setting them apart from other Gawker writers were not effective. Indeed, there was truth to Liam's claim that the viral beat "ups the ante" for everyone else: because each Gawker site's monthly traffic target was based on a rolling average of its traffic over the previous six months, traffic "hits" produced by viral-beat staffers contributed over time to ever-higher collective traffic targets for the sites on which they appeared.

Anthony and Rob were viral-beat writers who wrote for a semi-autonomous "subsite" of the larger Gawker site that Liam edited. This meant that uniques generated by posts on Anthony and Rob's subsite counted as traffic to Liam's site. But because the subsite operated largely independently, Liam had very little editorial direction over Anthony and Rob's work. Liam disliked when his site surpassed its traffic target due mainly to their posts. In our interview, he proudly described the month of February 2014, when his site surpassed their traffic target by 83 percent. This entitled the team to the maximum possible traffic bonus, equivalent to 20 percent of the site's total monthly budget. "And what was great about it," Liam explained, "was that we did it and it wasn't because of this viral shit that's on [Anthony and Rob's subsite]. It was because we have a whole bunch of really great posts." The following month, however, was a different story:

> [Anthony and Rob's subsite] just exploded in March, and like every damn thing it put up was all about, like, parents singing Disney songs to kids and so, I don't know, it's an embarrassment. And all those things did so well. And so we hit the 20 percent bonus again, but it was kind of like, it didn't feel like celebratory at all. Like, fuck, we hit the 20 percent bonus again and it wasn't because of us, it was because of Anthony and Disney characters and stuff.

For Liam, the fact that Anthony and other writers on the viral beat were discursively (and in the case of the subsite, organizationally) set apart from the larger editorial staff was insufficient to prevent the dirtiness of the traffic-chasing work from contaminating his entire site. Tellingly, Liam was fired from Gawker Media six weeks after our interview took place. In an email to the team announcing Liam's departure, a Gawker executive explained that he "did not integrate well" with the company.

At the *Times*, similar boundary-drawing between clean and dirty newsroom roles took place (though the term "traffic whore," or even "viral beat," would be highly unlikely to be used). As chapter 6 will discuss in more depth, at the time of my fieldwork *Times* editors had put in place a system of tiered access to metrics: editors had access to traffic data from both Chartbeat and Google Analytics, while reporters did not. Yet there were telling exceptions. Newsroom teams and staff members whose work product existed mainly or exclusively online (meaning it was not published in the print edition of the *Times*) seemed to play by an entirely different set of rules regarding metrics: access to analytics was freer and the permissible uses of such data were much more expansive. For instance, while editors and reporters alike categorically asserted that metrics did not drive story assignment for the print newspaper, metrics were one of the primary factors taken into account when creating features that would appear exclusively on the *Times* website, such as a tool that invited readers to try balancing the federal budget or an interactive Oscars ballot. Richard, a reporter who often worked with the growing interactive news team, described the decision-making process that led to the creation of an elaborate interactive feature for the website:

> After studying the idea for a while, they calculated maybe it would be worth doing, 'cause even though it would take a certain number of person-hours to build, it will get enough traffic to justify it. And so that's the type of decisions that [the interactive] group would make, because . . . the deep, sophisticated things they're only gonna build if they think they're gonna get a lot of traffic.

Later, when speaking more generally about the interactive team, Richard elaborated on the point: "Their job is to come up with these great things that are add-on components to the website just to build a lot of traffic. And that are, you know, obviously that are good and have journalism principles involved." The fact that Richard mentioned traffic first, and journalism principles second, when discussing interactive features stands in stark contrast to how interviewees almost uniformly discussed the print content of the paper, however fancifully, as being entirely disconnected from commercial considerations.

Similarly, decisions about which of the paper's many blogs should be maintained, and which should be shut down, were also made largely based on metrics. A post in 2013 announcing the *Times* leadership's much-criticized decision to discontinue its environmental "Green" blog, while not explicitly mentioning traffic, employed language about resources that was similar to Richard's: "This change will allow us to direct production resources to other online projects."[27] Sam, a reporter, attributed such decisions to "the economic straits of papers":

> One way you clearly see the impact [of economic pressures] is things like bottom-line-only blogs. . . . They open blogs, they closed a lot of blogs, you know, [they] just closed the Green blog. There they're totally responding to, you know, what the [audience] response to the blogs are. So, there it's a clear-cut thing.

Different standards of using metrics applied not only to online-only features of the *Times* but also to newspaper staffers who worked primarily on keeping up the website. Web producers—junior-level employees whose wide-ranging responsibilities included uploading articles into the *Times*'s content management system, creating multimedia features to accompany stories, cropping digital photographs, and adding tags to online articles—were given access to Chartbeat, though many of them were relatively young ("right out of college," as one senior staffer put it) and new to the paper. Several web producers wrote for the paper in addition to their production responsibilities, making them some of the only reporters who had regular access to the analytics tools. As Julian, a web producer, explained: "That stuff [metrics showing how many clicks a story gets] is not widely given out to writers, [but] it's not impossible to get ahold of. Producers have access to it, so I'm sort of in a situation where if I want to find out about this stuff I can."

These comments make clear that with the interactive news team, the blogs, and other online-only features, the *Times* had essentially cordoned off areas of the organization where the use of metrics was a, if not *the*, primary driver behind resource allocation. Thus, even in an age of "convergence" journalism that blends multimedia formats, the *Times* had in essence designated profane online-only enclaves within the otherwise sacred print newsroom. Within these particular spaces, metrics were allowed—even expected—to penetrate news judgments.

Like *Gawker*'s traffic-whoring experiment, the unrestricted access to metrics of online-only teams and staffers at the *Times* was part of a broader effort to leverage the instrumental benefits that metrics potentially could provide, while shielding the core of the editorial operation from their polluting influence. In the *Times*'s case, this print-and-online versus online-only division seemed highly intuitive to many of the journalists I interviewed because it reflected a broader truth: the print edition was the *Times*'s crown jewel and central to its long-standing organizational identity, while online-only features existed merely to supplement the reporting in the print edition and serve as a repository for things that wouldn't fit or didn't belong in print. The organization has gradually worked to shift to a "digital first" approach to publishing—by, for instance, actively courting digital-only subscribers and in 2015 reorienting the daily "Page 1" meetings, where the stories for the following day's front page were selected, to focus on the online rather than the print edition.[28] But even in recent years, the prioritization of print story formats, norms, and work rhythms was still rather stubbornly entrenched: as a 2017 internal report put it, "our largely print-centric strategy, while highly successful, has kept us from building a sufficiently successful digital presence."[29]

In this vein, a dichotomy that casts the online edition as profane and the print edition as sacred has persisted in the *Times*'s broader organizational self-presentation. For example, as of early 2020, the "newspaper" section of the *Times*'s online media kit for prospective advertisers boasted of the paper's prestige—noting its record Pulitzer Prize count and the fact that it "remains No. 1 in overall reach of opinion leaders"—but made no mention of the number of print subscribers, newsstand sales, or other print metrics.[30] By contrast, the "online" section of the media kit opened with the fact that nytimes.com attracts "78.1 million unique visitors each month."[31] The *Times*'s practices around metrics stemmed from the unequal distribution of prestige that those sorts of messages both reflect and perpetuate.

While explicitly traffic-driven editorial work was not considered particularly prestigious at either publication, it was not seen as meriting moral condemnation. On the contrary, interviewees at both organizations seemed to regard this sort of work as necessary for the newsroom to function optimally. At Gawker, there was wide acknowledgment (Liam's objections notwithstanding) that Anthony's commitment to and talent at the viral beat enabled his colleagues to pursue more "serious" stories that were unlikely to draw as many readers. Similarly, at the *Times*, reporters did not disdain their colleagues on interactive and other online-only teams for incorporating traffic considerations into their editorial judgment; indeed, these teams were widely recognized as helping the broader organization successfully adapt to the digital age.

Mary Douglas's conceptualization of dirt as "matter out of place" is helpful in understanding this relative absence of negative feelings about traffic-oriented newsroom roles and those who perform them. The mere presence of metrics in a newsroom was not considered to be inherently contaminating; rather, metrics threatened to pollute editorial integrity and judgment only if they breached established boundaries. However, as metrics became more thoroughly institutionalized in newsrooms, it was not always possible to limit use of the data to staffers in specific roles. There was increasing interest in optimizing the traffic performance of *all* content, including articles that were not produced expressly for the purpose of increasing traffic. Thus another set of boundaries emerged around clean and dirty uses of metrics.

Clean and Dirty Uses of Metrics

Many journalists I interviewed, particularly at the *Times*, spoke of a "line" between uses of metrics that were acceptable and those that were taboo. While not all staffers drew the line in precisely the same place, a general pattern emerged: using metrics to inform a story's "packaging" and promotion strategy was widely seen as permissible, even laudable, while using metrics to inform a story's subject or "content" was not. Cynthia, a *Times* reporter, explained that when thinking about the proper role of analytics in the newsroom, "I do draw a distinction between the format of the journalism you're doing and the content of the journalism you're doing." When asked to elaborate, Cynthia said:

> If you're deciding whether you're going to cover something in video or in print, either way, you're covering it. And we're just trying to figure out the way that it's most convenient for our users to consume. . . . But when it comes to the actual journalistic decisions getting made about what to cover and what not to cover, and how prominently to attract attention to it— those things I don't think should be governed by popular opinion.

Cynthia's colleague Amy, also a reporter, offered a similar perspective. She explained that she viewed certain uses of metrics as "uncontroversial," such as drawing on analytics to make decisions about the layout of the *Times* website and other aspects of news presentation: "Where do you put the thing on the page to make sure it attracts attention? How do we not bury our great content? How do we present it in a way that's visible and appealing?" Tim, a *Times* editor, told me that "we have begun on the news desk to look at metrics to identify stories that maybe either have a longer life span than we might have expected or are generating more interest than we might have expected"; such stories might then be placed on the home page or promoted on the paper's social media accounts. Tim also felt it was acceptable to use metrics when deciding matters like the time of day a story should be published on the newspaper's website to maximize its audience.[32] For instance, Tim explained that stories pertaining to East Asia were generally published at 9 p.m. Eastern Time, which allowed them to attract morning readers in Asia as well as Asian American readers on the West Coast of the United States who might visit the *Times* home page in the early evening.

Cynthia, Amy, and Tim saw the form and content of news as entirely distinct and easily distinguishable from one another: while the content of news was vital to the *Times*'s sacred civic mission, its form and mode of distribution were perceived as having little civic relevance of their own. If the form and distribution of a publication are considered to be mere vessels for editorial judgment rather than as *manifestations* of editorial judgment, metrics can unproblematically be used to guide decision making in these areas. In other words, the form/content boundary fosters the impression that, rather than reshaping the *Times*'s editorial sensibility, metrics are simply broadening the audience for that sensibility—or, as *New York Times* magazine writer Charles Duhigg has put it, "taking the vegetables and dipping them in caramel."[33]

Similar symbolic boundaries between a product's content, on the one hand, and its form and mode of distribution, on the other, have long existed in many cultural industries. In his study of labor in cultural fields, Bill Ryan notes that management of workers who produce creative content—such as composers, screenwriters, and journalists—was "remarkably benign," because heavy-handed labor rationalization was seen as counterproductive for creative work. But this relative autonomy was strictly limited to the production of creative goods; by contrast, the reproduction and distribution of cultural commodities was thoroughly mechanized.[34] Especially given this established historical precedent, the appeal of a boundary between content, on the one hand, and form/distribution, on the other, is clear: it allowed journalists to simultaneously feel that they were keeping up with technological change and reaping its benefits while also reassuring them that their professional judgment remained uncorrupted.[35]

However, choices about the form and distribution of news have never been neutral, nor are they irrelevant to discussions of how well the news media is fulfilling its role in democratic societies. Media scholars Kevin Barnhurst and John Nerone have argued that design elements like page layout, typography, and story format have both expressed and shaped modes of civic participation throughout U.S. history. For example, newspaper front pages in the late twentieth century were less cluttered than their late nineteenth-century counterparts, with more white space and stories that were arranged in a clear hierarchy of prominence. This shift aligned with the norms of the modern era, which favored order and standardization, as well as journalists' growing sense of themselves as an established profession with a responsibility to help their readers make sense of a chaotic world. Yet if the form of news is inherently political, we don't often think of it as such: once a style of news presentation becomes standard across the industry, it is taken for granted in ways that render invisible the normative values and assumptions embedded therein.[36] Similarly, processes of news distribution play a central—if overlooked—role in shaping how people congregate (or don't), imagine their communities, engage in political participation, and exercise freedom of speech.[37] In sum, the idea that news content can be neatly cleaved from news formats and modes of news distribution—and that the latter are neutral and normatively insignificant—has always been more a fantasy than a reality.

The untenability of the content versus form/distribution boundary has become even more apparent in the digital age. The algorithms that curate our personalized feeds on social media platforms, and which nearly all contemporary news outlets rely upon for distribution of their content, are now widely recognized as being inherently editorial and having enormous civic implications.[38] Furthermore, online-only news organizations have experimented with news form in controversial, even offensive, ways. To take one particularly high-profile example, after the ouster of Mohamed Morsi by the Egyptian military in July 2013, *BuzzFeed* published a piece titled "The Story of Egypt's Revolution in 'Jurassic Park' Gifs."[39] True to its headline, the post consisted of a scant 404 words of text summarizing Egypt's political upheaval, interspersed with GIFs from the classic Steven Spielberg film about an ill-fated dinosaur amusement park. For instance, the post used a GIF of a hatching dinosaur egg to symbolize Epypt's new constitution.

While undoubtedly optimized for clicks, the post might have been construed as an ill-conceived attempt to cover a complex subject in an attention-grabbing format that might attract readers who would be otherwise uninterested and uninformed about the situation unfolding in Egypt—as, in other words, "taking vegetables and dipping them in caramel." Instead, it provoked widespread outrage in the industry: *Slate* editor L. V. Anderson called the post "the worst thing [*BuzzFeed*] has ever done";[40] others pronounced it "the bottom of the barrel"[41] and "a new low" in journalism.[42] The general consensus was that the Egyptian conflict was too serious a subject to be covered in such a lighthearted, cheeky way.[43] *Slate*'s Anderson argued that "BuzzFeed's GIF-ification of Egypt's civil conflict belittles the pain of people whose lives have been upended by violence."[44] The backlash from other online news organizations against the *BuzzFeed* post illustrates, first, the infeasibility of a clear-cut normative distinction between news form and content in the age of social media distribution; second, the practical difficulty of drawing and maintaining consistent clean/dirty boundaries around uses of metrics; and, finally, how much those contested boundaries hinge on comparison with rival publications.

Clean and Dirty News Organizations

Within both the *Times* and Gawker, we have seen that clean/dirty boundaries around metrics sometimes proved flimsy: which metrics, roles, and practices were defined as clean or dirty periodically shifted in response to changes in organizational structure, dictates from management, and revenue pressures.

This could provoke feelings of insecurity in editorial staffers, especially when (as was most often the case) the boundaries shifted in the direction of being more permissive of metrics and as the areas of the newsroom that were protected from metrics' influence got smaller and smaller.

A common response to this internal instability was to construct a fourth type of discursive boundary about metrics that was *externally* focused, such that rival news organizations were unfavorably compared to one's own publication and cast as using metrics inappropriately. Journalists at the *Times*, for example, frequently drew positive contrasts between the *Times*'s approach to metrics and that of other publications. Nate, a reporter, criticized "places like *Huffington Post* and *Business Insider*" for publishing slideshows on topics such as, "you know, the top 35 people that wear glasses and live in Brooklyn." Because each "slide" the reader clicked on counted as a separate pageview, Nate saw such slideshows as a cynical ploy on the part of *Times* competitors to boost their traffic numbers. By contrast, he explained, "what the *Times* does [for slideshows] is that they have this interactive viewer where . . . you stay on one page and you just click through within the page. So [the *Times*] only get[s] one pageview, but you're seeing ten things." He drove home the distinction even further: "I think that, you know, these metrics-driven—I wouldn't even call them a news organization sometimes, but these metrics-driven *blogs*—[are] just creating nonsense."

Tim, a *Times* editor, felt similarly. In our interview he recounted a conversation with an editor from Aol who had told him that when a story attracted high traffic, "there was a big emphasis to get blog items about the story and to continue to just really milk the story. . . . We don't want to do that [at the *Times*, because] the next thing you know, we'll be writing about Lindsay Lohan and cats and dogs all the time." Tim drew an even starker boundary between the *Times* and *Gawker*: "There are sites like *Gawker* which really admit that they follow their metrics almost out the window in terms of that drives everything that's on there. We don't do that." When I prefaced a question to Cynthia, a *Times* reporter, by mentioning that the *Washington Post* had a real-time display of the paper's top-ranked stories on its newsroom wall, she was incredulous: "They have that at the *Washington Post*? . . . Oh god, this is so depressing to me." I asked Cynthia to explain why she felt that way, she responded, "I would like to think that would never happen [at the *Times*]. I hope I'm not being Pollyanna-ish."

Given the *Times*'s long-held organizational self-perception as the apex of journalistic professionalism in the United States, we might expect that newsroom employees would seek to set it apart from both historic rivals like the *Washington Post* and newer, digital-only outfits like the *Huffington Post* and

Gawker. Yet even Gawker Media staffers made similar normative juxtapositions between Gawker's approach to metrics and that of competing sites. Eddie explained that Gawker spurned the kind of "headline tricks, SEO [search engine optimization] tricks, tweet tricks" that he felt were embraced by the other sites like *Huffington Post* and *Upworthy*: "All those tricks work and they'll get you traffic. But more mature sites—Gawker media sites—realize that there has to be a balance between playing to the numbers but also paying attention to quality, and having some really simple rules in place as to what you will and will not do for traffic." Similarly, while Alison admitted to "praying" for a viral post to "fall in our laps," she said she refused to "actively hunt that stuff down, or else you start reading like *BuzzFeed*." Felix also cited *BuzzFeed* as an organization that used metrics in a way that Gawker wouldn't:

> I think that I would argue that our competitors, or some of our competitors, are working on a formulaic basis. I mean, like *BuzzFeed*. Or like that fucking bullshit, what's it called, *Upworthy*. *That* is a formula. That's, you leave a cliff hanger at the end of every headline so you have to click to figure out what the goddamn story's about. Or like "let's make eight hundred quizzes about these things, because these are the things people have emotional reactions to. People love reading things about *Clueless*, let's make ten more things about *Clueless*." We don't do that [at Gawker]. That is cynical.

I asked Felix to elaborate on what he meant by "cynical" in this context. He replied: "I think we're defining ourselves in a lot of ways against the underlying ethos that powers that."

CP: Which is—
FELIX: Which is cynicism, a sense that, like, all journalism is clickbait.

Felix acknowledged that Anthony and Rob's "viral beat" subsite was tasked with aggregating content explicitly for the purpose of garnering traffic. But he did not consider their work to be cynical because it was undergirded by genuine emotion: "Those dudes' posts are very clicky, but it's just like, this is their personality. . . . They're just people who like to laugh and they are legitimately astounded by this thing that they just saw on the internet. And that's what comes through in the post." The intro text on Anthony and Rob's subsite echoed this framing:

> Here you won't find fake and cheap viral crap. What we decide to publish are the things that really excite us, the stuff that we want to share with our

friends. . . . Many of our stories come from you, the readers who are not cynics, those of us who still wonder about the many great things that this world and its people give to us every day.

Although Gawker staffers like Felix and Alison saw *BuzzFeed*'s editorial approach as synonymous with clickbait and "cheap viral crap," *BuzzFeed* itself emphatically rejected this characterization, going so far as to publish a post in 2014 headlined "Why BuzzFeed Doesn't Do Clickbait." Ben Smith, who was *BuzzFeed* editor in chief at the time, argued that those who associate *BuzzFeed* with clickbait "confuse what we do with true clickbait," which was, in his view, a headline that baits the reader into clicking by overpromising on what the story, once clicked on, actually delivers. By contrast, Smith wrote, *BuzzFeed*'s headlines tend to be "extremely direct": for example, "'31 Genius Hacks for Your Elementary School Art Class' is just that."

While Gawker's definition of clickbait centered on the authenticity of the writer's intention, *BuzzFeed*'s focused on reader misdirection. The gulf between Felix's and Smith's opposing perspectives further illustrates the absence of a widely accepted definition of clickbait within the contemporary U.S. news media industry. Even more importantly, though, it shows how the very nebulousness of the term enables it to be mobilized in clean/dirty boundary-drawing efforts across the industry. In other words, "clickbait" has become a Rorschach test in which journalists see every news organization but their own.

Conclusion

Metrics confront journalists with a powerful mixed message. If they ignore the data altogether, they risk being seen as foolishly obstinate, patronizing toward their audience, and behind the digital times—in effect guaranteeing their professional obsolescence and possibly facing managerial censure or even job loss. But if they rely on metrics *too* much, they risk corrupting their sense of professional integrity and autonomy, and potentially sullying their reputation. To make matters more challenging, there is no widely agreed-upon normative standard within the profession for how to navigate between these two extremes.[45]

This chapter has shown that journalists respond to this uncertain and stressful situation by devising symbolic boundaries that designate some types of metrics, newsroom roles, and uses of metrics as clean, such that they do not contaminate the newsroom or the journalists who work in it, and some as dirty. As long as metrics stayed within their carefully prescribed confines—as long as they did not become "matter out of place"—the data, as well as the commercial pressures and work intensification it represents, was seen by journalists as something that could coexist relatively peacefully with their sense of professional autonomy and integrity.

Of course, the precise contours of these clean/dirty boundaries—that is, what counts as metrics being "out of place"—continually shift and can seem arbitrary to the outside observer. This becomes especially evident in journalists' efforts to draw a line between the content of news and its form/distribution, as well as the tendency to condemn rival news organizations' uses of metrics as craven and cynical while defending one's own use of metrics as appropriate and principled. However, the very act of *drawing* the line arguably matters more than *where* the line is drawn. Creating and maintaining clean/dirty boundaries around metrics gave journalists a sense of control—however minor—over what might otherwise seem like a clear managerial imposition on their editorial decision making, driven by structural economic forces that they were powerless to do much of anything about.

While these acts of boundary-drawing were a source of psychological reassurance, they could also become fodder for intra-organizational conflict. As we have seen, metrics are simultaneously ambiguous, in that they require labor to interpret, and consequential, in that their very existence speaks to deep questions about the management of journalistic work. For these reasons, metrics have the potential to disrupt (or reinforce) existing distributions of power in newsrooms. The next chapter will examine the power struggles that emerge within newsrooms over how access to metrics is distributed and who performs the interpretive labor required to make sense of them.

PART III

Managing Metrics

6

The Struggle to Monopolize
Interpretive Labor

Traffic gives power to people. It gives leverage to people. It gives backup.
Whereas in print, you never had that, right?

—JOSH, NEW YORK TIMES REPORTER

ON A SUNNY, late winter afternoon, I sat in the *Times*'s cavernous, light-drenched, and mostly empty cafeteria and conducted an interview with Parker, a staffer who had extensive experience with analytics. Parker had worked in various departments at the *Times* for years, and at the time of our first interview he had recently taken on a new role in newsroom operations. His mandate in this job was to help the paper's editorial staff develop uses for metrics that felt, in the parlance of the organization, "Timesian." To that end, Parker explained, he frequently fielded analytics-related queries from editors who wanted him to help them interpret what they were seeing on tools like Chartbeat or to apply his data fluency to answer their questions about historical traffic patterns.

When I asked for an example of such an interaction, Parker recounted an instance in which a sports editor had asked him to pull some historical data on the number of regular visitors to the *Bats* blog, the paper's erstwhile baseball blog. The editor said he needed the data quickly, by 5 p.m. that afternoon. The specificity and urgency of the request piqued Parker's curiosity, and he asked the editor why he needed that particular data on such a tight turnaround. The editor explained that he was assigning three reporters to cover the World Series game set to take place that night: two of them would write articles for the following day's paper, while the third (the "odd man out," as Parker put it) would cover the game exclusively for the *Bats* blog. The third reporter was unhappy with his blogging assignment—unsurprisingly, given that at the time blogs were known around the newsroom as repositories for content that, as one reporter put it, "basically wasn't worth it for the paper, but would be interesting to read to some members of [our audience]." Thus the sports editor wanted to share *Bats*'s traffic data, in order to show the unhappy reporter that his audience would in fact be much bigger writing for the blog than for the paper. "Editors want to manage the message [of metrics] a little bit," Parker explained. "It's easy to misinterpret this stuff, and information is ammunition."

Hearing Parker's story, I was struck by the way the sports editor had planned to use analytics—not to make any kind of editorial decision but rather to minimize his subordinate's discontent with a decision he had *already* made. Instead of metrics operating as an engine of rationalization in the Weberian sense, wherein work becomes routinized, systematized, predictable, and less dependent on the specialized skills and knowledge of particular individual or group, the sports editor sought to use metrics as a tool of rationalization in a *psychological* sense, in that a rational justification was formulated after the fact for a decision made on an intuitive basis.[1]

This chapter will examine when, how, and why editors mobilized metrics in the management of journalistic labor, and how the reporters they supervised responded. Chapter 4 showed that the meaning of audience metrics in journalism is often ambiguous. Data points don't come with particular takeaways attached. Rather, metrics accrue meaning through interpretive labor that seeks to answer questions about what qualifies as a high- or low-traffic performance, why a story got the traffic it did, and what actions should be taken as a result. As Parker's anecdote illustrates, the interpretive ambiguity of news analytics presented an opportunity for editors to bolster the legitimacy of their decisions—provided that they could, to borrow his phrase, "manage the message" of metrics successfully.

Yet the interpretive ambiguity of metrics also posed a potential threat to editors' authority. If reporters had access to metrics, they could craft alternative interpretations of the data and use these to contest editors' decisions about the assignment, placement, and timing of stories. This in turn could threaten to disrupt the traditional hierarchical newsroom structure, in which editors were the final arbiters of the nebulous quality that is "newsworthiness," as well as the primary dispensers of prestige, accolades, and admonishment among the reporting staff.

Put simply, the ability to interpret metrics—and have one's interpretation be widely accepted as legitimate and authoritative—is an important form of power in contemporary newsrooms. This chapter will look at how this power is distributed and examine the consequences for journalistic work. Although the *Times* and Gawker had organizational approaches to metrics that were highly dissimilar in many respects, we will see that editors in both newsrooms sought to control, as best they could, the circumstances in which their subordinates were exposed to metrics.

At the *Times*, editors contained the spread of metrics in the newsroom by implementing a system of tiered access to the data, according to which editors were able to consult analytics tools while reporters were not. *Times* editors' exclusive access to metrics allowed them to strategically disclose particular data points to reporters in order to accomplish managerial objectives—such as, per Parker's anecdote above, assuaging a reporter's displeasure with what he felt was a suboptimal assignment. Through this combination of data containment and strategic disclosure, *Times* editors sought to establish an interpretive monopoly over metrics. After all, reporters could not contest the meanings that editors assigned to metrics if they were unable to view the data themselves.[2]

By contrast, editors at Gawker were not able to limit writers' access to metrics because audience data was ubiquitous there: as discussed in previous chapters, enormous flat-screen monitors displaying real-time metrics were mounted on Gawker's office walls, staff traffic rankings were publicly available online, and every editorial employee had access to analytics tools. However, even in Gawker's metrics-saturated environment, we will see that editors sought to manage the message that the data communicated and to position themselves as a buffer between metrics and writers.

Editors' efforts to control reporters' access to and interpretation of metrics reflect not only their own desire (especially at the *Times*) to maintain their vaunted status in the newsroom pecking order but also the editor's unique (and understudied) position "as a profession 'in-between' management and journalism."[3] Editors' efforts to control metrics were only partially successful, however: writers challenged editors' interpretive monopoly in various ways, including by establishing a "black market" in which metrics surreptitiously circulated among reporters at the *Times*. The existence of these unofficial back channels for metrics contributed to the eventual decision to broaden access to metrics in the *Times* newsroom.

Data Containment

In the common spaces of the *New York Times* headquarters in midtown Manhattan, displays of any kind of metrics data were conspicuously absent. Unlike at Gawker, where vast swaths of wall were occupied by large flat screens displaying various real-time traffic rankings of stories and writers, some of the *Times*'s prominent wall space was covered with framed reprints of each of the paper's Pulitzer Prize–winning stories, of which it has published more than any other news organization.[4] The *Times*'s Pulitzer Wall, as it is known, was a point of pride for staffers, symbolizing the organization's formidable prestige.

Touring the *Times* offices for the first time in 2012, I wasn't expecting to see a Gawker-style Big Board on the wall: drawing attention to metrics via such a display would have been inconsistent with the organization's self-conception and its public face. I was, however, surprised to learn that although the *Times* maintained subscriptions to several analytics tools, including Chartbeat, the hundreds of reporters at the paper did not have access to metrics, even about stories they themselves had written. This policy of data containment was a deliberate choice on the part of masthead editors: two reporters told me they had explicitly asked for access to Chartbeat and their requests had been denied.

While a few reporters expressed indifference to seeing this type of data about their stories (one veteran reporter I had reached out to by email declined to be interviewed, saying she had never heard of Chartbeat), most voiced curiosity about the data. In some cases the interest in metrics was general. As Lucy, a reporter, put it: "I don't easily know how many people click on my stories . . . I would be curious to know that but I don't have a way of easily knowing." Amy, another reporter, echoed Lucy's curiosity about metrics: "I find that stuff fascinating, but I don't have any access to it in my current position." Other reporters, like Josh, had a clearer sense of precisely what kind of data they would like to see:

> I would love to know [by] what paragraph my readers start to give up on me, because you know they're not reading 'til the end, but we write it like they are, right? . . . And traffic [data] could unlock those answers. I mean, I'm sure editors have those answers somewhere. That sort of stuff I don't think we've really tapped into much, at least not in my tiny corner of the universe here.

Editors were aware that many reporters harbored curiosity about metrics but were reluctant to broaden access to analytics tools. The oft-given rationale was that editors did not want commercial considerations, as represented by metrics, to corrupt reporters' editorial judgment or jeopardize their professional integrity. Yet as my interviews at the *Times* progressed, it became clear that editors' motivations for restricting reporters' access to metrics were more complicated and had as much to do with preserving the newsroom's existing power structure—and editors' place at the top of it—as protecting the purity of reporters' journalistic judgment.

The *Times* print newsroom had traditionally operated as a rigid hierarchy with a set chain of command. As Parker put it: "The paper is like a military organization. It has generals, it has lieutenants and the general says we're [doing] whatever, and that's how it is." As the "generals" of the newsroom, editors assigned stories to reporters, guided reporting strategies and the development of editorial angles, and determined stories' placement and the timing of their publication. It was understood that editors made such decisions based on their specialized sense of "editorial judgment," which consisted of their instincts honed from years of experience in the news business. While reporters could question editors' dictates to a certain extent, editors had the ultimate say.

Yet the affordances of networked digital media made this rigidly hierarchical distribution of power harder to maintain at the *Times*. The amorphous timelines and oft-changing formats of online news allow for, and in some cases necessitate, more flexible arrangements and decentralized decision making. As Parker explained, "The web is much more collaborative [than print] because there's no deadlines. You have to get a paper on the doorstep by five in the morning, [and] if you talk back [to the editor], it ain't going to get on the doorstep. Whereas web deadlines are all the time and never." It's no coincidence that digital-native publications, including Gawker sites, tend to have fewer layers of editorial oversight and more horizontal organizational structures in the newsroom.

Metrics weren't the only manifestation of this shift, but they were a significant one. Editors' sense of "news judgment" is intuitive and inscrutable (and thus difficult for reporters to argue with). By contrast, metrics had the potential to be equally visible and accessible to all staffers in a newsroom. And because of metrics' interpretive ambiguity, a reporter could look at the same data as her editor and draw her own—possibly contradictory—conclusions.

As such, *Times* editors restricted reporters' access to metrics because they perceived the data as a potential threat, not only to the quality of the paper's journalism but also to their own managerial authority. As Ben, a *Times* editor who worked on the online-only interactive news team, explained when describing why the print editors closely guarded access to metrics:

> If you think about an editor, really the only thing an editor has—like their full job is based on their judgment. Because that's really what they do, is they just sit and use their judgment to edit stories and decide how important they are and where they should go on the site. And so replacing that with metrics of some sort is a massive threat to their livelihood and kind of value in the job.

That the newsroom's policy of data containment was partly driven by editors' effort to preserve their authority became especially clear in discussions about what was, at the time, the *Times*'s most high-profile metric: the most-emailed list (Fig. 6.1). The list of the top ten "most-emailed" stories was public and appeared prominently on the *Times* home page. It was, therefore, one of the only metrics to which reporters had regular access. However, editors had access to a supplemental list: they received a daily email showing *how many times* each story on the list had been emailed, while reporters did not. Unlike reporters, editors therefore knew that the number of times a story had to have been emailed in order to make the list was surprisingly small (when one editor showed me the list, the top-ranked story had been emailed only 987 times). Several editors explained to me that the list also skewed older than the *Times*'s general readership.[5]

The extra data to which editors had exclusive access led them to conclude that the most-emailed list was in fact a poor indicator of even the narrow thing it purported to be measuring, let alone of audience response more generally. When the most-emailed list came up in interviews, editors were often quick to point out its shortcomings as a metric. As a result, some editors told me they felt frustrated when reporters were, in the words of one editor, "constantly checking most-emailed" and becoming excited if their stories appeared on the list.

Despite their irritation that reporters did not understand the ways in which the most-emailed list was a poor measure of popularity or newsworthiness, editors were reluctant to share the extra data about the list more widely. Sandra, a reporter, told me that a desk editor had once called her over and shown her the email that contained the most-emailed numbers, and Sandra remembered being shocked at how few times the stories that made the list had actually been emailed. But she was unable to get regular access to this information: "I said, 'Why don't we circulate these [numbers]?' And I got back 'It's not a good idea, it bounces around too much.' I think there is some effort to tamp down how much people pay attention to most-emailed."

1. WELL
   How Walking in Nature Changes the Brain

2. Why Is It So Hard to Get a Great Bagel in California?

3. THE UPSHOT
   The Fundamental Way That Universities Are an Illusion

4. Drug Prices Soar, Prompting Calls for Justification

5. 36 Hours in Siem Reap

6. THE UPSHOT
   More Than Their Mothers, Young Women Plan Career Pauses

7. FEATURE
   Is This the End of Christianity in the Middle East?

8. OP-ED | JENNIFER WEINER
   'Hello Mother, Hello Daughter': Texts of Misery from Camp

9. REVIEW
   Paul Durand-Ruel, the Paris Dealer Who Put

FIG. 6.1. The *New York Times* most-emailed list as it appeared on the home page in late July, 2015.

I wondered why, if editors wanted to "tamp down how much people pay attention to most-emailed," they didn't share the numbers, especially given that these appeared unimpressive even to a relatively untrained eye like my own. But the size of the numbers was ultimately not the point. Editors wanted to decrease the attention paid to the most-emailed list, not solely because it was a faulty metric but because of the possibility that reporters would invoke data from the list to challenge editors' judgments, particularly about story placement.

An exchange with Tim, an editor, illustrates this. When asked why metrics were contained within the *Times* newsroom, Tim said, "they [top editors] don't want too many people involved with getting access to it." Tim spoke disapprovingly of reporters' excitement when their stories appeared on the most-emailed list. Indeed, he invoked their misplaced enthusiasm as an example of why the *Times* restricted reporters' access to metrics in the first place:

> It's more about the decision makers having that information than everybody having that information. The most-emailed list for instance has been around for a number of years on the website . . . because our readers are interested [in it]. But people in here don't fully understand that the most-emailed story is not being emailed that much. It's sometimes less than 2,000, number one, but people in here will say, "Oh my gosh, look! My story's number one on the most-emailed list, you should put it on the home page!" Well, no, that's not—we're not making judgments based on that, we're making judgments based on what's the right, what are the most interesting, or the most important stories for our readers.

Here Tim described a hypothetical reporter using metrics to gain professional advantage by trying to secure a more prominent placement for her story. Tim ostensibly rejected these types of requests because they relied on data from the most-emailed list, a metric he considered unreliable and unrepresentative of the *Times*'s readership ("People in here don't fully understand that the most-emailed story is not being emailed that much"). But Tim did not imply that citing a different metric would have been appropriate or preferable. Instead, he admonished the hypothetical reporter, reminding her that she was not a "decision maker." Crucially, Tim's annoyance was due not only to the hypothetical reporter's misinterpretation of the most-emailed list but also to her attempts to strategically *deploy* this misinterpretation to raise her own story's profile on the website—and, in doing so, challenge Tim's judgment about where particular stories should be placed.

There is an inescapable and seemingly puzzling circularity here. By denying reporters access to the numerical data for most-emailed stories, editors increased the likelihood that reporters would overestimate the importance of the most-emailed list. Tim then invoked *that very overestimation* as evidence that reporters should not have broader access to metrics. But Tim's perspective is less perplexing when understood as part of a broader effort to protect editors' status in the newsroom.

Indeed, Tim was far from the only editor to express a fear that, if given access to metrics, reporters would invoke data to challenge editors' authority and advance their own careers. Tara, a long-time Chartbeat employee, explained that during the development of the very first iteration of Chartbeat's newsroom analytics dashboard (then called Newsbeat), Chartbeat built a tiered permissions system that would allow reporters to see detailed metrics, but only for their own stories. However, many legacy news organizations— including the *Times*—elected not to use this feature because of a fear among editors that reporters would "abuse" the data.[6] As Tara explained:

> [Legacy news organizations are] typically giving [Chartbeat access] to, like, the top N percent. . . . So these are the guys [about whom they can say,] "We have no fear about them misusing data, abusing data." And "abusing" means that they don't know how to read it, therefore don't understand it, therefore are . . . gonna make the wrong, like, incorrect assumptions, or use it to their advantage. . . . I don't know how *real* that is, but it's definitely a fear.

Conversations about how metrics contribute to displacement and deskilling typically focus on workers. Yet Tara's comment illustrates how newsroom managers, too, were at risk of having their position undermined by metrics, if access to the data was universally distributed. *Times* editors' policy of data containment was their attempt to mitigate this risk.[7] Restricting the circulation of data within the newsroom allowed editors to monopolize the way in which it was interpreted and minimize the chance that reporters' rival interpretations would be used to challenge editors. For a time, data containment proved effective as a managerial strategy (although as we will see later in this chapter, it was not a sustainable approach to handling metrics in the long term).

By contrast, Gawker editors would not have been able to implement data containment even if they had wanted to. The company's top executives, including founder and CEO Nick Denton, mandated that several varieties of traffic metrics were accessible, not only to staffers in the office but also to the broader public. Some editors disagreed with this policy but were not in a position to change it. For example, as we saw in chapter 2, Andrew, a site lead, expressed a preference that access to metrics be more restricted, but he had little say over executive decisions about what data was made available and to whom.

While Gawker editors could not formally prevent reporters from accessing metrics as *Times* editors could, some nonetheless did try to *buffer* writers from certain metrics by neglecting to explicitly share them or tell writers where they could find them. Gawker editors' buffering efforts tended to focus on shielding staff from metrics that spotlighted the traffic performance of individual writers, as opposed to an entire site. As Andrew explained: "I'm always pushing away from the individual metrics to collective metrics. I think that's healthier overall for everything."

One such individual metric that editors largely declined to speak about with writers was the eCPM number. As discussed in chapter 2, Gawker calculated a cost measure called an eCPM for all editorial staffers, which was the measure of how many dollars employees earned in salary for every one thousand unique visitors their posts brought to the site. Writers were expected to maintain an eCPM no higher than $20; those whose eCPMs exceeded this number for a prolonged period were in danger of being fired. Although eCPM numbers factored into Gawker executives' decisions about employee compensation and personnel, most site leads did not discuss writers' eCPM numbers with them. As a result, while the eCPM numbers came up in nearly every site lead interview I conducted, writers rarely mentioned them. If I asked writers about eCPM, most seemed to have only a hazy understanding of what it measured and did not know their personal eCPM figure. While presiding over an editorial "all-hands" staff meeting, Noah, a high-ranking editorial executive, alluded to eCPM in an offhand fashion when discussing a different topic. A writer in the audience asked: "What does that mean?"

Seemingly puzzled, Noah replied: "What do you mean?"

WRITER: "What's eCPM?"
NOAH: "Oh, do you guys not know what eCPM is?"
WRITER: "No." [Laughter in room.]

Noah seemed surprised and slightly taken aback by this discovery. He explained what eCPM numbers measured and said that management wanted writers to maintain an eCPM of $20 or less—"which is actually pretty low, like, it's not that hard to hit that number. Most people within the company are actually well under $20. But that's the number that I use sort of internally to measure: is somebody playing the game of Gawker properly, or are they, you know, slacking?" Noah explained that he was trying to be "transparent" about the metrics with which management evaluated writers. Indeed, given the company's emphasis on transparency as a modus operandi, it was striking that site leads took deliberate measures to buffer writers from individual-level metrics, especially eCPM.

Why did they do so? Because the organizational structure of Gawker sites was less strictly hierarchical than that of the *Times*, Gawker editors' motivations for containing individual metrics like eCPM were distinct from those of their *Times* counterparts. Many Gawker editors felt that metrics that measured the performance of individuals were worse for morale than metrics, like the Big Board, that ranked sites and posts. Lisa said: "This is gonna sound weird, but I get worried when I see people that are on staff sinking down in the ratings and stuff, because, I mean, not like this is a place that people get fired from, but I imagine that they will be stressed out. And I don't want them to feel stressed out." Alison explained how she handled situations in which a writer had persistently stagnant individual traffic:

ALISON: I'll look and be like, okay, so-and-so has been flat for three months. I'm gonna not *say* that to her, but I'm going to actually pay more attention to her and work with her a little bit more closely—like kind of in a way where I don't even think they notice. But you know, I pay more attention.

CP: So you wouldn't [mention a writer's stagnant individual traffic] as feedback?

ALISON: No. But it kinda depends on the writer. But I don't like freaking them out, I don't. Let me be the freak about this. Let me do it.

Editors also sought to contain individual-level metrics because they feared these metrics could de-incentivize collaborative labor. Because Gawker sites were structured with far less editorial oversight than what was customary in a traditional newsroom, writers constantly needed to help each other with stories, angles, headlines, and images if sites were going to function smoothly. For this reason, editors preferred metrics that fostered cooperation and a sense of group belonging. Conversely, they aimed to downplay metrics that encouraged a more individualistic way of thinking about traffic. As Andrew put it:

It is less damaging to the reporter when they have a collective [traffic] goal rather than an individual goal, because there's more incentive to help each other out if there's a collective goal. And so I guess we're more socialist than capitalist or something, but it's designed to make it so that people actually feel like we are a team and we can achieve together.

Sitting in on the online group chat for Andrew's site, it was easy to see this type of collaborative work in effect. Before publishing a post, writers typically suggested three versions of a headline in the chat and asked their colleagues to weigh in on which was best. One writer used his Photoshop skills to make a funny image to accompany a post by another writer. Colleagues offered to assist each other with particularly labor-intensive posts. When asked, writers often provided each other thoughtful feedback in the chat on potential angles for posts.

While each of these interactions tended to be brief, taken together they consumed a significant amount of employee time over the course of the workday. It tracks, then, that editors would see individual-level metrics as a potential threat to their sites' collaborative workflow and seek to diminish their visibility to the writing staff.

The fact that editors in newsrooms as distinct as the *Times* and Gawker engaged in data-containment efforts (albeit in different ways and with different objectives) is striking. This finding suggests that controlling the circulation and interpretation of digital performance metrics has become a key aspect of managing contemporary knowledge workers. Yet, as the next section will illustrate, managing writers' exposure to metrics did not *always* entail discouraging them from paying attention to the data.

Strategic Disclosure

Although they withheld systematic access to metrics, *Times* editors would strategically disclose particular data points to reporters when they wanted to accomplish a specific managerial purpose or elicit a desired reaction.[8] As Arthur, an editor, succinctly put it: "If I need to prove a point, I go there."

For example, *Times* editors commonly invoked metrics in efforts to boost reporters' morale. Sam, a veteran reporter, said, "I have a few times gotten emails from an editor saying, 'Hey, we had great traffic on your story.'" After the publication of a massive, multistory feature on the war in Afghanistan that Cynthia, a reporter, had worked on, an editor had gone out of his way to show her traffic figures for the series: "An assistant managing editor at one point called me into his office and was like, 'Look how well this did!'" Despite editors' complaints that reporters were overly focused on the most-emailed list as an indicator of a story's success, editors regularly drew attention to that very list when doling out praise. As Sandra, a long-time reporter, explained: "It's absolutely routine now that when any desk head sends out their 'what a great job we're doing' [email], it will go, 'It was a great week, [so-and-so's] story shot to number-one-most-e-mailed in three and a half hours.'" This practice suggests that it was not invocation of the most-emailed list as a proxy for quality or popularity per se that editors found objectionable. Rather, it was the invocation of the most-emailed list *by reporters* that was seen as problematic, because it indicated that editors were losing control of the story that metrics were used to tell.

Editors also disclosed metrics to reporters when they believed doing so would help surmount managerial hurdles, many of which concerned the newsroom's halting adjustment to digital modes of news production and distribution.[9] My research at the *Times* took place during an illuminating moment of transition in this regard. It was becoming widely understood within the newsroom that the online edition and digital-only subscribers were central to the company's future—yet the *Times's* long-standing organizational culture and many high-ranking staffers still valued the print edition far above the digital one. Lucy explained that, for a reporter, "There's a cachet that being on the [paper's] front page has that nothing else can really measure up to." Editors generally agreed. As Randall told me:

> The newspaper is still considered . . . a marquee place for your story. The web, for all of its attributes, it is kind of a transient medium. . . . It's published but it's not a tangible product; it still doesn't carry . . . the same weight as a newspaper front-page story.

Randall went on to describe a long-standing tradition at the *Times* that illustrated the difference in prestige between the print and online editions: the first time a reporter wrote a story that appeared on page one of the print edition (known at the *Times* as A1), they were given an aluminum plaque of that day's front page as a keepsake to acknowledge the achievement. Digital milestones were not met with equivalent fanfare. Explained Randall: "Nobody wants to get a plaque that shows their story on the home page of the *Times.*"

The special weight the print edition carried was not merely symbolic. It was also manifested in organizational practices that had significant material implications for the writers' careers. In 2014, *BuzzFeed* published a leaked copy of the *Times*'s Innovation Report, a comprehensive and critical analysis of the paper's challenges transitioning to the digital age that was produced by a small group of *Times* staffers and not intended to be made public. The report noted that annual performance reviews often "lead off with" the number of times a reporter has had a story on A1, while making no mention of home-page placements or other online metrics, even for staffers who had been explicitly hired to focus on writing for the website.[10]

For editors, favoring the print edition (and the primacy of A1 more specifically) had obvious appeal: it was a way to maintain a connection to the paper's storied history at a time of upheaval. It was also a means of safeguarding their own status within the newsroom, since the job of selecting stories to go on A1 fell exclusively to editors. Lucy articulated it most clearly when she said that having one of her stories make A1 thrilled her because "you're being judged by a jury of your peers." Anointing A1 placements as the most significant form of performance evaluation thus signaled to reporters that the assessments of *Times* editors were paramount.

Yet valorizing the print edition and A1 also presented a managerial challenge, because the *Times* needed to feature a robust set of online-only offerings if it was to remain economically and culturally competitive in the digital age. This meant that, as a practical matter, most reporters had to regularly produce website content. But reporters were reluctant to write online-only material, having inferred correctly that writing for the print edition was considered by their editors to be more prestigious. Nate, a reporter, summarized the dilemma: "I think that one of the things that [editors] are struggling with right now is that the *Times* is trying to get more people blogging, but then you're also judged by this metric of your A1 stories."

As we saw in Parker's anecdote about the sports editor and the *Bats* blog, editors sought to resolve this tension by strategically invoking metrics. Editors' selective disclosure of particular data points aimed to increase reporters' interest in writing for the website without fundamentally changing the newsroom's print-focused allocation of prestige. For example, Tim described how he invoked select metrics in order to convince writers of the legitimacy and value of the website:

> One of the things that we've tried to do with [metrics] is to use it for other purposes [than to guide coverage and editorial decision making]. At the *Times* being on A1 is a hugely important thing and a huge accomplishment.

We're trying to impress upon people the value of being on the home page, too. And so if you can say, "Hey, thought you'd wanna know—your story was being read by 8,000 people at nine o'clock this morning, and remained number one on [the] readership list for eight hours" or something like that, then the point of that is just to try to emphasize to people the value of being on the home page. . . . [It] is a nice kind of feedback . . . you can give to someone.

Tim's use of metrics to emphasize to reporters the value of the home page seems somewhat surprising when we recall his frustration at reporters' requests for home-page placement when their stories made the most-emailed list. After all, such requests appear to indicate that these reporters *did* understand "the value of being on the home page"—why did Tim not approve of or reward them? What at first seems like a contradiction is actually consistent with the broader editor-reporter dynamic at the *Times*: editors saw metrics as useful and desirable when they could marshal them to serve strategic ends vis-à-vis reporters but counterproductive when reporters attempted to access and interpret this data themselves—especially when they did so to bolster their own status claims.[11]

The combination of data containment and strategic disclosure was disorienting for some *Times* reporters, who felt like they were receiving mixed messages. Josh complained: "There's a certain amount of schizophrenia, at least in this newsroom, about how to think about traffic. Like some days it seems to matter and some days it seems not to matter. And that annoys me, because I'd rather it be one way or the other." From Josh's perspective, there seemed to be a randomness to when metrics did and did not "matter" in the newsroom. But there was in fact a pattern: editors handled metrics in ways that allowed them to accomplish strategic managerial goals (such as boosting reporters' enthusiasm about writing for the website) without undermining their newsroom authority.

Gawker managers and editors also strategically invoked particular metrics to resolve mismatches between organizational aspirations and practical necessities. For example, for reasons that will be discussed in greater depth in chapter 7, Gawker executives (particularly Denton) wanted writers to participate more in the comments sections beneath their posts using Kinja, Gawker's proprietary publishing platform and content-management system (CMS). Increasing staffers' interactions with commenters was part of Denton's broader goal of transforming Gawker into a platform for "collaborative journalism," in which "the base unit of content [was] not a standalone article but an exchange between the author and the most insightful of readers."[12]

But many writers voiced skepticism about, if not outright hostility toward, Denton's expectation that writers increase their participation in reader comment threads. They worried that greater interaction with commenters would leave them less time to write new posts, which could, in turn, depress their site's number of unique visitors and thus their chance of getting a monthly bonus. As Andrew explained: "As soon as you sort of sniff out that [interacting with commenters] actually has nothing to do with traffic, it becomes very hard for the writer or reporter to pay any attention to it." Liam seconded this point: "If I leave a whole bunch of comments in Kinja, that doesn't affect site traffic, which therefore does not translate into a bonus." The fact that the traffic-based monthly bonus was based on unique visitors (as opposed to, say, pageviews or time spent) made it seem especially detached from interaction with readers: unique visitors is a metric that rewards bringing *new* audiences to a site, whereas nearly all commenters were already-devoted readers. (If a reader visits a Gawker site every single day for a month, she may be responsible for hundreds of pageviews or minutes spent, but she only counts as a single unique.)

In an attempt to incentivize writers' engagement with commenters, management first introduced a "Kinja bonus," modeled after the uniques bonus. Yet the Kinja bonus did little to shift writers' motivations. This was partly because the Kinja bonus was capped at 2 percent of a site's monthly budget, far short of the uniques bonus, which was capped at 20 percent. The large disparity between the size of the two bonuses reflected the fact that, Denton's interest in writer-reader interaction notwithstanding, advertisers—the company's primary source of revenue—continued to look mainly at uniques when deciding whether to buy space on Gawker sites.

In addition, there was also no transparent or straightforward way of determining who deserved the Kinja bonus, due in part to the formidable challenges of quantitatively measuring "interaction." The Kinja bonus's opacity led both writers and site leads to question its legitimacy and fairness. "It was never clear how it was measured," complained Liam. Andrew elaborated further: "How is [good Kinja participation] judged? Well, they don't actually have a way to count this yet."

When the Kinja bonus failed to produce the desired result of getting writers to engage more in comment threads, Gawker management pivoted to a different tactic: the strategic disclosure of a new metric. Midway through my fieldwork at Gawker, a writer forwarded me an email that Noah had sent to the entire staff of this writer's site. The email had the subject line, "Author Participation Numbers," and read: "I want everyone to be in at least 80% of their threads interacting. That ideally means commenting yourself, but failing that at least recommending other [people's] comments. In April, the following people didn't hit those numbers. (Or rather, really missed them by a lot.)" Noah had pasted a spreadsheet into the email that listed, by name, several writers who had failed to meet the 80 percent target and showed by exactly how much they had fallen short. He concluded the email with an exhortation to "Pick up the pace!"

The writer who forwarded this email to me was one of the staffers Noah had admonished in front of his colleagues—though if he was ruffled by it, he didn't let on. "I don't think [the 80 percent target] is unreasonable at all," he wrote to me. "In fact, Noah's being pretty reasonable in this email. But it's the first time anyone not in management has seen a measurement of author Kinja participation." Like the *Times* editor who shared previously secret metrics about the readership of the *Bats* blog when he needed to boost a reporter's enthusiasm for his blogging assignment, Noah divulged the Kinja participation metric when doing so was deemed necessary for achieving a form of behavior modification that was proving difficult to bring about by other means. Noah's strategic disclosure of the Kinja participation metric seemed to work as intended: "What effect is it having?" the writer's email to me continued. "I'm [now] participating [in the comments] on every post [I write]. It's not hard. I just didn't know until now the exact boundaries of the expectation."

These examples from the *Times* and Gawker illustrate how editors strategically disclosed metrics as a way of coping with the managerial predicaments presented by inconsistent, competing, or shifting organizational goals and values. In both newsrooms, managers wanted to induce a new behavior in staffers that conflicted with a deeply ingrained aspect of the organization that executives were unwilling or unable to deprioritize. At the *Times*, editors wanted to incentivize reporters to write web-exclusive content without diminishing the prestige of the print edition; at Gawker, executives wanted writers to interact with commenters without sacrificing the high numbers of unique visitors that were a key selling point for advertisers.

Given the time-intensive nature of each of these goals, achieving them simultaneously required getting employees to work harder. It comes as no surprise that managers' deployment of carefully selected metrics at crucial moments proved useful in this regard: as we saw in chapter 2, analytics-driven rankings have habit-forming properties that make them powerful tools for extracting increased productivity from workers while minimizing resistance.

Through data containment and strategic disclosure, editors at both organizations tried to manage the flow of metrics in a way that allowed them to take advantage of the data's usefulness for accomplishing managerial objectives while keeping at bay any potential threat that metrics posed to their authority (at the *Times*) or staff morale and collaborative work routines (at Gawker). These strategies were easier to put in place at the *Times*, where editors had far greater leeway to dictate reporters' access to metrics. Yet, while some *Times* reporters willingly accepted editors' control over the flow of metrics within the newsroom, others were frustrated by editors' withholding of metrics and devised unofficial methods of accessing traffic data about their stories.

The Black Market for Metrics

In March 2014, the *American Journalism Review* reported that editors at the *Verge*, a popular technology site, restricted reporters' access to metrics. This was striking for a tech publication, especially one owned by Vox Media, which had a reputation as a cutting-edge digital media company. The *Verge* reporters interviewed for the story said they felt the policy, while sometimes frustrating, was ultimately for the best. But the site's top editor, Nilay Patel, said that despite the policy it was still all but impossible to prevent reporters from accessing traffic data through various under-the-radar methods. "It's like a black market," Patel explained. "It gets spread around whether I like it or not."[13]

The *Times* manifested a similar pattern; editors were simply unable to mediate reporters' every exposure to metrics. As at the *Verge*, something of a "black market" for analytics existed in the *Times* newsroom. Reporters circumvented the paper's restrictive policies about metrics in three ways. First, tech-savvy reporters explained that they monitored audience response to their stories using various online tools such as bit.ly, which enabled users to shorten a URL and monitor how many times it was being shared on Twitter and other social platforms, or Topsy, which provided data about how a piece of content was being discussed on social media sites.

Second, some reporters had access to metrics simply by accident. For instance, Josh described having "lucked into" a Google Analytics account for a brief period: "I don't think I was ever supposed to get one, but I did." Others, like Nate, had previously inhabited roles with access to metrics and had simply kept their log-ins when they transitioned into full-time reporting roles:

> The only reason I have access to the metrics is because I still have tools that I used when I worked in [a tech-focused department], and so I can go in and see kind of what's going on. . . . But most reporters wouldn't know their story got 20 pageviews or 20 million.

Third, some reporters leveraged their social relationships in the newsroom to access metrics on an informal, ad hoc basis. Since losing his accidental Google Analytics account, Josh obtained traffic data via his friendship with a colleague who had access to metrics:

> I don't have an account, but I do like to look over the shoulder of the guy that sits in front of me who does, and he and I have great conversations about what the traffic means and what the traffic patterns are and where our traffic's coming from, you know, all that sort of [thing]. Cause he's a web producer, so he has access to it and sees it.

Cynthia also highlighted the role of newsroom gossip in spreading information about traffic. She explained that while the metrics disclosed by editors were always positive ("I think an editor would only pull me aside to give me good news [about traffic]"), she heard negative traffic-related news from other reporters or web producers in a way that was "more gossipy": "like, 'Oh, I heard people aren't watching the videos [on the website].'"

In sum, *Times* reporters had found ways to leverage technical know-how, administrative oversights, and social relationships to access metrics, albeit in an unsystematic way. Indeed, when making the case to top editor Dean Baquet in 2014 that the *Times* should broaden access to metrics, Betsy and the rest of the Innovation Report team made the argument that reporters were *already* devising methods for accessing metrics, but doing so in haphazard ways over which editors had no oversight or control. "For a long time we thought metrics was like a bad word in our newsroom, but in fact we're using accidental metrics all the time," Betsy told me. "People use these proxy metrics [like Topsy and the most-emailed list]. [But] we have not chosen them strategically in the newsroom." Betsy's argument was akin to that of parents who view teenagers' drinking as inevitable and therefore sanction it in their home, where at least they can supervise. While Betsy personally felt that broader access to metrics would be greatly beneficial for the organization, she explained that a slightly paternalistic argument was more likely to be effective with the *Times*'s masthead editors: "My work here is persuasion. It's retail politics."

Betsy's persuasion efforts ultimately paid off: the *Times* began rolling out Chartbeat access more widely in the newsroom not long after the release of the Innovation Report in 2014. Eventually, the *Times* even developed its own bespoke analytics tool, Stela, with which staffers throughout the newsroom were encouraged to become familiar. The *Times*'s eventual decision to reverse course and broaden access to metrics suggests that data containment and strategic disclosure are not viable as long-term managerial strategies. Yet perhaps they did not need to be: these tactics played a key role in facilitating the initial introduction of metrics to the *Times*, when editors' anxiety about analytics as a potential force of displacement was at its highest. Once a firm precedent had been set that editors would be the ones to "manage the message" communicated by metrics, the data presented less of a status threat and thus could be more broadly shared.

Conclusion

If previous chapters have argued that interpretive labor is required to assign meaning to ambiguous newsroom metrics, this chapter has shown the various ways editors attempted to control or even monopolize that process. Through data containment, editors at both the *Times* and Gawker sought to curtail their supervisees' exposure to metrics. Editors could then strategically disclose particular metrics to accomplish managerial aims such as boosting morale, motivating particular kinds of behavior (e.g., writing online-only content at the *Times*), and intensifying work (e.g., by prodding Gawker writers to interact with commenters while also keeping their post count up).

In these efforts to manage the circulation and interpretation of metrics, we see how editors occupy what sociologist Erik Olin Wright called "contradictory locations within class relations." To Wright, managers and supervisors have divided loyalties and interests: "they are like capitalists in that they dominate workers; they are like workers in that they are controlled by capitalists and exploited within production."[14] Indeed, many news editors start as rank-and-file reporters and tend to relate strongly to this group and its work. At the same time, however, as managers editors are usually ineligible to join editorial unions, and high-ranking editors have more contact with media owners and business-side executives than does anyone else in the newsroom. Editors' efforts to control the circulation of metrics and monopolize the interpretation of the data reflect the indeterminacy of their position in the journalism labor process and newsroom power structure. We can imagine that managers in other knowledge-work fields might find themselves in a similarly precarious spot and seek to leverage metrics to safeguard their nebulous authority.

However, this chapter has argued that an interpretive monopoly over metrics proved difficult for editors to establish at Gawker and to maintain at the *Times*. At Gawker, top executives opted for near-full transparency about newsroom metrics both within the organization and publicly, thus undermining editors' efforts to buffer writers from what they deemed to be excessive exposure to metrics. At the *Times*, curious reporters developed a number of strategies to informally access data about their stories' traffic performance—which, as the book's conclusion will discuss further, eventually helped lead to a broadening of metrics access in the newsroom. This suggests that while tight managerial control over workers' access to and interpretation of performance metrics may be initially feasible in certain contexts, it ultimately becomes unsustainable for managers within organizations. Still, taken together, the practices of data containment, strategic disclosure, and the black market for metrics illuminate the degree to which metrics have become an important piece of terrain on which newsroom power struggles unfold—and they are likely to remain so.

7

The Autonomy Paradox

At the end of the day, we can do what we want here. We can write whatever we want. We can take the site wherever we need to go.

—ALISON, GAWKER MEDIA SITE LEAD

DURING MY FIELDWORK at Gawker, I encountered a phenomenon that was common enough that media reporter Peter Sterne gave it a name: "the Gawker boomerang." In a 2015 article, Sterne noted that at least half a dozen Gawker editorial staffers had recently left the company to accept other journalism jobs, only to eventually return to Gawker.[1] It was hardly surprising that employees frequently left Gawker: the digital media field is known for high levels of turnover, and earlier chapters have illustrated how Gawker's relentless pace of work and intensive system of metrics-driven evaluation contributed to chronic stress. Nor did Gawker staffers seem to have trouble finding other jobs: the digital journalism skills they'd honed at Gawker, especially the ability to produce a high volume of engaging copy quickly, were in high demand.

Yet, like Sterne, I too was surprised by how many staffers, including those who complained about Gawker's stressful work environment, either had chosen to return there after stints at other publications or had turned down plum job offers at legacy media companies where traffic pressures were not so intense. Why did staffers come back to Gawker, or stay as long as they did?

When I posed this question in interviews, the answer was nearly always the same: writers and editors said they cherished the freedom and editorial autonomy they felt Gawker provided. When I asked Andrea, a writer, to name her favorite thing about her job, she responded: "The amount of freedom that I get, and also just sort of feeling as if we do these sort of things that other sites wouldn't dare to do, or would be too afraid to run or whatever." Sadie, a writer, told me she had turned down two job offers from prestigious legacy magazines after she published a particularly lauded post. She offered the following explanation for her decision:

> [At Gawker] you're really visible and you're allowed to be yourself. And I think that's one of the great things about writing for any of the Gawker sites, is that they encourage you to have an opinion and to have a voice. Whereas at [one of the magazines whose job offer she'd declined] they'd be like, "Be yourself, but be yourself through us."

Alison's career trajectory is particularly instructive here. An early Gawker employee, Alison initially had left the company after a year because she felt "too burned out" by the grueling publication schedule and relentless traffic pressure. She took a job at a well-regarded magazine where she had long dreamed of working, and which lacked the daily intensity to which she had attributed her feelings of burnout at Gawker. But Alison found her new boss to be too editorially and stylistically restrictive: "I got there and [the editor in chief] was like 'No, no, no, we don't do that, we don't say these things, we don't dress this way. We do this, we do that.' Very rigid. [The editor] likes things a certain way and I hated it." Alison left that magazine after just eight months to become the second-in-command editor for the website of another high-profile magazine. She had "loved" that job and stayed for several years. Even so, partly because of the lack of emphasis on analytics (and particularly the lack of a real-time analytics tool like Chartbeat, which she had become accustomed to using heavily at Gawker), "I felt like I was spinning my wheels. The feedback I would get would be from my bosses and they'd say, 'That's good.' But I still felt like I didn't know if I'd succeeded with something. The traffic is an instant measure of my job performance." Eventually she accepted an offer to come back to Gawker as a site lead; four years later, when I began my research, she continued to occupy this position.

Staffers' perception of editorial autonomy at Gawker emerged repeatedly and strongly in my interviews, as well as in public statements staffers have made about the company.[2] The pattern was undeniable, yet I struggled to reconcile it with the ways in which metrics-saturated organizational cultures like Gawker's are typically conceptualized: as oppressive, deskilling, and disempowering to workers. I came to think of this as the "autonomy paradox": how could knowledge workers perceive themselves to be autonomous in their labor process while, at the same time, they were hyperaware that their work performance was incessantly tracked by real-time analytics?

The mystery deepened when Gawker became the first major digital news outlet to unionize in 2015—mere months after an article in the *Washington Post* had confidently asserted that "Internet journalists don't organize" in part because young digital journalists see "management as an ally."[3] The purpose of this chapter is to make sense of the autonomy paradox by uncovering the sometimes surprising ways in which performance metrics can become intertwined with—and in Gawker's case, even reinforce—knowledge workers' perceptions of professional autonomy and group solidarity.

Diverging Conceptions of Journalistic Autonomy at the *New York Times* and Gawker

What is journalistic autonomy? In chapter 1, we saw that it is a surprisingly difficult concept to define. Professional autonomy, the broader category into which journalistic autonomy is often put, is typically considered to consist largely of freedom to carry out one's work with minimal interference from those external to the field. Consider, for instance, sociologist Pierre Bourdieu's field theory approach, according to which social fields are situated between two opposing poles. The "heteronomous" pole encompasses economic and political capital that is derived from external sources. In journalism, this might manifest as "circulation, or advertising revenues, or audience ratings."[4] The autonomous pole, by contrast, encompasses what Bourdieu called "specific" capital: the types of honors and recognition that are particular to a field, bestowed by other inhabitants of the field according to that field's own unique internal logic.[5] The Pulitzer Prizes, which are awarded by a group of distinguished journalists who convene at the prestigious Columbia Journalism School, are the paradigmatic example of specific capital in the journalism field. To Bourdieu, autonomy in fields of cultural production was not the freedom to do whatever one wants but rather the state of being beholden to standards, institutions, and individuals *within one's field*, as opposed to outside influences and pressures.

Though *Times* journalists did not invoke Bourdieu, many of them characterized journalistic autonomy in a way that aligned with a field theory perspective. Stories should be assessed only according to their "news value," *Times* staffers told me, and news value was best determined by journalists and their colleagues. As Amy, a veteran reporter, put it:

I've never heard anybody use data . . . say, the way that it's used in Hollywood. Like, oh, we tried that kind of story and it didn't get traffic, so let's not assign it—that kind of data and analytics. Hollywood says, oh, no, no, no, we had a romantic comedy with a thirty-something redhead and it didn't sell, so we're not going to do this movie. Everything [at the *Times*] is assessed on a journalistic value.

Indeed, many staffers expressed pride in the fact that they worked at the *Times* because of the way they perceived the organization to privilege internal assessments of "journalistic value" over external indicators such as analytics and audience popularity. For example, Cynthia explained to me that the premium the *Times* put on journalistic value aligned with the "idealistic reasons" that she had entered the news media field in the first place.

To reporters at the *Times*, then, the exercise of autonomous journalistic judgment was not only compatible with but also relied upon the supervision and guidance of higher-ranking editors. For example, we can recall from chapter 6 that Lucy felt that having one of her stories chosen for the paper's front page was particularly meaningful because "you're being judged by a jury of your peers." When I asked Sam, a veteran reporter, if he thought about whether a story was likely to be read by a wide audience when he was pitching or writing it, he responded, "No. I never think of that. During a story I always think of whether I think it's interesting or important." I followed up: "How do you think about what makes a story interesting or important?" Sam responded:

> Whether it's interesting or important to me! Like anything, it's just a subjective judgment. If I find something interesting, I'm assuming it may be something other people would. But also, I'm not the final word on it. You know, an editor is approving a story too. . . . So, if *I* think something is interesting and *they* think something's interesting, then I'm making the assumption that enough readers will think it's interesting.[6]

A version of Sam's conception of journalistic autonomy, according to which the most important assessments of newsworthiness come from him or his editor, is common to many professions. In academia, for instance, the peer review process is the ultimate arbiter of whether new research is well-conducted and worthwhile.

However, the idea that a profession is autonomous when it is free from external influences is an awkward fit for journalism, a field whose primary normative reason for existing is to communicate with a *public*. If a field's autonomy is determined by its degree of insularity, then an "autonomous" journalism field not only risks irrelevance but also shirks its vital civic responsibilities. Instead, in chapter 1 we saw that the press is always necessarily separated from some institutions and dependent on others: to achieve press freedom, then, the question is not how to eliminate all external influences on the press but rather how to configure the press's "separations and dependencies" in such a way that the press can serve the role it needs to for a healthy self-governing public.[7]

Seen in this light, Gawker staffers' professions of autonomy, despite being heavily monitored by metrics, start to make more sense. Unlike their counterparts at the *Times*, who valued their colleagues' opinions above those of any outsider, Gawker writers did not necessarily want their performance judged primarily by a "jury of their peers." Indeed, part of Gawker's founding ethos was that it would be, in the words of former *Jezebel* editor Jia Tolentino, "a media organization that is founded on hostility to the powerful and is run with almost no internal hierarchy."[8] Nick Denton, Gawker's founder and owner until 2016, believed that legacy journalists' desire for "respectability" led them to self-censor in a way that was overly deferential to the wealthy, famous, and powerful. Following Denton's lead, Gawker staffers tended to be suspicious of authority, even when the authority figure was their own editor.

In sum, for *Times* journalists, editorial autonomy meant the freedom to follow personal and intra-organizational criteria for newsworthiness while largely free from the influence of external pressures. By contrast, Gawker writers saw top-down editorial authority and internal organizational rules (about, e.g., appropriate tone and writing style) as threatening their autonomy just as much as—if not even more than—market pressures as represented by metrics. As the phenomenon of the "Gawker boomerang" illustrates (and as examples below will corroborate), many Gawker staffers *preferred* to be, in essence, managed by metrics.

Managed by Metrics

The extent to which many Gawker writers preferred metrics-driven performance evaluation to its editor-led counterpart became clear in 2015, when Gawker appointed a new top editor to oversee all the sites: Tommy Craggs, who had previously been the long-time site lead of *Deadspin*, Gawker's sports-focused site. In an attempt to deemphasize metrics in the company's organizational culture, Craggs eliminated the long-standing traffic-based bonus and replaced it with a new system: at the end of each month, site leads submitted collections of what they felt had been their site's strongest posts. A group of top editorial staffers—which winkingly called itself "the Politburo"—pored through these submissions, reviewed them "Zagat-style" on a shared spreadsheet, and collectively decided which sites merited a bonus based on the reviews. In an interview, Craggs told me he had hoped that the new system—which, with its heavy reliance on the considered judgment of top editors, more closely resembled the performance evaluation process at the *Times*—would alleviate writers' traffic-related stress and allow them to take risks with time-consuming reporting projects that might not attract a lot of traffic. According to a field theory framework, Craggs's system afforded considerably more professional autonomy than the traffic-based form of evaluation it was replacing, by emphasizing internal or "specific" capital over economic capital.

Yet at Gawker the shift proved controversial. Site leads (who, unlike writers, were given access to the Politburo's review spreadsheet) questioned the Politburo's ability to fairly and accurately assess the quality of posts. "My case to them," Craggs explained,

> was, "Look, last year, Facebook [from which the majority of traffic to Gawker sites was referred, effectively] determined your bonus. Do you trust [the] Facebook [algorithm] more than you trust me and the members of the Politburo, who've been working at Gawker Media for a while, and who know what kinds of stories are good?" And the funny thing is, I think some people privately, to themselves, said, "Yeah, we probably trust Facebook more than the sports guy."[9]

In other words, faced with the prospect of having their work judged not by mass popularity as measured by metrics but rather by a "jury of their peers" and superiors, many Gawker staffers favored the former.

Gawker's rebellious, anti-authoritarian organizational culture undoubtedly plays a role in site leads' skepticism about the Politburo system. As noted above, antipathy toward those possessing power, money, social status, and authority was a defining feature of Gawker's editorial ethos. As historian Theodore Porter has pointed out, "trust in numbers" tends to blossom in contexts where trust in established experts and elites is lacking.[10] Thus it is perhaps to be expected that Gawker journalists would "trust" metrics-driven evaluation of their work more than an elite organizational body like the Politburo. Still, my fieldwork made clear that Gawker staffers had several additional reasons for preferring to be managed largely by metrics.

First, metrics-driven management afforded stylistic autonomy that more traditional forms of editorial oversight typically would not. Compared to most other professional journalists, writers at Gawker sites faced minimal editorial—let alone business-side—oversight in terms of the tone, style, or content of their stories. Typically, legacy publications have extensive style guides that all writers and editors are expected to follow, but Gawker had no such official company document. (As a writer for *Deadspin* explained in a post: "We generally don't believe in rigid rules around our journalism, to say nothing of style best practices. Instead, if somebody has a style question they are unsure about, they drop it into our work chatroom and whoever is around discusses it.")[11] Alison explained that while she or her deputy editor reviewed and approved all post ideas from writers, "when it comes to close reads or line-editing [of posts], I don't have time for it." It is illuminating to compare this to the *New York Times*, where every story goes through multiple levels of editorial oversight, and whose famous style guide clocks in at 368 pages and is published as a trade paperback. Stories written in the first person, expressing the author's personal perspective, and using slang and profanity were common at Gawker and virtually unheard of in the news pages of the *Times*.

Furthermore, Denton's self-professed ethos of "radical transparency" meant that stories, arguments, and criticisms that would be kept internal at other firms were regularly made public by staffers at Gawker without fear of retribution—as long as the traffic stayed high. A particularly illustrative incident occurred in January 2012, when then-*NBC Nightly News* anchor Brian Williams wrote Denton a casual email calling for more *Gawker* posts on the weekends and mocking pop singer Lana Del Rey's performance on *Saturday Night Live* (which aired on NBC, the same network as Williams's news broadcast). Denton forwarded the email to *Gawker*'s then-editor A. J. Daulerio in order to "stress that influential readers expected us to publish at weekends." Daulerio promptly posted the full text of the email on *Gawker* with the headline: "Brian Williams Says Gawker Should Have Torched Lana Del Rey."[12] Denton, embarrassed, admitted he had "yelled at" Daulerio in the aftermath of the post, but in hindsight he approved of Daulerio's attempt "to prove his editorial independence, display his general badass-ness and hold me to the principle of radical transparency."[13]

There are countless other incidents similar to this one in Gawker's history. In 2014, a group of anonymous commenters began repeatedly posting short looping video clips (or GIFs) of violent pornography in the comments sections of *Jezebel*, Gawker's feminist site. After privately complaining to management about the problem for months and receiving no meaningful response or solution, staffers published a post on *Jezebel* titled "We Have a Rape GIF Problem and Gawker Media Won't Do Anything about It."[14] Staffers also openly and passionately disagreed with each other in public comment threads, on topics ranging from unionization to Gamergate. In an all-hands meeting that occurred during my fieldwork, Noah, an executive, told editorial employees they were free to "trash [Gawker Media's CMS] on Twitter" if they wanted—a rather extraordinary statement for an executive to make, and one of which staffers took ample advantage.

By contrast, it is nearly impossible to imagine *Times* staffers voicing such unvarnished criticism about their employer in a public forum. And while metrics-delegated management was not the sole reason that such open dissent was tolerated at Gawker, it was undoubtedly a significant contributing factor. Indeed, the airing of intra-organizational dirty laundry often brought in impressive traffic: as of June 2015, *Jezebel*'s post about the "Rape GIF Problem" had garnered 682,037 pageviews and 285,359 uniques.

Being managed by metrics afforded logistical autonomy as well. Gawker staffers had a relatively high degree of control over when, how, and from where they performed their work. For example, during the beginning of Alison's second stint at Gawker, she was working full-time out of the company's New York office while her long-time boyfriend was living in the Midwest. Eventually, this long-distance arrangement came to feel unsustainable to her. "When I got engaged, [I felt] I had to finally move my stuff," Alison explained in one of our interviews. Without asking permission from Denton, she began spending part of each week in the Midwest and working remotely on those days. Alison recalled feeling extremely anxious about what might happen once her move became known, but she soon discovered she needn't have been. "The [rent of the] apartment we got in [the midwestern city] was based on the possibility that Nick [Denton] was going to fire me when he found out. And [when I finally told Nick], he was like, 'No, of course not. *The numbers protect you.*'"

Alison's story illustrates the ways in which many typical managerial duties were essentially outsourced to metrics at Gawker. Alison had assumed, not unreasonably, that her boss might be displeased that an employee (especially one responsible for managing a team of NYC-based employees, as she was) had unilaterally and secretly decided to move halfway across the country, cutting her days in the office from five per week to two or three in the process. But Alison had underestimated the extent to which Denton relied on metrics to assess workers' job performance. During her tenure as a site lead, the site she managed had exceeded its management-set traffic target every month, often by large percentages. For Denton, those high numbers were enough to "protect" her from facing serious consequences or even admonishment for her unauthorized move.

Denton's "the numbers protect you" ethos also hints at the ways in which metrics-driven management and workers' perceptions of autonomy can coexist. Of course, Denton's pronouncement implied a threat in addition to reassurance: if high numbers protect one's job security, then it follows that low numbers could imperil it. But for the moment, Alison's site's high traffic afforded her certain freedoms over aspects of her working conditions that improved her quality of life, such as her ability to live in the same city as her fiancé.

In addition to allowing for logistical and stylistic autonomy, metrics could function as an important alternative form of performance evaluation for Gawker writers—particularly women and people of color—who feared that their work would be systematically undervalued by two key constituencies: top editors and commenters. As of late 2015, Gawker's editorial team was 71 percent male and 77 percent white, and the highest ranks of the newsroom were largely dominated by white men. In a reported piece on Gawker's "problem with women," former staffer Dayna Evans called diversity a "blind spot" for the company. Evans noted a "pervasive feeling" among female staffers that male editors tended to favor young male writers over their female counterparts with higher salaries, more promotions, and choicer story assignments. While Evans acknowledged that the differential treatment was likely often unintentional, the end result was that women were relegated to performing the thankless, "invisible labor" of ensuring the daily functioning of Gawker sites, while their male colleagues reaped accolades. "At workplaces where men are the bosses," Evans wrote, "it is hard to overcome unconscious bias. . . . Value is determined by the people in charge." Ashley Feinberg, a Gawker writer quoted in Evans's article, echoed this point: "Your value at Gawker is defined by how well your interests line up with those of the people in power."[15]

Seen from this perspective, the appeal of metrics as an *alternative* form of assessing value—and proving it to potentially dismissive or skeptical supervisors—becomes clearer.[16] Metrics could serve as evidence of professional worth and worthiness for writers whose work was at risk of being overlooked and underappreciated in the evaluative schemas of their so-called "peers." Indeed, several female staffers told me they took it upon themselves to carefully compile their traffic data when they were preparing to request a raise or promotion. This tactic was not fail-safe: Evans recounted the story of a female acting editor in chief of *Gawker* who was passed over for the permanent position in favor of a man despite the fact that, under her leadership, *Gawker* had the "highest traffic day in its history." Still, in examining the accounts of Evans, Feinberg, and others I interviewed at Gawker, it begins to become clear how metrics-delegated management could feel meaningfully linked to greater editorial autonomy for particular subsets of writers.

In addition to providing an alternative form of valuation when faced with bosses with unconscious biases, metrics functioned as a form of psychological armor for coping with commenters. While Gawker's famously engaged and committed commenters were the envy of other media sites struggling to energize or engage their audiences, intense acrimony existed between commenters and writers at Gawker. When asked for her thoughts on commenters, Alison said: "I hate them. So much. I fucking hate them. I've always hated them. They're the worst." Lisa described the commenters as "kind of a nightmare," adding, "I show [my boyfriend] stuff from the commenters, and he's like, 'Oh, that's so terrible. How do you deal with that?' And he's a *comedian*."

Just as women and staffers of color were disproportionately at risk of having their contributions undervalued by management, they also were targeted by demeaning and harshly critical comments more often than their white male colleagues, some of which veered into harassment and threats. Michelle, a Black writer, explained, "You have to read a lot of commenters where people are like, you're a cunt, you're a fucking idiot, you're the worst person I've ever heard, I want to kill you, blah blah blah." Andrea, a Latina writer who wrote for a site with a mostly white male staff, described how comments about her work were more negative than those about her colleagues':

> The severity [of the comments] that I get, or the sorts of comments that I get on pretty much every article, I don't necessarily see on other people's articles. . . . I'll click on someone else's article and like for no reason a commenter will be talking about me and how I should be fired, or something like that. That doesn't happen on my articles—[commenters] talking about other writers.

In the face of this onslaught of negative (and sometimes explicitly sexist and racist) comments, some staffers pitted comments and metrics against each other, using the latter to protect their sense of professional self-worth. On the day of our first interview, Alison noted that her site was enjoying a day of "gangbusters" traffic. It had come at a good time, she explained, because the day had gotten off to an inauspicious start: "I woke up and I looked at [Twitter on] my phone and I was like, you have to be kidding me. Like [someone had tweeted], 'Oh, I used to love [Alison's site] but it's been really downhill since [tags Alison's Twitter handle] took over.' That's what I see at 7:30 in the morning." Later in our interview, as we discussed Chartbeat, Alison said,

> We broke 9,000 [concurrent visitors] earlier today, so that was awesome. I take screen cap[ture]s of that. That is a reminder that I can do this. . . . It doesn't matter if I have someone screaming at me [on Twitter] at 7:30 in the morning. I'm good at my job. . . . And if [my site] was really downhill, more and more people wouldn't be reading it![17]

In Gawker staffers' tendency to view commenters as "a nightmare" and "the worst," we see echoes of the past—but with a twist. Print-era media scholarship remarked upon journalists' practice of ignoring letters to the editor and dismissing those who wrote them as "insane."[18] These print-era journalists, along with many of the contemporary *Times* staffers I interviewed, preferred instead to rely almost exclusively on the opinions of their colleagues and editors to gauge their job performance. Like their print counterparts, Gawker staffers distrusted comments (arguably the digital version of letters to the editor) and commenters. But as we have seen, they were *also* reluctant to rely solely on each other's assessments for validation, because doing so would be at odds with Gawker's self-conception as a rebellious, anti-elitist company willing to break the norms of "legacy" journalism. Instead, when faced with hostile audience commentary, they often turned to metrics for reassurance.

In sum, rather than pitting journalism insiders against journalism outsiders, as was common at the *Times*, Gawker staffers like Alison pitted one representation of the audience (comments) against another (metrics). Staffers thus conceptualized commenters not as vivid instantiations of the audience they otherwise only saw as numerical representations in Chartbeat and Quantcast but rather as an *un*representative sliver of the much broader audience that was measured by analytics tools. Andrew described the commenters as "the one percent of the one percent of the people who are reading [a post]"; Michael, a writer, emphasized that commenters were a "fraction" of the audience.[19] It was empirically true that the vast majority of readers on any Gawker post did not comment. But staffers' juxtaposition of the commenting audience and the quantified one is noteworthy for how it establishes a diametric opposition between commenters, on the one hand, and the audience represented by analytics tools like Quantcast and Chartbeat, on the other—and positions the

latter as a far more significant and legitimate representation of the "true" audience. Metrics have been characterized as casting the audience as an abstract,
inert, "largely consumptive aggregate."[20] But for Gawker staffers facing hostile
or even discriminatory comments, the very abstractness of metrics allowed
them to serve as a source of professional reassurance.[21]

So far, we have seen how management-by-metrics afforded Gawker staffers
particular variants of logistical, stylistic, and editorial autonomy that did not
exist at the *Times*. In addition, metrics could serve as a form of leverage for
writers whose work was at risk of being systematically undervalued by editorial management, as well as reassurance against negative and at times abusive
audience comments.

Yet perhaps the most important reason Gawker staffers preferred to be
managed by metrics was a more troubling one: metrics-driven management
didn't *feel like management*. Recall that chapter 2 discussed the ways in which
the Chartbeat dashboard built a relationship directly with the managed
worker—the rank-and-file journalist—such that when journalists felt addicted
to the tool, they perceived it as a personal failure of willpower rather than the
result of managerial pressure. In a similar vein, chapter 3 argued that Chartbeat
refrained from making explicit algorithmic recommendations in its dashboard
in order to avoid being seen as overly prescriptive by journalists who had been
conditioned to expect a degree of professional autonomy in their work.

Gawker staffers' consistent professions of autonomy, even as they labored
under a regime of intensive metrics-driven surveillance and management,
show the effects of these user-experience design decisions on the part of
Chartbeat. Put another way, it isn't completely accurate to say that Gawker
staffers explicitly preferred metrics-driven management to editorial management; they were, instead, a group of journalists who resisted being managed
in general, and Chartbeat was designed not to feel like management at all.

There is a broader takeaway here. Because of their historical association
with Taylorist scientific management, metrics are often seen as facilitating direct, top-down managerial control. But direct managerial control would inspire open rebellion at a place like Gawker—or, we can surmise, in many
knowledge-work contexts where workers have the expectation of maintaining
a high degree of control over their labor process. The case of Gawker illustrates
how digital performance metrics, when designed in a particular way, actually
distance themselves from Taylorist associations.

Chartbeat is aligned instead with a more indirect form of management that
has been variously called "responsible autonomy," "operational autonomy," or

"soft management." This style of management puts "an emphasis on the personal and individual freedoms now able to be exercised within the loose confines of a more 'enabling,' playful and decentered set of work relations."[22] Under soft management, workers are afforded higher status, greater responsibility, and more leeway in how they carry out their work on a day-to-day basis than they would be under a scientific managerial regime.[23]

With their relentless, unforgiving performance rankings, analytics dashboards would seem to be at odds with a soft managerial approach. Yet in the case of Gawker, metrics actually *facilitated* a looser managerial style. Because Chartbeat was designed to be habit-forming, it was an effective tool to encourage editorial workers to, in effect, manage themselves. Part 1 showed that as Gawker writers and editors became immersed in metrics, they engaged in "self-exploitation" by pushing themselves to work ever harder and blamed themselves when they felt they were checking metrics excessively or failing to get the traffic they'd hoped for.[24] At the same time, metrics also provided a firm managerial backstop: as Denton's "the numbers protect you" comment illustrates, Gawker executives felt they could afford to be relatively hands-off with employees, so long as the metrics continued moving in the right direction.

While soft management is typically associated with a "de-Taylorized" work environment, the case of Gawker complicates this idea.[25] With the help of Chartbeat and Quantcast, Gawker was a workplace in which neo-Taylorism existed in a symbiotic relationship with soft management: neo-Taylorist measures like unique-visitor targets and eCPM numbers were the hard "backstop" that made a soft management style acceptable to executives; and soft management, in turn, made metrics-driven neo-Taylorism adequately palatable to workers.

Gawker's metrics-abetted "soft" managerial approach has much in common with what Michel Foucault called "governmentality," in which the need for explicit coercion is obviated by self-surveilling, self-policing subjects. As sociologist Mark Banks has put it, "While critical theory approaches have suggested that cultural workers are *forced* to accept capitalist relations of production as a consequence of their powerlessness in the face of corporate power, 'Neo-Foucauldian' or 'governmental' approaches suggest that workers are trained to accept and reproduce *for themselves* the precise conditions of their subordination."[26]

Does this mean Gawker staffers were, in essence, deluded when they professed their autonomy or chose to return to Gawker after a stint at another company? This is an important question, and not one with an easy answer. Some scholars, particularly those partial to a neo-Foucauldian framework, have cautioned against taking people's perceptions of autonomy at face value, while others argue that workers' experience of their work must not be dismissed as a clouded or distorted picture of their "real interests."[27] The most sensible way to adjudicate between these diverging perspectives is to consider workers' percep- tions of their autonomy while also examining "the social conditions under which they make decisions and . . . how meaningfully different their choices are."[28]

Certainly, the workplace environment at Gawker seemed to indicate that staffers did not have as much freedom to make decisions as they felt like they did. Yet there are two crucial caveats that must be considered. First, the same could be said of the *Times* staffers who professed autonomy. Indeed, multiple scholars have pointed out that some of the very components of traditional journalistic professionalism embraced by the *Times* and rejected by Gawker (e.g., "both sides" objectivity, dismissal of external influences, and valuing editors' opinions above all others) arose as ideological mechanisms of labor control in news- rooms. Media scholar Anthony Nadler characterizes journalistic professional- ism as the outcome of a "negotiated peace between journalists and media owners in which 'journalists gain their independence and in exchange they give up their voice.'"[29] Tellingly, the American Newspaper Publishers Association, a trade group of media owners, supported the classification of journalism as a profes- sion by the National Labor Relations Board, while the Newspaper Guild (now called the NewsGuild), which represented journalists, opposed it, "because such a classification would mean less protection for journalists as workers."[30]

Second, as the next sections will illustrate, two incidents occurred—one toward the end of my fieldwork and the other after it had wrapped up—in which Gawker staffers worked to change the conditions of their work. First, staffers resoundingly rejected a new metrics-driven leaderboard that they felt unfairly put them on par with unpaid commenters. Second, in 2015 Gawker editorial workers voted overwhelmingly to form a union—the first at a prominent digital media outlet. Both developments suggest that metrics-driven self-exploitation and self-blaming have limits, even in a data-saturated environment like Gawker.

Contested Classification:
The Rejection of the Kinja Leaderboard

Shortly before the commencement of my fieldwork, Gawker executives in- stalled a new metrics-based ranking on the editorial floor of the company headquarters. Prominently displayed across several large flat-screen moni- tors in the center of the office, the new leaderboard ranked by name the top 90 individual users of Kinja (Gawker's publishing platform and content

The Top Kinja Users ⊘

#		Name	#		Name	#		Name	#		Name
1	→	Alan Henry 6,968,178	11	↑73	Kristin Wong 2,352,275	21	↑1	Brian Ashcraft 1,755,972	31	↑29	David Nield 1,322,542
2	↑1	Melanie Pinola 4,066,272	12	↑18	George Dvorsky 2,184,506	22	→	Barry Petchesky 1,755,053	32	↑11	Meredith Woerner 1,297,075
3	↑97	Leah Finnegan 3,601,978	13	↓5	Casey Chan 2,169,574	23	↓2	Kevin Draper 1,733,749	33	↓20	Nathan Grayson 1,293,420
4	↓2	Whitson Gordon 3,508,777	14	↓5	Esther Inglis-Arkell 2,146,439	24	↑24	Sam Biddle 1,663,658	34	↓28	Rob Bricken 1,256,080
5	↑60	Tessa Miller 3,283,915	15	↓4	Adam Dachis 2,062,638	25	↑6	Eric Ravenscraft 1,616,974	35	↓3	Rich Juzwiak 1,222,894
6	↑8	Timothy Burke 3,186,639	16	↑36	Samer Kalaf 1,996,056	26	↓3	Maddie Stone 1,560,443	36	↓9	Mark Shrayber 1,175,144
7	→	Patricia Hernandez 3,011,744	17	↑27	Jason Schreier 1,979,304	27	↓3	Gabrielle Bluesto... 1,521,321	37	↑131	Michael Hession 1,164,717
8	↑4	Jay Hathaway 2,395,873	18	↓1	Tyler Rogoway 1,925,344	28	↓18	Shep McAllister, ... 1,521,093	38	↑3	James Whitbrook 1,104,509
9	↓5	Thorin Klosowski 2,394,940	19	↓3	Charlie Jane And... 1,924,017	29	↓24	Andrew Liszewski 1,374,258	39	↑66	Wes Siler 1,092,685
10	↑9	Luke Plunkett 2,376,931	20	↓5	Tom Ley 1,814,494	30	↑6	Robbie Gonzalez 1,339,238	40	↑10	Carlos Zahumens... 1,078,390

● ● ●

FIG. 7.1. The Kinja leaderboard.

management system with which we became familiar in chapter 6) according to how many unique visitors their posts had drawn to Gawker sites in the previous 30 days.

Had it not been for the installation of what became known as the Kinja leaderboard, and the backlash it occasioned, I might have thought there was no limit to the metrics-based commensuration that Gawker staffers would accept, or even embrace. Unlike their counterparts at the *Times*, it seemed intuitive to Gawker staffers that individual posts—even when they appeared on different sites and covered radically different subjects—were commensurable on the basis of metrics like pageviews and uniques. Similarly, Gawker staffers voiced no opposition to the policy that all of the company's sites be held to the same monthly target rate of traffic growth. And although the Big Board, the real-time display that ranked posts across the Gawker network based on concurrent visitors, caused stress, I almost never heard Gawker writers and editors criticize it on the grounds of fairness. They also did not object to the monthly site-level uniques bonus.

Unlike these accepted forms of metrics-based performance evaluation, the Kinja leaderboard faced immediate, vocal, and intense criticism from writers and editors alike.[31] In interviews, Gawker staffers often accounted for this discrepancy by arguing that the Kinja leaderboard was a biased—and therefore illegitimate—form of commensuration. As Lisa put it: "There are people who have an advantage because their site's baseline traffic is just higher and more people look at the site every day." Alison echoed this point: "That [leaderboard] means nothing to me. Like if you're gonna put our writers—you're gonna measure them against writers on sites that have double [my site's] traffic, that's not fair. That's stupid." To Lisa and Alison, individual writers did not seem sufficiently alike to commensurate if they wrote for sites that had different amounts of "baseline traffic."

Yet this criticism of the Kinja leaderboard could also apply to the Big Board, which was widely accepted as a legitimate form of commensuration within Gawker. After all, if one site had three times the baseline traffic of another, its posts were arguably substantially more likely to achieve high numbers of concurrent visitors and appear on the Big Board, just as its writers were more likely to be ranked highly on the Kinja leaderboard. When I asked Alison about this seeming inconsistency, she replied that unlike the Kinja leaderboard, the Big Board

> is a level playing field. These aren't uniques. This is the number of people on the site at any given time. So it doesn't matter if [another Gawker site] is three times the size of [my site]—there are 7,000 people on [my site] *right now*, and on that particular post. And there's no other post in the company that has that many people on it. So I feel like that's fair. . . . That's fair because that's not even about uniques. It's about statistics, very straightforward.

Alison's invocation of terms associated with fairness and objectivity—"level playing field," "very straightforward"—to compare the Big Board favorably to the Kinja leaderboard indicates that she saw the former as a legitimate form of commensuration while the latter was not. Yet it remained unclear why she had this perception.

Over the course of my fieldwork, it became evident that staffers' discontent with the Kinja leaderboard stemmed not primarily from its method of commensuration but from what it symbolized.[32] Specifically, they objected to the leaderboard's criteria for inclusion—not *how* the leaderboard ranked staffers but rather *who* was eligible to be included on it the first place. Unlike the Big Board and the site bonuses, which applied only to posts written by paid editorial staff members, the Kinja leaderboard did not distinguish between paid staff and unpaid contributors. Anyone could make a Kinja account for free and write comments on Gawker sites or stand-alone posts elsewhere in the Kinja network. All Kinja account holders, whether they were Gawker staff or not, were eligible to be ranked on the Kinja leaderboard.

This broad eligibility criterion was a deliberate choice on the part of Denton, who had poured tremendous financial resources into Kinja in hopes that it would become the first "truly interactive news platform."[33] The idea was to elevate Gawker's existing commenters—as well as, ideally, adding experts, sources, and tipsters to their ranks—to the same status as the company's paid editorial staff. Denton described wanting to "erase this toxic Internet class system" that divided writers, editors, commenters, and sources into discrete groups and replace it with a more egalitarian, meritocratic alternative.[34]

In practice, what this meant was that every Kinja account holder was christened a "contributor," and everything written on Kinja—whether by a paid staffer or a contributor—was a "post." (At one point, the terms "comment" and "commenter" were even banned at the company and employees incurred a $5 penalty whenever they slipped, though this policy was not still in effect at the time of my research.)[35] Paid staffers were expected to engage in thoughtful and spirited discussion in the comments sections of their posts whenever possible. There was even a short-lived plan to remove bylines on posts in order to underscore the idea that no individual's contribution was more significant than anyone else's. (After staff protest, individual writers' bylines were preserved on their posts but were supplemented by the number of people who had written a comment on the post [e.g., "Hudson Hongo and 179 others"] in order to create the impression that a conversation was occurring.) Of all these changes, the new leaderboard was perhaps the most potent symbol of, as Liam put it, "the deprioritization of the author in Kinja."

Denton's vision for Kinja was an effort to concretize—and profit from—ideas about participatory and citizen journalism that had circulated since the popularization of the internet, when several scholars and media commentators predicted the collapse of the long-standing boundary between media producers and media audiences.[36] To many observers, Gawker seemed just the type of company where such a vision could be fully realized. It had long been known for its cadre of highly engaged and committed commenters, a handful of whom so adeptly channeled Gawker's witty, irreverent voice that they were eventually hired to write full-time for Gawker sites. Even more importantly, Gawker's company ethos had always incorporated a strong awareness of the audience: in part due to Gawker's years-long emphasis on traffic, editorial staffers were highly sensitized to readers' reactions to their work. Furthermore, unlike their counterparts at the *Times*, Gawker staffers also tended to believe that there existed a high correlation between the quality or importance of a story and the audience's reaction to that story. As Andrew put it:

> [Nick Denton] has essentially built a company around the belief that gut instinct, the truth that gnaws at you to express [it], is the same as [what]

the biggest number of people will be interested in. . . . And I think [that equation] is actually a very healthy and enlightening and, in a way, journalistically pure mantra that allows us to be so stat-focused without losing a sense of what is right and true and noble about journalism.

However, Gawker's audience-focused orientation notwithstanding, Denton's emphasis on Kinja's participatory affordances was deeply and almost universally unpopular among the editorial staff. As a group of mostly young writers trying to gain a foothold in the competitive New York online media world, staffers wanted to build their reputations as professional journalists, editors, and writers. Thus they tended to be resentful of Denton's aspiration to break down boundaries between writers and audiences. Some believed Kinja was a product not of Denton's idealism but of his cynicism. John Cook, who for a time had been the editor of *Gawker*, told the *New York Observer*: "Nick has always loved to subtly and not so subtly insult his employees. He thinks of us as glorified commenters."[37] Gawker's fired editorial director wrote in a scathing post (on Kinja, of all places) that for all of Denton's idealistic-sounding comments about interactivity and collaborative journalism, Kinja was "mostly a bulwark against needing to pay writers to create content."[38]

In practice, non-staff Kinja contributors almost never appeared on the leaderboard: because they were not writing for core Gawker sites, their posts rarely attracted enough uniques to make the list of top Kinja users. Still, the mere fact that non-staff were eligible to appear on the board was a symbolically powerful act of reclassification that represented a major threat to staffers' status and their long-term employment prospects at the company. Contrast this with Gawker's traffic pressures—which, while stress-inducing to staffers, preserved their elevated position vis-à-vis commenters—and it becomes clearer why staff rejected the Kinja leaderboard as an illegitimate form of commensuration.

Sociologist Wendy Espeland has argued that commensuration is defined in part by its "radical inclusiveness" that can "create relationships between virtually any two things."[39] But of course, commensuration is not *inherently* radically inclusive—those who design and implement systems of numerical comparison must make decisions about which individuals, organizations, or entities will be ranked. They must classify who or what does and does not belong in a particular set; these classificatory choices reflect values and priorities. By choosing to include non-staff contributors along with paid staff in the Kinja leaderboard, Gawker management communicated a powerful message: staff and non-staff writers were, at least in theory, interchangeable.

Classification can have profound social consequences: as Geoffrey Bowker and Susan Leigh Star put it, "For any individual, group or situation, classifications and standards give advantage or they give suffering. Jobs are made and lost; some regions benefit at the expense of others."[40] Though jobs were not lost due to the blurring of boundaries between author and audience in Kinja during my fieldwork, the leaderboard was a vivid reminder of how they *could* be. Even Gawker staffers who ranked highly according to the Kinja leaderboard's individualized system of commensuration felt their jobs could still be jeopardized as a result of the *classificatory* system it represented, in which paid staff could one day theoretically become obsolete. For young writers trying to make a name for themselves in a struggling industry, this was a demoralizing and fear-inducing prospect. It was also an additional mechanism by which quantitative metrics became central to staffers' conceptions of professional self-worth and contributed to the intensification of their work. If Gawker employees had no inherent qualitative value as professional journalistic practitioners, their best option to distinguish themselves from unpaid "Kinja contributors" was to generate traffic numbers so high that no non-staff contributor would be likely to match them.

Yet staffers' resounding and vociferous protestations against the Kinja leaderboard had consequences, too: by early 2015, the Kinja leaderboard had been removed from the office displays (though it remained available online); the eight large flat screens that had previously displayed it instead showed the home pages of each of Gawker's eight core sites. The editorial executive who had overseen the implementation of the leaderboard had been replaced, and his successor explained that the leaderboard had been taken down because it "sent a lot of bad messages." Through all this, the Big Board's position was unchanged: it remained prominently displayed on both the editorial and business floors of the Gawker headquarters.

Though the rejection of the Kinja leaderboard was striking as a form of worker resistance in a (seemingly) thoroughly governmentalized workplace, it paled in comparison to what happened next: in 2015, Gawker became the first major digital media company to unionize.

Building Collective Identification: The Gawker Media Union

In early June 2015, Gawker's editorial employees voted overwhelmingly to form a union with the Writers Guild of America East (WGAE)—the first at a prominent digital media outlet.[41] True to form, Gawker staffers made public many of their internal deliberations regarding the union, including in an impassioned and sometimes contentious thread where staffers shared—in by-lined posts—how they were voting on whether to unionize and why. The decision to publicize the union debate alarmed some of the WGAE organizers Gawker was working with, who worried that doing so might cede power and leverage to management. But Nick Denton, for his part, told reporters he was "intensely relaxed" about the union drive, while executive editor Tommy Craggs said he was "politically, temperamentally and, almost, sentimentally supportive" of it.[42]

The union drive took place after the conclusion of my fieldwork at Gawker. Nevertheless, I followed it closely, as it seemed like an important new chapter in the ongoing saga of what I had come to think of as the "autonomy paradox" of the metrics-driven knowledge workplace. On the one hand, Gawker was the paradigmatic case of a governmentalized workplace, in which—with the help of real-time performance metrics hanging, quite literally, over their heads—workers had thoroughly internalized an individualistic "discourse of risk."[43] As we have seen throughout this book, Gawker staffers often felt personally responsible not only for their own traffic successes and failures but for those of the company as well. Perhaps for this reason, Gawker's union drive surprised many observers of the digital media industry. As media scholars Nicole S. Cohen and Greig de Peuter put it in their book on digital media unions, Gawker's vote to unionize "belied assumptions about digital-first newsrooms like Gawker: laid-back workplaces staffed by young writers who are underpaid but happy to be employed, fueled by a techno-libertarian ethos more common to tech startups than to legacy media outlets, housed in offices that look more like nightclubs than newsrooms."[44]

On the other hand, this chapter has shown that Gawker staffers repeatedly and strongly emphasized the autonomy they experienced in their jobs. The union drive should give pause to anyone tempted to dismiss their collective perception of autonomy as nothing but a manifestation of neoliberal ideology. The nascent union's efforts soon bore fruit: in March 2016, the Gawker staff ratified a three-year contract, which covered issues like severance pay, salary minimums, health benefits, and protections for editorial independence.

There are many lessons to be drawn from the story of Gawker's union drive: about the evolution and maturation of the digital media industry, about the relationship between legacy news media outlets and their digital "upstart" counterparts, about the economic conditions of the twenty-first-century press. For our purposes, though, I will focus on one in particular: how to make sense of the union drive in light of Gawker's metrics-infused labor process, and what this might mean for understanding the role of metrics in knowledge work moving forward.

Namely, we must consider the possibility that it is not a coincidence that the digital media company with a reputation for being the most metrics-driven was also the first to unionize. I do not mean this in the sense that editorial workers were so dissatisfied with metrics-driven working conditions that they organized to change them: while workers detested the Kinja leaderboard, it had been taken down by the time the union drive began. And as we have seen, Gawker staffers did not reject other forms of metrics-based performance evaluation, such as the Big Board. In fact, the eventual union contract did not mention metrics at all.

Rather, the relationship between metrics and unionization at Gawker seems more complex and, in some ways, counterintuitive. There are several reasons why Gawker's metrics-driven labor process and organizational culture may have been unexpectedly compatible with a union drive. From a management perspective, Denton's "intense relaxation" about the union drive was actually of a piece with his "the numbers protect you" managerial ethos. As long as the traffic kept coming, Denton had little reason to interfere in the unionization process. And come it did: the thread where staffers discussed how they were voting on the union drive garnered over 156,000 pageviews.[45] As Cohen and de Peuter explain, "the idea to report on the drive (and, later, debate publicly how workers were voting on the union) was encouraged by Gawker top brass, who saw a brand-reinforcing opportunity to generate traffic."[46]

It is difficult to say what role, if any, metrics may have played in the drive to organize among Gawker's editorial workers, but we can speculate on a few possibilities. First, metrics-driven rankings may inadvertently and gradually have helped to build a sense of solidarity that can serve as the initial spark for organizing efforts.[47] Metrics dashboards use a handful of numerical standards to commensurate writers who are otherwise dissimilar in terms of the beats they cover, the sites they write for, their levels of experience, their identity characteristics, and so on. As we have seen, this form of commensuration can turn competition inward, as coworkers become focused on "beating" each other in the traffic game. But while metrics can be individualizing and alienating in day-to-day work, over the long term they may also serve as an inadvertent reminder to writers that, when it comes to editorial working conditions, they are all fundamentally in the same boat (or, shall we say, on the same leaderboard).

Denton's metrics-driven managerial approach, according to which writers could post "whatever they wanted" so long as it drew traffic, also facilitated an airing of shared grievances about management that may have helped build support for organizing to secure greater workplace protections. For instance, *Jezebel*'s public post about the site's "Rape GIF problem" drew expressions of support from male staffers at other sites who had not otherwise known the extent of misogynist harassment their female colleagues were facing.

Furthermore, in an industry in which unpaid internships are common and writers are sometimes offered "exposure" instead of monetary remuneration, metrics are stark, ever-present reminders of writers' economic value to the companies for which they work. In addition, if professional ideology can inhibit the development of class consciousness among knowledge workers, then Gawker's rejection of the trappings of traditional journalistic professionalism may have made staffers more readily able to identify *as workers*.[48]

In exploring potential elective affinities between a metrics-saturated knowledge workplace and a union drive, I do not mean to suggest that Gawker's organizational approach to metrics was the main—or even a primary—reason the editorial staff unionized. As Cohen and de Peuter point out, several other factors (including growing societal attention to economic inequality and digital journalists' experiences covering social justice movements such as Occupy Wall Street, Black Lives Matter, #MeToo, and the 2016 Bernie Sanders presidential campaign) may have fueled the development of a greater class consciousness among digital journalists, as well as a vocabulary with which to talk about it. As one journalist interviewed by Cohen and de Peuter explained, digital journalists become open to unions because "it's just very obvious to most of us that the way the economy works right now does not work for us."[49]

But if nothing else, analytics tools may make this reality even more obvious than it would have otherwise been. Metrics are a vivid reminder of the harsh economic realities of the digital publishing landscape—both in the way that they rank journalists against one another and in the sense that they reflect a situation in which one's audience (and by extension, one's job) is largely dictated by the unaccountable and inscrutable algorithms of enormous technology platform companies. It is not far-fetched to think that constant exposure to metrics might, over time, increase journalists' understanding of these grim structural circumstances and their motivation to try to improve them.

Conclusion

This chapter has examined the ways in which newsroom metrics intersect with journalists' perceptions of autonomy. Diverging conceptions of autonomy manifested at the *New York Times* and at Gawker. At the *Times*, editorial autonomy was seen as achievable only *within* the traditional normative confines, standards, and expectations of the journalism profession. Staffers also tended to conceptualize autonomy as freedom from influences external to the organization. This meant that in the paper's hierarchical structure, the opinions of other internal actors, especially *Times* editors, were considered the best barometers of news judgment. Meanwhile, the relationship between autonomy and metrics was cast as inversely proportional, such that if metrics became a more prominent and influential newsroom presence, journalistic autonomy would decrease.

At Gawker, by contrast, autonomy meant freedom *from* many of the traditional strictures and norms of the journalism profession and its established sources of authority, even when that meant being beholden to metrics instead. To writers and editors at Gawker, quantified measures of audience popularity were not necessarily in conflict with journalistic autonomy. Insofar as metrics afforded Gawker staffers a sense that they needn't adhere to traditional office arrangements, stylistic rules, or the expectations of powerful actors (including at their own company), the data was seen as compatible with—or even actively fostering—autonomy. Put simply, many Gawker staffers felt that the company's emphasis on metrics afforded them greater control over their work than more intensive editorial oversight would have. Staffers also turned to metrics for reassurance, corroboration, and validation when their work was denigrated by hostile commenters or undervalued by skeptical or biased editors.

Workplace performance metrics are typically associated with top-down, explicit managerial control. But because of the way Chartbeat was designed and deployed at Gawker, management-by-metrics didn't *feel* like management at all. In this way, metrics fostered a "soft" management style, in which workers are given greater leeway over their daily work environment but are in return expected to police their own performance.

Seen this way, the picture at Gawker looks rather bleak, as though what staffers experienced as autonomy was simply an illusion that persuaded them to acquiesce to their own exploitation. Yet the second half of the chapter discussed two instances that complicate this narrative: the staff's overwhelming repudiation of the Kinja leaderboard, which staffers interpreted as a managerial effort to disempower and eventually replace paid staff, and the unionization drive, in which editorial staffers organized to secure improved working conditions. There is no question that metrics operated as an effective form of managerial discipline and control at Gawker—but only to a point. Metrics did not prevent Gawker's editorial workers from pushing back against the company's management; indeed, I have suggested that Gawker's metrics-driven managerial regime may have indirectly and unintentionally contributed to a climate conducive to organizing.

What do these findings mean for the relationship between metrics and autonomy in cases of knowledge work beyond journalism? Throughout the book, we have seen that metrics can be a powerful individualizing force. They can foster competitive dynamics among workers and lead them to feel personally responsible not just for their own successes and failures but for the company's. And yet, metrics may also *inadvertently* cultivate a sense of shared grievance, collective identification, and class consciousness among knowledge workers—themes which the conclusion will explore in more depth.

Conclusion

THERE IS NO OTHER field of cultural production that does more than journalism to inform citizens about social issues and civic affairs, set the public agenda, and hold powerful figures and institutions accountable.[1] But maintaining the kind of robust and lively media system that is crucial to sustaining a healthy democracy is highly resource-intensive. Ever since U.S. media organizations transitioned away from political party patronage in the 1830s, they have been almost entirely dependent on market forces, largely in the form of advertising and subscription revenues, to sustain their work. This approach has never guaranteed editorial independence: advertiser pressure, both direct and indirect, can distort coverage and lead to self-censorship.[2] For a time in the mid- to late twentieth century, however, economic, political, and technological forces aligned such that news businesses could do aggressive, expensive reporting *and* turn a profit. In that favorable climate, the perils of relying on a heavily commercialized media system to fulfill journalism's vital civic role—although ever-present—were easy enough to ignore.

That's not the case anymore. As critical media scholar Victor Pickard has pointed out, "Systemic problems typically remain overlooked until shocks to the status quo render them more visible."[3] In the contemporary media landscape, shocks to the status quo are mounting. At a time when a handful of technology platform companies dominate advertising and media distribution, the idea of reliably profitable journalism seems at best fraught, and at worst something close to an oxymoron.

There are exceptions, of course: a select few marquee news brands like the *New York Times* are successfully transitioning from an advertising-dependent business model to one that draws the bulk of revenue from paying subscribers. But the overall picture looks bleak. Local newspapers are shutting down and scaling back at an alarming rate, and as yet no alternatives have managed to fill the void: recent studies have shown that local papers continue to provide the majority of original news reporting in the communities they serve.[4] Online-only news outlets, until recently hailed as the visionary digital upstarts that had mastered social media distribution and figured out how to work *with* tech platforms symbiotically, are also struggling: some have folded entirely while others, such as *BuzzFeed*, *Vox*, and *Vice*, have cut staff. The current state of affairs raises disturbing questions about whether we are confronting a case of market failure, in which the market-driven digital media landscape, as it is currently configured, cannot reliably sustain the kind of public-interest journalism that democracy requires.[5]

This crisis is not attributable to audience analytics—the news industry would be in turmoil with or without metrics. Yet while metrics have not *caused* the news industry's financial woes, neither have they cured them. Early promises from the analytics industry that paying close attention to metrics was the path to long-term financial stability and prosperity for digital publishers have mostly failed to come to fruition. Many of the outlets that most strongly pursued this strategy have run into trouble: Gawker no longer exists in anything resembling its original form, while *BuzzFeed* laid off 15 percent of its workforce in 2019 and closed its national news desk. (News organizations that have implemented a paid subscription model have generally fared better, but, as journalism analysts have noted, this model is likely not scalable industry-wide.)[6] If metrics-driven journalism was supposed to be a Faustian bargain, in which journalists ceded control over their labor process and relaxed their editorial standards in exchange for securing the news industry's financial viability, the devil has yet to deliver on his end.[7] Just as the rise of market research did not solve the problem of declining newspaper readership in the 1980s and 1990s, the proliferation of metrics has not fixed the structural problems of digital news publishing.[8]

In sum, newsroom analytics are not the root cause of the digital media industry's problems, and they are also not the solution. So, then, what are they? Metrics are best understood as a *symptom* of relentless and intensifying economic pressures. But this does not mean that metrics are inconsequential—far from it. Just as symptoms of an underlying disease can produce distinct effects on a patient's health and quality of life, this book has shown that analytics tools are reshaping journalists' work in fundamental ways. The intensely habit-forming user interface of real-time metrics dashboards like Chartbeat—coupled with a pervasive awareness of the stakes of low traffic for individual journalists and news organizations alike—enlists journalist-users as players in what I've called the "traffic game." The traffic game requires contemporary journalists to compete against their colleagues and themselves in an attempt to boost their articles' views, time spent reading, and social media engagement. Thus, like other tracking tools by which managers monitor and evaluate worker performance, newsroom metrics extract increased productivity from journalists. Because the traffic game is endless, so, too, becomes the work of editorial optimization.

The work intensification facilitated by real-time metrics benefits management at media companies at the expense of journalists themselves, who often struggle with feelings of stress and exhaustion. Crucially, though, the habit-forming user experience of a tool like Chartbeat can make the work speed-up *feel* to editorial workers like a matter of individual agency rather than managerial coercion. We saw this in the Gawker writers who described their "addiction" to Chartbeat as a failure of personal willpower rather than as a direct consequence of managerial pressure to drive up traffic.

There is an important lesson here about the process by which once unthinkable regimes of quantitative accountability become institutionalized in knowledge-work contexts far beyond journalism. The most impactful analytics tools are not likely to be those that impose rigid and unforgiving numerical targets, because such a blunt approach can provoke vociferous resistance among the rank and file.[9] Instead, the tools that win the consent of knowledge workers are likely to be those that perform deference to the workers' judgment, declare allegiance to their professional norms, and manufacture moments of reenchantment.

I have argued that such tactics enable novel performance metrics to "get in the door" of expert fields instead of being resisted or rejected outright. For this reason, tools like Chartbeat serve to rationalize knowledge work by, among other things, pushing workers to work harder and faster than they otherwise would.

Yet we also have seen that there is more to this story. Analytics companies like Chartbeat engineer knowledge workers' consent and compliance by leaving space for interpretive ambiguity in the numbers themselves, thus allowing users to exercise a degree of autonomy in making sense of and acting on the data. The book's later chapters explored how journalists leveraged this ambiguity to serve their own ends, such as Gawker writers invoking metrics to lobby for raises and promotions, or *Times* editors carefully managing reporters' exposure to metrics as a way to solidify the newsroom's long-standing hierarchical power structure. In sum, many of the very technological affordances that initially made Chartbeat palatable to journalists—thus paving the way for the rationalization of journalistic work—have also limited the tool's deskilling power.

———

Most ethnographic studies represent only a snapshot of a particular setting or phenomenon. Field sites, especially in the tumultuous business of digital media, do not remain static in the years it takes the researcher to analyze data and write, edit, and publish a manuscript. This does not diminish the value of ethnographic work, but it does underline the importance of reflecting on developments that have transpired at the site after the conclusion of fieldwork and considering how they speak to one's findings and analysis.

In the spirit of such reflection, I want to note once again that the bulk of my research was conducted from 2011 to 2015, with the most intensive period of fieldwork ranging from mid-2013 to mid-2014. This was a particular moment—albeit a pivotal one—in the ongoing story of newsroom metrics. Analytics tools were present in most U.S. newsrooms by this point but had not yet become fully institutionalized: as this book has shown, organizational actors were actively negotiating what these tools signified and what role they should have in editorial work. This was an optimal moment to explore one of this book's central questions: How do performance analytics get taken up in knowledge-work fields? But the uniqueness of the time period also raises questions about what happens once performance data *is* institutionalized and more fully integrated into knowledge-work settings. To that end, the following sections briefly examine key developments that have transpired at each of my field sites in the years since the conclusion of my research. My intention here is not to provide an exhaustive account of everything that has happened at these companies since I left the field. Rather, I aim to provide a concise overview of the shifts that are most relevant to the analytical themes and arguments I have taken up in this book.

Chartbeat

At the time of my fieldwork, Chartbeat emphasized the descriptive affordances of its analytics tools (e.g., the ability to show users the amount of reader attention earned by each story across a range of metrics) but was hesitant to play a more explicitly *prescriptive* role (i.e., to recommend that users follow a particular course of editorial action in light of analytics data) lest journalist-users feel that the dashboard posed a threat to their autonomous professional judgment. We have seen how Chartbeat's performance of deference helped the company earn journalists' acquiescence and preempt their resistance during the crucial period in which many reporters and editors were first encountering analytics in their work.

The picture looks somewhat different a few years on. Chartbeat (and analytics in general) are now more solidly institutionalized in newsrooms: that is, metrics have become a fixture whose presence is largely taken for granted by journalists. In this context, Chartbeat no longer shies away from playing a prescriptive role to the extent it once did: the company has begun to offer strategic consulting services to newsrooms as an "add-on" to its suite of analytics tools. Although this idea was occasionally floated by Chartbeat staffers during my fieldwork, at the time it was rejected because of fears that it would come off as a technology company's unwelcome intrusion into the exercise of editorial judgment. Chartbeat's subsequent foray into consulting suggests that analytics companies' performance of deference to knowledge workers' judgment becomes less necessary over time, as metrics become more firmly entrenched in the labor process.

Not everything has changed, however. In late 2017, Chartbeat tweaked its logo from an image that was meant to evoke a needle on a dial to a similar image that was meant to resemble a flag. In the company blog post announcing the change, Chartbeat's CEO wrote: "The industry is rallying together, standing behind truth and accuracy. Our logo has evolved from a dial to a flag that we plant squarely in support of quality publishers everywhere."[10] Thus, while Chartbeat has deemphasized the performance of deference to journalistic judgment, at the height of the Trump era it doubled down on the profession of allegiance to traditional journalistic norms and values.

The *New York Times*

During the period of my research at the *Times*, staffers' orientations to analytics tended to correlate with one's position in the newsroom's organizational hierarchy. Editors, wary that metrics would contaminate reporters' news judgment and provide fodder for challenges to editors' authority, restricted reporters' access to metrics. Editors thus enjoyed an interpretive monopoly over the data, which allowed them to strategically disclose particular data points to reporters in order to achieve managerial goals. Meanwhile, reporters' responses to this editor-determined arrangement ranged from approval to indifference to exasperation. Those who chafed most at editors' restrictions had established technological and social workarounds that allowed them to obtain partial access to metrics.

Partly in response to the "black market for metrics" that had begun to emerge in the newsroom, the *Times* began to gradually broaden access to analytics tools, including Chartbeat, to a wider swath of the newsroom staffers in the years after the bulk of my interviews had concluded. This process culminated with the in-house development of Stela, the *Times*'s bespoke internal analytics tool, and its rollout to the entire newsroom in September 2015. In many respects, Stela was functionally similar to Chartbeat and other third-party analytics tools: it measured engagement proxies such as a story's social media likes, comments, and shares, kept track of tweaks to headlines and any correlated shifts in traffic, and displayed data on readers' geographic location, referral sources, and the type of devices they used to access stories. In a striking echo of Chartbeat's marketing, one of the *Times* staffers who spearheaded the creation of Stela emphasized that he wanted the tool to make analytics feel "approachable . . . simple and fun to use."[11]

Stela's most unique feature, then, may not have been a technological one at all but rather the fact that Stela was an analytics tool developed exclusively by and for the *Times*—and thus perhaps seemed more domesticated and unthreatening than a third-party tool ever could. Indeed, the team behind Stela worked with a designer to ensure that the internal dashboard used "*Times* typefaces and is structured to match the look and feel of the *Times* brand."[12]

Of course, the vast majority of news organizations do not have the resources to build a bespoke analytics tool even if they were inclined to do so. But the *Times*'s investment in Stela underscores a broader finding from this book: the process of institutionalizing quantitative performance analytics in knowledge-work fields requires an enormous amount of discursive, emotional, and aesthetic labor—and the more prestigious the profession and organizational context, the more such work is likely to be required.

Gawker

To say that Gawker Media has experienced tremendous upheaval since the conclusion of my fieldwork is an understatement. In May 2016, the company filed for bankruptcy after a Florida jury ordered it to pay $140 million in damages to professional wrestler Hulk Hogan (real name Terry Bollea), who had sued for invasion of privacy after *Gawker* published excerpts of a sex tape featuring him. It later came to light that Hogan's expensive legal counsel had been secretly paid for by libertarian Silicon Valley billionaire and Facebook board member Peter Thiel, who harbored a long-standing grievance against *Gawker* for its coverage of his sexual orientation and business dealings.[13] The media conglomerate Univision purchased all Gawker Media sites except for *Gawker* in August 2016 and renamed them the Gizmodo Media Group. *Gawker* was shuttered; the media company Bustle Digital Group purchased its domain name in 2018 and made moves to relaunch the site in some form, although the timeline and status of those plans remain uncertain at the time of this writing.

There are many lessons embedded in the lawsuit that sealed Gawker's fate. The saga speaks to, among other things, the increasingly unchecked power of billionaires to curtail speech and shape the public sphere to their liking, as well as the public's plummeting trust in journalism and the role it may have played in the jury's willingness to side with Hogan. For our purposes, though, perhaps the most significant chapter of the story came in 2019, when Univision combined the Gizmodo Media Group with a handful of other digital titles (including satire sites the *Onion* and *Clickhole*, as well as the Black news and culture site the *Root*), christened the new bundle G/O Media, and sold it to a private equity firm called Great Hill Partners.

Soon after the sale, editorial staffers at former Gawker sites immediately began to clash with the company's new owners—and these conflicts revolved in large part around the issue of metrics. When Great Hill CEO Jim Spanfeller told G/O Media editorial leaders that he expected them to double, and then quadruple, their sites' pageviews, many staffers bristled. Their resistance did not stem from the notion that metrics were a poor indicator of journalistic job performance: Gawker veterans were no strangers to managerially imposed traffic targets and the expectation of continual audience growth; throughout this book, we have seen that many of them internalized and even endorsed these things. As Megan Greenwell, the erstwhile editor in chief of *Deadspin*, Gawker's sports-focused site, put it in a post published on the day of her resignation from G/O Media, "The journalists at *Deadspin* and its sister sites, like most journalists I know, are eager to do work that makes money." She went on to note that *Deadspin*'s traffic numbers were already "large and growing" and that she had "tunneled obsessively into the details of those traffic numbers" throughout her eighteen-month tenure running the site.

Greenwell's objection, then, was not to newsroom metrics but rather to the way Great Hill Partners seemed to conceptualize the relationship between traffic, audiences, and profit. Greenwell criticized Spanfeller for his apparent belief that "he could simply turn up the traffic (and thus turn a profit), as if adjusting a faucet, not by investing in quality journalism but by tricking people into clicking on more pages."[14] The conflict intensified a few months later, when Spanfeller fired Greenwell's replacement, Barry Petchesky, when he refused to limit *Deadspin*'s coverage strictly to sports stories, leading the entire *Deadspin* editorial staff to quit in protest. In a *New York Times* op-ed about his firing, Petchesky noted that *Deadspin*'s traffic was the highest it had ever been, and others pointed out that the site's stories about politics and culture regularly outperformed its sports coverage in metrics. Yet this did not seem to matter to Spanfeller and the private equity firm. If companies like Great Hill Partners have their way, Petchesky wrote, "everything you liked about the web will be replaced with what the largest number of people like, or at least tolerate enough to click on and sit through three seconds of an autoplay ad."[15]

It is ironic, bordering on surreal, to see Gawker veterans like Petchesky issue warnings about the dangers of traffic-driven journalism that are nearly identical to the criticisms legacy media commentators used to direct at Gawker. And as Greenwell and Petchesky would likely be the first to acknowledge, newsroom metrics are and always have been linked to money: in a media system that was less intensely commercialized and profit-driven, metrics might well play a lesser or at least different role.[16] Even so, over the course of Gawker's existence as an independent company, the journalists there worked to carve out a space in which metrics could coexist with (or even, as chapter 7 argued, foster) their conception of editorial autonomy.

The conflict between Spanfeller and former Gawker staffers underscores a central theme of this book: the meaning of metrics—not only the numbers themselves but also what their presence in a newsroom symbolizes and signifies—is ever-ambiguous and therefore ripe for ongoing negotiation and contestation. As digital performance analytics continue to proliferate in expert fields, power struggles in the workplace will increasingly revolve around questions of which organizational actors have the ability to interpret metrics and have their interpretations be considered legitimate, authoritative, and influential. In the case of the journalists of what is now G/O Media versus the executives of Great Hill Partners, the journalists appear to have lost that battle.

Yet there are bright spots: most notably, the trend toward unionization that started at Gawker in 2015 and has since swept through more than sixty digital newsrooms.[17] While major legacy print publications like the *New York Times* and the *Washington Post* have long been unionized, just a few years ago it seemed unlikely that unions would gain a foothold in online news organizations. At a *BuzzFeed* company meeting in 2015, Jonah Peretti, the company's founder and CEO, was asked to comment on the possibility of his editorial staff unionizing. Peretti responded that unionization was beneficial "if you're working on an assembly line" but would be inappropriate for a "flexible, dynamic company" like BuzzFeed, which seeks to attract "the very best talent" and enjoys "an alliance between managers and employees."[18]

Peretti's comments were in line with much of the prevailing digital news industry discourse at the time. Digital newsrooms were, after all, staffed with a rising cohort of millennial journalists who had been conditioned to expect a career characterized by frequent job changes, a lack of long-term institutional affiliations, and the promise of "exposure" in lieu of monetary compensation.[19] Some commentators predicted that this job market precarity would foster a cutthroat individualistic sensibility in young digital journalists, manifesting in a singular fixation on building a "personal brand" whose value could be attested to by individual-level metrics like follower counts and article pageviews.[20]

Yet these predictions have thus far proven largely wrong. In 2019, the staff of *BuzzFeed News did* unionize—as have editorial employees at *Vice, Vox, HuffPost, Slate, Salon,* and many other online news organizations. It is, of course, difficult to tease out the complex mix of causal factors that are contributing to the wave of unionization in digital newsrooms. But it bears noting that some of the very digital newsrooms whose journalists were most deeply steeped in metrics—Gawker chief among them—were among the first to organize.

This book has examined how modes of quantitative performance evaluation that were originally deployed on the industrial factory floor have migrated into the knowledge-work settings in the digital age, as well as the ways they are evolving in the process. I have argued that in order to engineer the consent of journalists, newsroom metrics had to be both powerfully habit-forming and interpretively ambiguous. Once metrics become deeply institutionalized in journalism, they are capable of intensifying journalistic work, extracting increased productivity, fostering competitive dynamics between colleagues, and producing feelings of alienation.

Yet perhaps in their relentless insistence that the value of journalistic work can be quantitatively monitored and assessed, newsroom metrics are also unexpectedly clarifying. Traffic rankings, displayed on the newsroom wall, simultaneously symbolize journalists' economic value to the companies for which they work and their structural precarity. Put another way, newsroom metrics may remind journalists of their status *as workers*—and the ways in which, contra Peretti, the assembly line and the contemporary digital newsroom are actually not so different. Paraphrasing Marx, communication scholar Dan Schiller writes that while large-scale industry led to the exploitation of workers, it also produced a "*shared experience* of labor," which "not only encouraged a common class-consciousness but also engendered, through the use of common tools, a workaday awareness of the efficacy of collective action."[21] This is the great irony of newsroom metrics: individualistic and alienating as they often seem and feel, they may inadvertently foster a sense of shared struggle and solidarity in today's digital journalists.

Might the same be true in other knowledge-work fields where metrics are being widely implemented? Moving beyond the case of journalism, this book suggests that digital performance metrics facilitate a dialectical relationship between managerial control and knowledge workers' autonomy. Because knowledge workers *expect* to have substantial control over their labor process and working conditions, analytics tools that measure their performance must be designed in such a way that they do not feel like an overbearing form of managerial surveillance and coercion. These design decisions, which include forming relationships directly with managed workers and performing deference to their sense of specialized expertise, are effective in that they motivate workers to work harder without ever feeling like they are being forced to do so. At the same time, however, the design decisions that engineer knowledge workers' consent to analytics tools also render metrics ambiguous in their meaning and prescriptions. These ambiguities, in turn, can open opportunities for knowledge workers to leverage metrics to achieve their own individual and collective ends, sometimes in opposition to management.

Critical scholars in the 1990s and 2000s lamented the rise of "enterprise values" in creative and cultural fields, according to which workers assume individual risk on behalf of their companies and intensify their own work, thereby participating in their own subordination. So pervasive was the enterprise mindset among creative and knowledge workers that collective action was, for many observers during this period, difficult to imagine.[22]

It is not yet clear whether "enterprise values" are falling into broad disfavor among knowledge workers—and, if so, what role digital metrics may be playing in this process. Two things are evident, though. First, just as many have feared, metrics are likely to reshape the labor process in fields where they take root, speeding up knowledge work and rendering it more rationalized. However, metrics also make it harder for knowledge workers to ignore that what they do *is work*, however creative, prestigious, and autonomous it may seem, and however passionately they may feel about it. That heightened awareness—especially if it leads to demands for greater dignity, stability, and equity in the workplace—is a reason to be cautiously hopeful about the future.

ACKNOWLEDGMENTS

Whenever I get a new book, the first thing I do is read the acknowledgments. I love getting a glimpse at the community that sustained and propelled an author as they brought their book from idea, to research, to draft after draft, to—at long last—the object I hold in my hands. It was daunting to write this because my own community feels so vast, and so extraordinary, that I fear I will never be able to adequately express my appreciation. Still, I've done my best: here goes.

I owe an enormous debt of gratitude to the employees of Chartbeat, the *New York Times*, and Gawker Media who shared their time, insights, and experiences with me. Their generosity, patience, and thoughtfulness made this research possible. I particularly would like to acknowledge those who took the time to speak with me on multiple occasions, answered my many questions over IM and email, let me shadow them, or otherwise went far above and beyond to help me understand their work. I wish I could thank them by name, but I hope they know who they are.

The research upon which this book is based deeply benefited from the mentorship and friendship I enjoyed in the Sociology Department at New York University. It is hard to overstate my gratitude to Eric Klinenberg. Eric pushed me to take intellectual risks and pursue opportunities I never would have gone for on my own. His influence has made me a bolder, more confident scholar and person; our conversations over the years have sharpened my thinking and fortified my arguments. Eric has helped me navigate career decisions big and small with patience and good humor, and continues to provide me the most wonderful work home-away-from-home at the Institute for Public Knowledge.

A number of the ideas and questions pursued in this book were developed over lengthy, caffeine-fueled conversations with Gabriel Abend. One would be hard-pressed to find a smarter, more generous collaborator and mentor; I'm grateful that Gabi invested his time and rigorous analytical mind in my work. Many of the themes in this book have been profoundly shaped by Michael

Schudson—in the form of both his indispensable body of scholarship and our spirited conversations and email exchanges on subjects ranging from the nature of journalistic autonomy to the future of the news industry. Rodney Benson expertly guided my earliest forays into media sociology and has since provided thoughtful comments on countless drafts and presentations. Iddo Tavory provided perceptive comments on many of the ideas here, especially regarding the production of analytics. I'm grateful to the many other faculty members at NYU who have advised, challenged, and cheered me on over the years, especially Craig Calhoun, David Garland, Jen Jennings, Colin Jerolmack, Lynne Haney, and Steven Lukes.

My time at NYU and since has been immeasurably enriched by the friendship, care, and dazzling minds of an amazing group of fellow graduate students. "Support group breakfasts" at Veselka with Liz Koslov and Shelly Ronen buoyed me when I most needed it. Max Besbris is a true-blue friend and treasured collaborator. Life would be far less fun without Daniel Aldana Cohen's sparkling wit, intellectual provocations, and energetic dance moves. Working long hours side by side in a windowless, closet-sized room for years on end will turn people into either good friends or mortal enemies: with Adaner Usmani and Issa Kohler-Hausmann, it luckily turned out to be the former. (Issa gets a special shout-out for allowing me to stay in her New Haven guest room for *checks notes* two years.) I am lucky to have learned from and enjoyed the company of so many others, especially Hillary Angelo, Jen Heerwig, Max Holleran, Jeannie Kim, Tara Menon, Eyal Press, Anna Skarpelis, and David Wachsmuth.

I am grateful to the many scholars and thinkers who have taken the time to read my work and discuss ideas. Early conversations with Chris (C. W.) Anderson convinced me that a worthy book could be written on newsroom metrics. Fred Turner deserves special thanks as a long-time supporter of my work and the person who first introduced me to labor process theory. In an astounding act of generosity, Rachel Sherman read an early draft of the entire manuscript and talked through it with me for three hours; our conversation helped me sharpen the main argument. Julia Ticona was an invaluable source of camaraderie, accountability, and editorial troubleshooting in our Zoom writing dates during the final stretch. My work as a research assistant for Eli Pariser oh-so-many years ago sparked my interest in many of the questions that drive this book; I feel so lucky for his friendship and happy whenever our paths cross. Caitlin Zaloom taught me how to do good interviews (stop interrupting so much!) and remains a go-to source of advice on just about anything. Angèle Christin is one of my favorite people to trade ideas with; I'm thankful for her brilliant scholarship and genuine kindness. There are so many others who have deepened and enriched my thinking over wine, coffee, or email over the years, especially Mike Ananny, Matt Carlson, Mark Coddington, Brooke Erin Duffy, Herbert Gans, Jack Katz, Dave Karpf, Karen Levy, Seth Lewis, Frank Pasquale, Ben Shestakovsky, and Nikki Usher.

I am fortunate that several institutions and individuals have provided all manner of support for this project—financial, logistical, intellectual, and moral. The Tow Center for Digital Journalism at Columbia University provided funding and a platform from which to communicate some of my findings to practitioners in the digital media field. I am especially grateful to Emily Bell for her early vote of confidence in this project and for helping me obtain access to field sites. I also thank Taylor Owen and Fergus Pitt for their guidance and feedback throughout the research. Jack Balkin afforded me precious time and space to develop my ideas as a postdoctoral fellow at the Information Society Project at Yale University. The ISP community, especially Valérie Bélair-Gagnon, Colin Agur, and Rebecca Crootof, provided useful guidance and insightful feedback on the book proposal. I have been lucky to workshop multiple sections of this book at the Data & Society Research Institute; I am always bowled over by the community there. Tom Roush and LaVon Kellner generously lent me their guest room to use as a work space during the final push; I could not have asked for a more peaceful writing retreat during quarantine.

My fantastic colleagues at the Rutgers School of Communication & Information have been unwavering in their support. I am so lucky to have Melissa Aronczyk as a generous and wise mentor and delightful friend. My colleagues in the Department of Journalism & Media Studies are an all-around pleasure to work with (and, just as importantly, chat with) and have welcomed me warmly since day one. Conversations with Vikki Katz, Chenjerai Kumanyika, Jeff Lane, Khadijah White, and others have been an amazing source of camaraderie and guidance as I navigate the sometimes choppy waters of academic parenthood. As chairs, Susan Keith and Amy Jordan have gone above and beyond to make sure I had the time and resources I needed to get this book across the finish line. I'm grateful to Jonathan Potter, Mark Aakhus, and Dafna Lemish for championing my work and helping to plot my career trajectory. Marisol Porter, Narda Acevedo, and Karen Novick have provided indispensable administrative support and patiently answered my many questions.

I am grateful for the Program for Early Career Excellence (PECE) at Rutgers, which has provided structure and loads of helpful resources—thanks especially to Beth Tracy, Bernadette Gailliard, and Karen McCarthy. PECE also connected me to a wonderful peer group of scholars from across our vast university whom I might not have otherwise met: Stacey Greene, Lori Hoggard, Trinidad Rico, and especially Lauren Leigh Kelly, accountability buddy and friend extraordinaire. My deepest thanks also to Lisa McGahren, who has given clear-eyed and concrete advice, celebrated my victories, and talked me through difficult moments with calm and compassion.

The team at Princeton University Press has been terrific. I am especially grateful to Meagan Levinson for her incisive editing (especially her eagle-eye for jargon), her sense of humor, and her care and efficiency while shepherding this book to publication. Mark Bellis, Jackie Delaney, Dayna Hagewood, and Annabelle Sinoff were so helpful and responsive throughout the process. My sincere thanks to Jenn Backer for her vigilant copyediting and her kind patience in answering even my most obsessive questions, and to Fred Kameny for his thoughtful and meticulous indexing. I appreciate the anonymous reviewers of my proposal and full manuscript for supporting the project while also posing tough questions and pushing me to make it better. Thanks also to Jing Wang, who provided thorough and thoughtful research assistance, and Jayde Valosin, who wrangled my citations on a tight deadline.

My profound gratitude goes to my friends and extended family. My aunts Jane Banks and Marian Petre have doled out smart advice about building a career in academia. My network of family friends have cheered me on through thick and thin, especially Christine Doudna, Rick and Michael Grand-Jean, Molly and Greg Heller, and Sarah Lazin. I am beyond grateful for my in-laws Lori Brand and Lorin Karic, my brother-in-law Jesse Brand, my niece Willa and my nephew Eli—who have supplied me with a steady stream of babysitting help, home-cooked food, wine, laughter, comfort, and love over the years. I want to extend a special thanks to Anna Johnson, who is not only my beloved sister-in-law but also my dear friend and sounding board about everything from life in academia to baby sleep (as well as my favorite fitness instructor). I am outrageously lucky to have the friends I do: to a T, they are kindhearted, wise, honest, hilarious, and loyal. In particular, I would be grievously lost without Kate Axelrod, Jane Levin Cascio, Naomi Ekperigin, Isabel Jay, Annie Mathews, Mira Rapp-Hooper, and Lauren Stossel.

In acknowledgments, it is something of a cliché to say that the book wouldn't exist without the help of certain people. And yet, having finished this book during a global pandemic with a baby, a preschooler, and next-to-nonexistent childcare, I can confidently say that in this case, the cliché is quite literally true. Were it not for the following people, you would not be reading these words: full stop.

First, I want to thank Oscar Petre Brand and Josie Isabel Brand. If I ever managed to finish this book, I wasn't sure if it would be because of my children or in spite of them, but I'm leaning toward because. Frustrating as it sometimes was to have my writing interrupted because a small person urgently needed me to peel off a yogurt lid "the right way," build a stack of blocks for them to knock over, or pretend to be a peregrine falcon, these moments kept me from lapsing into excessive self-seriousness and grounded me in a way that I very much needed. Thank you, my skoodledoots; I love you the biggest much I've ever seen.

This book is dedicated to my parents, Ann Banks and Peter Petre. They provided our family a port in the Covid-19 storm, without which everything about this time would have been immeasurably more painful and difficult. But that is the least of what they have given me. They have edited countless drafts of my writing, made me the very best pancakes, and created magical experiences for my children. They have carried me during the worst moments and cheered me on during the best. Just about everything good in my life, including this book, is thanks in no small part to their steadfast love and confidence in me.

Finally, words cannot do justice to the gratitude I feel for Ari Brand: my great love, my champion co-parent, my confidante, my most reliable source of laughter, my anchor, my partner in all things. On our wedding day, you vowed to support me and do whatever you could to make my dreams happen—and wow, have you delivered. I love you. Team teamwork forever.

Methods

From the earliest stages of conceiving this project, it was clear that my questions about the processes by which newsroom analytics were produced, interpreted, and used would best be answered by in situ research. The purpose of this appendix is to provide insight about the process (and struggles) by which I obtained access to each of my field sites and the methods I employed to study them.

Chartbeat

The process of obtaining access to Chartbeat illustrated the challenges of conducting ethnographic research in corporate environments. I had interviewed two Chartbeat staffers, Tara and Steve, in the early stages of my research in 2011. Our interview had gone well and I wrote to them subsequently to see if I could shadow them in the office. Not hearing back, I followed up several times but eventually moved on. Then, in the summer of 2013, contacts at Columbia University's Tow Center for Digital Journalism put me in touch with Pete, a high-ranking staff member, via email.

My initial dealings with Chartbeat were consistent with the company's carefully cultivated low-key vibe. Pete seemed highly receptive to the project and put me in touch with Molly, another staff member who was to help facilitate my entree into the site. At my initial meeting with her, I was told I would be welcome to spend as much time as I wanted in the office but that I first had to meet with Melanie, another executive who was away on vacation. Melanie, who was trained as a lawyer and whose job title on the Chartbeat website included the descriptor "resident adult," was warier of me and my proposed research than Pete or Molly had seemed to be. She insisted I sign a blanket nondisclosure agreement and said I would not be permitted to do the research unless Chartbeat could review it and prevent publication if the company saw fit. When I offered to make the company anonymous, she countered, reasonably, that doing so wouldn't be much help because Chartbeat was distinctive in the analytics industry and would be easily identifiable to anyone familiar with it (she also said that if I ended up having positive things to say, she would want me to use Chartbeat's name). Melanie repeatedly said she wasn't worried I was going to find out something bad but maintained that she had to protect the company and prevent its reputation from being potentially damaged in the eyes of clients or investors.

At our first three meetings (the third of which was also attended by the company's lawyer), Melanie maintained that unless Chartbeat could have full veto power over my work, I would not be permitted to do the research there. I felt that these conditions would jeopardize my independence as a researcher to an unacceptable degree, so after deliberating and consulting several fellow ethnographers, I proposed a compromise. While I would not grant Chartbeat advance review or veto power over my analysis, I would agree to four conditions: first, I would not share the names or analytics data of any Chartbeat clients that were not already public; second, I would guarantee anonymity to individual Chartbeat staff members and assign pseudonyms when they were quoted or otherwise referred to in published materials; third, I would allow the company to review all direct quotes and transcribed anecdotes from my time at the office prior to publication and retroactively remove from the record any they did not want to be made public; finally, I would give Chartbeat the option to decide at the conclusion of my research whether the company wanted me to use its real name or a pseudonym.

While the first and second conditions were standard for ethnographic work of this type, I was initially apprehensive about the third condition and, to a lesser extent, the fourth. However, it was clear from the protracted access negotiation that the study would not take place otherwise, so I decided to move forward despite my reservations. Luckily, my fears proved to be unfounded. Melanie left the company shortly after we reached our agreement, and her colleagues proved considerably more comfortable with my presence, undoubtedly in part because they got to know me over the course of months of fieldwork. Of the dozens of quotes and field-note excerpts I offered to the company for review, Chartbeat only removed two altogether and cut a single line or phrase from six. None of these edits substantially changed the presentation of my findings, because all of my analytical arguments are based on multiple data points. If the company denied permission to use a particular quote, I was able to draw on alternative evidence to corroborate the argument.

I was also given permission to use the company name, so long as I didn't use employees' real names or link them to their specific teams or job titles (Chartbeat was small enough that some employees could be identifiable from their teams or titles alone). Instead, I was asked to identify employees only as working either on the business side (i.e., the executive team, sales, marketing, and product) or on the development side (i.e., user experience, research, design, and engineering), so that is what I have done.

As noted in the introduction, I conducted fieldwork in Chartbeat's offices from August 2013 through January 2014, during which I observed internal meetings, user-experience product-testing sessions, client trainings, social events, and the rhythms of daily office life. While I had initially envisioned visiting the office on a set schedule, this quickly proved impractical because relevant meetings and conversations happened at all times and often without much advance planning or notice. At the beginning of my fieldwork, it was agreed that the best approach would be for me to "squat" at an empty desk in the office so that I could be pulled into meetings as appropriate. While spending hours of unstructured time in the office at the beginning of the fieldwork was awkward (I wrote in my field notes that I often felt like the new kid in the high school cafeteria), it gave me a feel for the company culture, work routines, and atmosphere.

The later stages of fieldwork were more structured. Over time I formed relationships with a few key staff members, who would invite me in advance via email to attend or call in to specific meetings and events. These included: weekly all-staff meetings (called "Pulsechecks"), which occurred every Tuesday at noon, with catered lunch provided by the company; user-testing calls, in which Chartbeat employees would share with clients a prototype of the new dashboard and record their feedback (in exchange for a $50 Amazon gift card); periodic check-in meetings for the team working on the revamped dashboard; occasional social events, such as the company holiday party; in-person meetings with a client; training calls with clients after the launch of the revamped dashboard; and professional development events, such as a coding skills workshop and a "competition lunch" in which staffers compared notes on Chartbeat's rival analytics companies.

Because Chartbeat employees carried their laptops around the office and nearly always had them open in meetings, I was usually able to take comprehensive notes on my own laptop without seeming out of place or causing a distraction. This was especially convenient when sitting in on meetings, where I was often able to capture what was said close to verbatim. Upon leaving the office after each visit, I augmented my field notes, adding details that I had been unable to capture while at the office (e.g., offhand social interactions for which I didn't have my laptop on me), and free-wrote about emerging themes.

I also conducted 22 interviews and in-depth conversations with 16 employees who worked on a range of teams across the company. Specifically, I interviewed three staffers from the sales team, two from tech support, four from branding and marketing, three from product development, three from user experience and research, and one from engineering. The purpose of these interviews was to gain a candid understanding of Chartbeat employees' perceptions of the company and feelings about their work. Formal interviews were taped and transcribed; for informal conversations, I wrote detailed notes as soon after the fact as possible. Throughout the fieldwork, I wrote periodic thematic memos, which then guided my focus in subsequent field visits. After concluding my time in the field, I developed a preliminary coding frame based on my memos and notes, and used the qualitative data analysis program Dedoose to code interview transcripts and field notes. I continued to revise the frame as new themes emerged throughout the coding process.

The *New York Times*

My research at the *Times* consisted primarily of in-depth interviews. Suspecting (correctly, as it turned out) that it might be difficult to obtain official permission to conduct research in the newsroom, I began by leveraging my personal and professional networks to contact individual reporters and editors, rather than reaching out first to high-ranking staff as I did at Chartbeat and Gawker. To recruit interview subjects, I initially relied on snowball sampling, finding that a colleague's introduction (usually via email but occasionally also in person in the newsroom) increased the odds that someone would respond to my interview request. Later in the process, I expanded my sample by cold-contacting reporters, usually through the *Times*'s "reader mail" feature. I found that media and technology reporters were most likely to respond to these queries, possibly because their beats overlapped somewhat with my research topic.

In January 2014, I met a former senior *Times* editor through an academic presentation on the results of my research at the *Times*. He was interested in my findings and, when I mentioned that I'd like to supplement my interviews with observation, offered to pass along a description of my proposed fieldwork to a small group of *Times* editorial executives. After doing so, he was told that my being granted ethnographic access was not likely, and his attempts to follow up were met with non-response, which he advised me to take "as evidence of a lack of interest in your proposal." Despite this disappointing setback, I was heartened by the fact that *Times* staffers were generally quite forthcoming in interviews. In addition, two internal documents—the 2014 Innovation Report and a PowerPoint presentation on metrics that was presented to executive editor Dean Baquet and shared with me by an editor—provided material against which to compare what I was hearing in interviews.

Between 2011 and 2015, I conducted 25 semi-structured interviews with 22 newsroom staffers. Subjects performed a variety of roles in a range of departments and desks: I interviewed eight reporters (seven of whom were full-time employees, one of whom was a regular contributor), eight editors (including two who had left the *Times* by the time of our interview), one web producer, two columnists, and three staffers who inhabited more strategic positions related to newsroom operations. Interviews lasted between 25 and 105 minutes; the majority were approximately 45 minutes long. I began with questions about the subject's professional background and her current role and daily responsibilities at the *Times*, and subsequently transitioned to the issue of metrics. As the subjects knew from my recruitment email that I was interested in the topic, many of them brought up metrics on their own. If they did not, I would remind them of my general research interest before segueing into questions about their relationship to audience data. I began with broad questions about subjects' orientation toward audiences (e.g., "What kind of relationship do you have with your readers?") and then moved to the more specific (e.g., "How many times have you consulted an analytics tool today?"). Where applicable, I often found it helpful to refer to specific stories that subjects had recently written or edited (e.g., "Do you know what the pageviews were for story X? What sources, if any, did you consult to find this out?"). These probes encouraged subjects to discuss their specific practices, rather than lofty abstractions, with regard to audience data.

In addition to my interviews, I moderated two public panels on the topic of metrics at Columbia University's Tow Center for Digital Journalism that featured *Times* staffers: James Robinson, then the director of newsroom analytics, and Samantha Henig, then a "digital deputy" for the styles, home, travel, and real estate sections. I also closely followed public discussion about the *Times*—including academic research, media coverage, white papers and reports, and conference panels.

Gawker

My initial entree into Gawker came via Chartbeat. Gawker was a long-time client of Chartbeat's, and the two companies had a close relationship: Chartbeat's famous Big Board, the leaderboard that ranked news stories according to the number of concurrent visitors visiting them in real time, was initially built specifically for Gawker. While most news organizations did not want their analytics shared, Gawker allowed Chartbeat to use its real data to demo the dashboard during trainings with new and prospective clients. Toward the end of my fieldwork at Chartbeat, a couple of staffers who knew I was interested in studying media companies asked where I might like to go next. When I mentioned Gawker, one of them put me in touch with Gawker's chief technology officer, who in turn facilitated my introduction to Noah, an editorial executive. Noah granted me access to do research at Gawker (and use the company's name) at the conclusion of our first meeting.

Unlike Chartbeat, no one at Gawker ever raised the concern that I might write something damaging to the company's reputation. Rather, Noah's concerns were twofold: first, that individual employees be made to understand that participation in the research was strictly optional; second, that I would face logistical difficulties in attempting to use traditional ethnographic methods (such as shadowing employees) because so many of the relevant interactions happened in online settings. These reservations notwithstanding, Noah was curious to see what I would find, especially upon hearing that I would be conducting interviews anonymously. As he put it in his email introducing me to the editorial staff: "I look forward to the results of [Caitlin's] work. I think it will tell us a lot about how analytics affect our journalism, style, and happiness in our work."

While the process of obtaining access to Gawker was substantially easier than it had been at Chartbeat, actually conducting observational research proved to be more difficult for precisely the reason Noah had anticipated. Though most of Gawker's editorial staff worked together in a large room at the company's Nolita headquarters, in-person meetings and even conversations were relatively rare on the editorial floor. Even if there had been lots of in-person interaction to observe, I did not have a reliable perch from which to observe it: unlike at Chartbeat, where I was given an empty desk in the middle of the office, affording me a prime vantage from which to observe workplace goings-on, Gawker's editorial floor was crowded to the point where some staffers had been asked to work from home. There was no surplus desk space for a visitor.

I devised various stratagems to address these methodological challenges. First, I conducted 28 interviews with a broad swath of editorial staff—including five site leads, three lower-ranking editors, sixteen writers, two editorial fellows, and two editorial executives—as well as two with employees on the business side. While, per Noah's wishes, I emphasized that participation was strictly optional when emailing staff to ask for interviews, editorial employees were generally eager to speak with me and had a lot to say on the subject of metrics. Interviews lasted between 30 and 120 minutes; longer interviews (between 80–110 minutes) were typical.

I also observed in-person meetings whenever possible: these included meetings restricted to site leads as well as editorial "all-hands" meetings, of which I received links to video recordings after the fact. In addition, I analyzed the company's internal memos, with particular attention to those concerning metrics (some of these were provided to me by staffers, some were published on Gawker sites, and others were leaked online).

Finally, I spent a total of five days "sitting in" on the online group chats of two of Gawker's core sites. One was considered a big Gawker site, ranking in the top four of the company's eight core titles on the measure of monthly unique visitors, while the other was considered small and ranked in the bottom four. My time in these group chats, which took place on a collaborative work program called Campfire, helped me to develop a situated understanding of daily editorial processes at Gawker and to see whether employees interacted with metrics differently depending on the size of their site's audience. The lead editors for each of these sites also corresponded with me during and after my Campfire visits over email and instant message; these one-on-one exchanges helped to contextualize what I was observing in the group chats.

A Note on Preserving Informant Anonymity

In keeping with sociological convention and IRB protocol, I have assigned pseudonyms to all research subjects. As for other details, such as job titles, I have worked to strike a balance between providing important contextual information and omitting any details that could potentially compromise my subjects' anonymity. In some cases, individuals and sites requested to be referred to in a particular way: for instance, as noted above, Chartbeat asked that I not share job titles (because of the small size of staff teams) but rather refer to employees as being on either the "business" or "development" side of the organization. When individuals and organizations did not voice a preference,

I used my best judgment. For example, when I refer to or quote a writer at a particular Gawker site, I identify the site if (1) that information is relevant, and (2) the site had enough writers that I could name it while preserving the individual's anonymity. But when I quote a "site lead," I do not name the site, because each site had only one lead and that person would be easy to identify. In addition, in most instances where journalists discussed particular stories they wrote or edited, I refer only to the general subject matter rather than the specific subject or headline of the story.

A Guide to the Chartbeat Publishing Dashboard

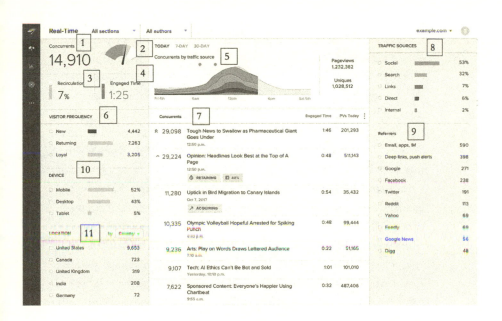

1. The **concurrents count** shows the total number of browsing sessions currently open to the site. The concurrents count includes any browser window where the user has shown some activity (e.g., clicking, scrolling, or moving the cursor) within the past two hours. Browser windows with no user activity for two consecutive hours are considered inactive and are excluded from the concurrents count until the user resumes activity.[1] Though the concurrents count technically tracks browsing

sessions, not individuals, the concurrents count was treated as a proxy for the number of concurrent visitors to a site.

2. The **concurrents dial** is another way of displaying concurrent browsing sessions. The dial's needle rises and falls as browsing sessions to the site begin and end. The gray shaded portion of the dial illustrates the typical range of concurrents for that day and time.

3. **Recirculation** is the percentage of a site's browsing sessions that were referred by another page on the site. It is used as an indication of the extent to which readers tend to click on another page on the site after the first article they look at.[2]

4. **Engaged time** is the average number of seconds or minutes visitors spend "engaging" with content on the site. To develop this measure, Chartbeat conducted an experiment using its own employees and participants on Amazon's Mechanical Turk as subjects. It instructed participants to focus on reading an article or watching a video, and used a tracker to monitor their actions (i.e., moving their mouse or tapping a key) as they read. From this data, Chartbeat discovered that when people are actively reading or watching something, they usually do not go very long (often around one second, almost never more than five seconds) without performing some sort of action on their device. Thus Chartbeat counted a user as "engaged" on a site if she had interacted with it in some way in approximately the last five seconds.

5. **Concurrents by traffic source** is a color-coded graph that shows users where most of their concurrent visitors are coming from over time (e.g., social media, search, direct, etc.).

6. **Visitor frequency** sorts concurrent visitors into three buckets: "new" visitors are those visiting the site for the first time in at least 30 days; "loyal" visitors are those who have visited the site during at least 8 of the past 16 days; and "returning" visitors are those that fall somewhere in between these two.

7. **Top pages** is a list of the site's top-performing articles according to various metrics (this screenshot shows top-performing pages by concurrents, but it is also possible to sort top pages according to other metrics, such as Engaged Time).

8. **Traffic sources** shows the percentage of the site's total traffic that is driven by various categories of referrers (such as search engines and social media platforms).

9. **Referrers** breaks down sources of traffic into specific sites and apps and shows how many referrals each has made to the site within a given period.

10. **Device** shows which devices audience members are most commonly using to access the site.

11. The **location** metric shows how many concurrents are viewing the site from different countries. Users can "pivot" onto a particular country if they want to see metrics (such as engaged time and referral sources) specific to that area.

NOTES

Introduction

1. Nicholas Carlson, "LEAKED: AOL's Master Plan," *Business Insider*, February 1, 2011, https://www.businessinsider.com/the-aol-way.

2. TechCrunch, "Paul Miller and the Five Rules of Stunt Resignation," February 19, 2011, https://techcrunch.com/2011/02/19/aol-way-or-the-highway/.

3. Dan Mitchell, "The AOL Way: Broken, Battered, and Hopeless," *Fortune*, February 2, 2011, http://fortune.com/2011/02/02/the-aol-way-broken-battered-and-hopeless/.

4. Anthony Ha, "The New 'Aol Way': It's All about the Numbers," *Venturebeat*, February 1, 2011, https://venturebeat.com/2011/02/01/the-aol-way/.

5. See Harry Braverman, *Labor and Monopoly Capital: The Degradation of Work in the Twentieth Century* (New York: Monthly Review Press, 1974). For more on Taylorism and routinization in service work contexts, see Robin Leidner, *Fast Food, Fast Talk: Service Work and the Routinization of Everyday Life* (Berkeley: University of California Press, 1993).

6. See Vincent Mosco, *The Political Economy of Communication*, 2nd ed. (London: Sage, 2009); Bill Ryan, *Making Capital from Culture: The Corporate Form of Capitalist Cultural Production* (Berlin: DeGruyter, 1991); and David Hesmondhalgh and Sarah Baker, *Creative Labour: Media Work in Three Cultural Industries* (London: Routledge, 2011). The oft-discussed "paradox" of managing knowledge workers is also discussed further below.

7. As Mosco puts it, "The image of the crusading professional journalist or the high tech entrepreneur overwhelms the less romantic reality of a media and high-tech world, most of whose workers toil under conditions that industrial workers of the past would recognize. There is an understandable tendency to emphasize the individual creative dimensions of media production which distinguish this sector from the many occupational sectors that share the characteristics of industrial production. . . . There are substantial grounds for this view, principally based on the relatively high level of conceptual thought that this industry requires. This is the chief reason why print workers and their trade unions have historically occupied a privileged position in the workforce. But the emphasis on individual creativity only obscures a complex process of production, one that, however unevenly, has come to look more like the labor process in the general economy" (*The Political Economy of Communication*, 139–40).

8. In their overview of the big data phenomenon, internet scholar Viktor Mayer-Schönberger and journalist Kenneth Cukier anticipate that "the biggest impact of big data will be that data-driven decisions are poised to augment or overrule human judgment"—a development that they see as largely positive. Viktor Mayer-Schönberger and Kenneth Cukier, *Big Data: A Revolution*

That Will Transform How We Live, Work, and Think (Boston: Houghton Mifflin Harcourt, 2013), 141. Economist and legal scholar Ian Ayres echoes this claim: "We are in a historic moment of horse-versus-locomotive competition, where intuitive and experiential expertise is losing out time and time again to number crunching." Ian Ayres, *Super Crunchers: Why Thinking-by-Numbers Is the New Way to Be Smart* (New York: Bantam Books, 2007), 10.

9. E.g., legal scholar Frank Pasquale has argued that when expert judgment is replaced by data-driven computational methods, something important is lost—namely, professionals' experience-honed ability to wrestle with deep "conflicts of values and introspection that algorithms are ill suited to address." Frank Pasquale, "Professional Judgment in an Era of Artificial Intelligence and Machine Learning," *boundary 2* 46(1) (2019): 73–101, 83.

10. For more on the concentration of media ownership in the United States, see, e.g., Robert McChesney, *The Problem of the Media: U.S. Communication Politics in the Twenty-First Century* (New York: Monthly Review Press, 2004); Victor Pickard, *Democracy without Journalism? Confronting the Misinformation Society* (Oxford: Oxford University Press, 2019); and Eric Klinenberg, *Fighting for Air: The Battle to Control America's Media* (New York: Metropolitan Books, 2007).

11. Pickard, *Democracy without Journalism?*

12. Justin McCarthy, "Trust in Mass Media Returns to All-Time Low," Gallup, September 17, 2014, http://www.gallup.com/poll/176042/trust-mass-media-returns-time-low.aspx.

13. Jim Norman, "Americans' Confidence in Institutions Stays Low," Gallup, June 13, 2016, https://news.gallup.com/poll/192581/americans-confidence-institutions-stays-low.aspx.

14. Theodore Porter, *Trust in Numbers: The Pursuit of Objectivity in Science and Public Life* (Princeton: Princeton University Press, 1995).

15. Media scholar Rodrigo Zamith has argued that there is value in distinguishing between these terms in certain contexts—such that "analytics" refers to particular systems or types of software that track web traffic (such as Google Analytics or Chartbeat), while "metrics" describes particular measurements *within* those systems (such as pageviews or unique visitors). Yet for simplicity's sake I have elected to use the two terms interchangeably, following the convention of scholars such as Angèle Christin (among others) as well as my research participants. Rodrigo Zamith, "Quantified Audiences in News Production: A Synthesis and Research Agenda," *Digital Journalism* 6(4) (2018): 418–35; Angèle Christin, *Metrics at Work: Journalism and the Contested Meaning of Algorithms* (Princeton: Princeton University Press, 2020).

16. For more on the challenges of measuring unique visitors accurately, see chapter 2, note 5.

17. James G. Robinson, "The Audience in the Mind's Eye: How Journalists Imagine Their Readers," *Tow Center for Digital Journalism*, June 26, 2019, https://www.cjr.org/tow_center_reports/how-journalists-imagine-their-readers.php, p. 48. For more on the development of audience information systems in media industries, see Philip Napoli, *Audience Evolution: New Technologies and the Transformation of Media Audiences* (New York: Columbia University Press, 2011).

18. Though see these exceptions: Nicole S. Cohen, "At Work in the Digital Newsroom," *Digital Journalism* 7(5) (2018): 571–91; Nicole S. Cohen, "From Pink Slips to Pink Slime: Transforming Media Labor in a Digital Age," *Communication Review* 18(2) (2015): 98–122; Nicole S. Cohen, *Writers' Rights: Freelance Journalism in a Digital Age* (Montreal: McGill-Queen's University Press, 2016); Nicole S. Cohen and Greig de Peuter, *New Media Unions: Organizing Digital Journalists* (London: Routledge, 2020); Mel Bunce, "Management and Resistance in the Digital Newsroom," *Journalism* 20(7) (2019): 890–905; Caitlin Petre, "Engineering Consent: How the Design and Marketing of

Newsroom Analytics Tools Rationalize Journalists' Labor," *Digital Journalism* 6(4) (2018): 509–27; and Chang-de Liu, "De-skilling Effects on Journalists: ICTs and the Labour Process of Taiwanese Newspaper Reporters," *Canadian Journal of Communication* 31(3) (2006): 695–714.

19. See, e.g., Rodrigo Zamith, "On Metrics-Driven Homepages: Assessing the Relationship between Popularity and Prominence," *Journalism Studies* 19(8) (2018): 1116–37; Pablo Boczkowski and Eugenia Mitchelstein, *The News Gap: When Information Preferences of the Media and the Public Diverge* (Cambridge, MA: MIT Press, 2013); and Angela M. Lee, Seth C. Lewis, and Matthew Powers, "Audience Clicks and News Placement: A Study of Time-Lagged Influence in Online Journalism," *Communication Research* 41(4) (2012): 505–30.

20. See, e.g., Christin, *Metrics at Work*; Angèle Christin, "Counting Clicks: Quantification and Variation in Web Journalism in the United States and France," *American Journal of Sociology* 123(5) (2018): 1382–1415; Nikki Usher, "Al Jazeera English Online: Understanding Web Metrics and News Production When a Quantified Audience Is Not a Commodified One," *Digital Journalism* 1(3) (2013): 335–51; Phil MacGregor, "Tracking the Online Audience: Metric Data Start a Subtle Revolution," *Journalism Studies* 8(2) (2007): 280–98; C. W. Anderson, "Between Creative and Quantified Audiences: Web Metrics and Changing Patterns of Newswork in Local US Newsrooms," *Journalism* 12(5) (2011): 550–66; Edson C. Tandoc and Ryan J. Thomas, "The Ethics of Web Analytics: Implications of Using Audience Metrics in News Construction," *Digital Journalism* 3(2) (2015): 243–58; Edson Tandoc, "Journalism Is Twerking? How Web Analytics Is Changing the Process of Gatekeeping," *New Media & Society* 16(4) (2014): 559–75; Nicole Blanchett Neheli, "News by Numbers: The Evolution of Analytics in Journalism," *Digital Journalism* 6(8) (2018): 1041–51; and Folker Hanusch, "Web Analytics and the Functional Differentiation of Journalism Cultures: Individual, Organizational and Platform-Specific Influences on Newswork," *Information, Communication & Society* 20(10) (2017): 1571–86. In an illustrative example of the state of the literature, Zamith lists several theoretical lenses scholars have used to analyze the role of metrics in news production (e.g., isomorphism, diffusion of innovation, field theory, institutionalism, and the social construction of technology), but labor process theory is not included (Zamith, "Quantified Audiences in News Production," 424).

21. For instance, Zamith looks at metrics and analytics and how they manifest "across the ABCDE of news production: attitudes, behaviors, content, discourse, and ethics." Working conditions and labor are not included as a core aspect of news production (though the use of metrics for employee evaluation is mentioned glancingly) (Zamith, "Quantified Audiences in News Production," 419). Similarly, Hanusch looks at how analytics are changing "journalistic practices, norms and values" but does not explicitly analyze working conditions (Hanusch, "Web Analytics and the Functional Differentiation of Journalism Cultures," 1572). These are but two examples of a broader tendency in journalism studies, which has led some scholars to call for more attention to working conditions and labor process in journalism scholarship; see Cohen, "At Work in the Digital Newsroom"; Cohen and de Peuter, *New Media Unions*; Henrik Örnebring, "Technology and Journalism-as-Labour: Historical Perspectives," *Journalism* 11(1) (2010): 57–74; Hanno Hardt, "Newsworkers, Technology, and Journalism History," *Critical Studies in Media Communication* 7(4) (1990): 346–65; and Marianne Salcetti, "The Emergence of the Reporter: Mechanization and Devaluation of Editorial Workers," in *Newsworkers: Towards a History of the Rank and File*, ed. Hanno Hardt and Bonnie Brennen (Minneapolis: University of Minnesota Press, 1995), 48–74. Relatedly, other scholars have noted a relative

neglect of labor issues in communication scholarship more generally; see Christian Fuchs, *Communication and Capitalism: A Critical Theory* (London: University of Westminster Press, 2020); Ryan, *Making Capital from Culture*; Hesmondhalgh and Baker, *Creative Labour*; and Mosco, *The Political Economy of Communication*.

22. See Cohen, *Writers' Rights*; Pickard, *Democracy without Journalism?*; Klinenberg, *Fighting for Air*; and Emily J. Bell, Taylor Owen, Peter D. Brown, Codi Hauka, and Nushin Rashidian, "The Platform Press: How Silicon Valley Reengineered Journalism," *Columbia Journalism Review*, March 29, 2017, https://www.cjr.org/tow_center_reports/platform-press-how-silicon-valley-reengineered-journalism.php.

23. Hesmondhalgh and Baker, *Creative Labour*, 17. There is, of course, a robust debate about what constitutes high-quality and low-quality cultural products in general, and news in particular, which is addressed in greater depth in chapter 2. For now, it suffices to say that however one chooses to define high-quality news, it seems quite likely that good working conditions would support its production, while bad working conditions would hinder it.

24. Max Weber, "Science as a Vocation," in *From Max Weber: Essays in Sociology*, ed. H. H. Gerth and C. Wright Mills (Abingdon: Routledge, 2009), 129–58; Michel Foucault, *Discipline and Punish: The Birth of the Prison* (New York: Random House, 2012); Michel Foucault, "Governmentality," in *The Foucault Effect: Studies in Governmentality*, ed. Graham Burchell, Colin Gordon, and Peter Miller (Chicago: University of Chicago Press, 1991), 87–104; Ian Hacking, "Making Up People," in *Reconstructing Individualism: Autonomy, Individuality, and the Self in Western Thought*, ed. Thomas C. Heller, Morton Sosna, and David E. Wellbery (Stanford: Stanford University Press, 1986), 161–71; Porter, *Trust in Numbers*; Wendy Nelson Espeland and Michael Sauder, "Rankings and Reactivity: How Public Measures Recreate Social Worlds," *American Journal of Sociology* 113(1) (2007): 1–40.

25. Mark Coddington, "The Wall Becomes a Curtain: Revisiting Journalism's News-Business Boundary," in *Boundaries of Journalism: Professionalism, Practices and Participation*, ed. Matt Carlson and Seth C. Lewis (Abingdon: Routledge, 2015), 67–82.

26. See Mark Deuze, *Media Work* (Cambridge: Polity Press, 2007). See also Christin, *Metrics at Work*; Timothy Marjoribanks, *News Corporation, Technology, and the Workplace: Global Strategies, Local Change* (Cambridge: Cambridge University Press, 2000), 4, 9–10; and Pablo J. Boczkowski, *Digitizing the News: Innovation in Online Newspapers* (Cambridge, MA: MIT Press, 2005).

27. Michael Burawoy, *Manufacturing Consent: Changes in the Labor Process under Monopoly Capitalism* (Chicago: University of Chicago Press, 1979). For an example of this line of thinking applied to journalism, see Marjoribanks, *News Corporation, Technology, and the Workplace*.

28. Hesmondhalgh and Baker, *Creative Labour*, 31.

29. Vincent Mosco and Catherine McKercher, *The Laboring of Communication: Will Knowledge Workers of the World Unite?* (Lanham, MD: Rowman & Littlefield, 2009), 24.

30. In this book, I analyze journalism as a form of creative labor that falls under the broader umbrella of knowledge work. Scholars have offered several definitions of knowledge work, ranging from the narrowest (knowledge work must be directly creative; artists, engineers, and university professors would be in this category) to the broadest (knowledge work includes anyone involved in any aspect of the production and distribution of knowledge, including call center workers and factory workers who manufacture networked electronic devices). The definition I employ is somewhere in the middle in terms of breadth.

31. See, for instance, Dan Schiller, "Labor and Digital Capitalism," in *The Routledge Companion to Labor and Media*, ed. Richard Maxwell (New York: Routledge, 2016), 6–7.

32. Hesmondhalgh and Baker, *Creative Labour*, 59. Similarly, Banks analyzes "cultural work" as that which occurs in industries "involved in the production of 'aesthetic' or 'symbolic' goods and services; that is, commodities whose core value is derived from their function as carriers of meaning in the form of images, symbols, signs and sounds" (Mark Banks, *The Politics of Cultural Work* [Houndmills: Palgrave Macmillan, 2007], 2). See also Ryan, *Making Capital from Culture*.

33. For more on the contradictions and tensions of industrial cultural production, see Hesmondhalgh and Baker, *Creative Labour*; Banks, *The Politics of Cultural Work*; and Ryan, *Making Capital from Culture*.

34. Banks, *The Politics of Cultural Work*, 6. Or, as Ryan puts it in *Making Capital from Culture*, "installation of creative management represents an attempt by capitalists to impose hierarchic control based on formal (legal) authority, on an otherwise irrational labor process—to increase the degree of subsumption via the medium of management. The organizational purpose of artistic and creative direction is to ensure achievement of prescribed outcomes and goals, but that process necessarily demands negotiation and compromise with the very workers management are supposed to govern. This is what gives the creative stage of production its indeterminacy" (122). For a more optimistic perspective that sees the art-commerce relation as a potentially generative set of interactions, see Deuze, *Media Work*.

35. See Gina Neff, *Venture Labor: Work and the Burden of Risk in Innovative Industries* (Cambridge, MA: MIT Press, 2012); Banks, *The Politics of Cultural Work*; and Paul duGay, *Consumption and Identity at Work* (London: Sage, 1995).

36. As Ryan puts it: "Creation in a corporate context represents a complex grid of systems of control and avenues of freedom" (*Making Capital from Culture*, 30).

37. Salcetti, "The Emergence of the Reporter."

38. Hesmondhalgh and Baker, *Creative Labour*, 66.

39. Mike Ananny, *Networked Press Freedom: Creating Infrastructures for a Public Right to Hear* (Cambridge, MA: MIT Press, 2018), 53. Ananny conceptualizes the press as similar to museums, public schools, and libraries—public-facing institutions responsible for facilitating the free speech—both speaking and listening—upon which democratic self-governance relies.

40. Hesmondhalgh and Baker, *Creative Labour*, 66.

41. Max Weber, *The Protestant Ethic and the "Spirit" of Capitalism* (New York: Penguin, 2002 [1905]).

42. Wendy Nelson Espeland and Mitchell L. Stevens, "A Sociology of Quantification," *European Journal of Sociology* 49(3) (2008): 401–36.

43. Ibid., 408.

44. Espeland and Sauder, "Rankings and Reactivity."

45. John W. Meyer and Brian Rowan, "Institutionalized Organizations: Formal Structure as Myth and Ceremony," *American Journal of Sociology* 83(2) (1977): 340–63.

46. Paul J. DiMaggio and Walter W. Powell, "The Iron Cage Revisited: Institutional Isomorphism and Collective Rationality in Organizational Fields," *American Sociological Review* 48(2) (1983): 147–60.

47. Christin, *Metrics at Work*.

48. As Christin puts it, "much of the coverage of algorithms and digital metrics has split between technological utopianism and dire warnings," both of which "take the efficacy and power of algorithms for granted" in problematic ways (*Metrics at Work*, 3–4).

49. See, e.g., Ayres, *Super Crunchers*; Mayer-Schönberger and Cukier, *Big Data*.

50. See, e.g., Frank Pasquale, *The Black Box Society: The Secret Algorithms That Control Money and Information* (Cambridge, MA: Harvard University Press, 2015); Pasquale, "Professional Judgment in an Era of Artificial Intelligence and Machine Learning"; Jerry Muller, *The Tyranny of Metrics* (Princeton: Princeton University Press, 2019); David Beer, *Metric Power* (London: Palgrave Macmillan, 2016); and Shoshana Zuboff, *The Age of Surveillance Capitalism: The Fight for a Human Future at the New Frontier of Power* (New York: Public Affairs, 2019).

51. Braverman, *Labor and Monopoly Capital*.

52. Ibid., 282. See also Mosco and McKercher, *The Laboring of Communication*, 35; David Knights and Hugh Wilmott, *Labor Process Theory* (Houndmills: Macmillan, 1990), introduction. For applications of the deskilling argument applied specifically to journalists, see Liu, "Deskilling Effects on Journalists"; Revati Prasad, "An Organized Work Force Is Part of Growing Up: Gawker and the Case for Unionizing Digital Newsrooms," *Communication, Culture & Critique* 12(3) (2019): 359–77.

53. Burawoy, *Manufacturing Consent*, xi.

54. For a critique of Burawoy along these lines, see Dan Clawson and Richard Fantasia, "Beyond Burawoy: The Dialectics of Conflict and Consent on the Shop Floor," *Theory and Society* 12(5) (1983): 671–80. For a synthetic discussion of the literature on the dialectical relationship between worker resistance and managerial control, see Robert A. Brooks, *Cheaper by the Hour: Temporary Lawyers and the Deprofessionalization of the Law* (Philadelphia: Temple University Press, 2011), chap. 1.

55. The aim of this section is to provide a brief overview of my sites and methods. Chapter 1 includes a more comprehensive discussion of the institutional context and history of each of the three sites, while appendix A delves into my research methods and the process of obtaining access to each site.

56. As is probably apparent by now, this book focuses almost exclusively on editorial, rather than advertising, analytics. When I refer to "staffers" or "employees" at Gawker or the *Times* in the pages that follow, it is safe to assume I am referring to editorial staff unless otherwise noted. There are several reasons for my focus on editorial contexts. First, as noted earlier, my goal is to examine an influx of analytics in a field that has multiple aims, rather than a single end for which it is optimizing. While the advertising employees of news publishers inhabit organizations that see themselves as having democratic as well as commercial aims, the advertising staffers generally do not have to reconcile these aims in their daily work the way editorial staff members do. Second, I was interested in studying a field in which quantitative performance measures were relatively new. While data that gauges the reach of advertising campaigns has become far more sophisticated in recent years, the print news advertising market has been using data about subscriptions and newsstand sales for decades. The third reason is simply one of feasibility. The field of organizations involved in measuring online advertising is far more crowded and complex than its editorial counterpart.

Because most news organizations still maintain a wall between advertising and editorial, it was not difficult to mirror this boundary in my fieldwork. Even so, we will see that advertising and editorial frequently overlap indirectly. After all, in theory the goal of news-room analytics is to expand audiences, in hopes that greater prestige, access to sources, and eventually revenue will follow. The metrics according to which many newsrooms measure their traffic—pageviews and unique visitors—are the same metrics that are the currency of the online advertising market. In this way, metrics are an important—perhaps the primary—way that business considerations penetrate the daily work of a contemporary newsroom.

57. Chartbeat *Media Kit*, 2015, https://static2.chartbeat.com/images/marketing_ng/media _kit/media_kit.pdf.

58. Nikki Usher, *Making News at the New York Times* (Ann Arbor: University of Michigan Press, 2014).

Chapter 1: Digital Journalism

1. Banks, *The Politics of Cultural Work*, 2.

2. John Hartley, *Popular Reality: Journalism, Modernity and Popular Culture* (London: Arnold, 1996), 32, as quoted in Deuze, *Media Work*, 142.

3. For general discussions of the normative role of the press in democracy, see, e.g., Ananny, *Networked Press Freedom*; Michael Schudson, *Why Democracies Need an Unlovable Press* (Cambridge: Polity, 2008); and Clifford G. Christians, Theodore L. Glasser, Denis McQuail, Kaarle Nordenstreng, and Robert A. White, *Normative Theories of the Media: Journalism in Democratic Societies* (Urbana: University of Illinois Press, 2009).

4. Ananny, *Networked Press Freedom*, 11. See also Anthony M. Nadler, *Making the News Popular: Mobilizing U.S. News Audiences* (Urbana: University of Illinois Press, 2016), 20. Nadler argues that the "news media serves as a critical civic architecture for contemporary democracies."

5. Matt Carlson, *Journalistic Authority: Legitimating News in the Digital Era* (New York: Columbia University Press, 2017), 33.

6. See, e.g., Rodney Benson and Erik Neveu, eds., *Bourdieu and the Journalistic Field* (Cambridge: Polity, 2005).

7. Michael Schudson, "Autonomy from What?" in *Bourdieu and the Journalistic Field*, ed. Rodney Benson and Erik Neveu (Cambridge: Polity, 2005), 219.

8. Ananny, *Networked Press Freedom*.

9. Herbert J. Gans, *Deciding What's News: A Study of CBS Evening News, NBC Nightly News, Newsweek, and Time* (Evanston, IL: Northwestern University Press, 2004 [1979]). Still, see Zamith, "Quantified Audiences in News Production"; Napoli, *Audience Evolution*; and Nadler, *Making the News Popular*. Zamith, drawing on Napoli, notes that journalists' understanding of the audience became progressively more data-based throughout the twentieth century, mainly via three "waves of rationalization." The first, in the 1930s, occurred when advertisers demanded concrete evidence of their ads' effectiveness, and newspapers began investing in reader surveys as a result. The second, in the 1970s, was an attempt to leverage the affordances of emerging computational technologies to collect statistical data about audiences. The third wave, occurring in the early twenty-first century, further rationalizes audience understanding via the deployment of digital analytics.

10. Gans, *Deciding What's News*, 230. For more on journalists' disinterest in audience research and feedback in the pre-internet era, see Gans, *Deciding What's News*, 229–36; Philip Schlesinger, *Putting "Reality" Together: BBC News* (London: Routledge, 1978), 134; Robinson, "The Audience in the Mind's Eye"; and Dwight DeWerth-Pallmeyer, *The Audience in the News* (New York: Routledge, 2009 [1997]).

11. Andrew Abbott, *The System of Professions: An Essay on the Division of Expert Labor* (Chicago: University of Chicago Press, 1988), 8.

12. Carlson, *Journalistic Authority*, 43. See also Michael Schudson and Chris Anderson, "Objectivity, Professionalism, and Truth-Seeking in Journalism," in *The Handbook of Journalism Studies*, ed. Karin Wahl-Jorgensen and Thomas Hanitzsch (New York: Routledge, 2009), 88–101.

13. Deuze, *Media Work*, 169.

14. As Deuze explains, "Outside forces are kept at bay primarily by the rather self-referential nature of newswire, as expressed through the tendency among journalists to privilege whatever colleagues think of their work over criteria such as viewer ratings, hit counts or sales figures." Ibid.

15. As Michael Schudson and C. W. Anderson put it, journalists "are almost always hired hands, not independent operators." Schudson and Anderson, "Objectivity, Professionalism, and Truth-Seeking in Journalism," 97.

16. Lou Ureneck, "Newspapers Arrive at Economic Crossroads," *Nieman Lab*, June 15, 1999, https://niemanreports.org/articles/newspapers-arrive-at-economic-crossroads/.

17. Banks, *The Politics of Cultural Work*, 40 (see also 6–7). See also Hesmondhalgh and Baker, *Creative Labour*; Ryan, *Making Capital from Culture*. Ryan explains that "creative management is remarkably benign; cultural workers such as studio announcers, composers, screenplay writers and journalists, are initially briefed by creative management but then complete their work with minimal supervision" (110–11).

18. Örnebring, "Technology and Journalism-as-Labour," 62.

19. See Schudson and Anderson, "Objectivity, Professionalism, and Truth-Seeking in Journalism," 96.

20. Gans, *Deciding What's News*, 234.

21. For an in-depth exploration of news aggregation, see Mark Coddington, *Aggregating the News: Secondhand Knowledge and the Erosion of Journalistic Authority* (New York: Columbia University Press, 2019).

22. See, e.g., Pickard, *Democracy without Journalism?*; Margaret Sullivan, *Ghosting the News: Local Journalism and the Crisis of American Democracy* (New York: Columbia Global Reports, 2020).

23. More than 60% of the total money spent on digital advertising in 2017 went to either Google or Facebook, and Amazon and Snap are also rapidly gaining ground as attractive destinations for advertisers. Alexandra Bruell, "Rivals Chip Away at Google's and Facebook's U.S. Digital Ad Dominance, Data Show," *Wall Street Journal*, March 19, 2018, https://www.wsj.com/articles/rivals-chip-away-at-googles-and-facebooks-u-s-digital-ad-dominance-data-show-1521457321.

24. The news analytics company Parse.ly has found that news organizations rely on external referrers, such as search engines and social networking sites, for nearly half of their traffic. Parse.ly, "Referral Trends in the Parse.ly Network," *Parse.ly blog*, n.d., https://www.parse.ly/resources/data-studies/referrer-dashboard/.

25. Matthew Zeitlin, "The Digital Media Bloodbath: Hundreds of Jobs Lost," *BuzzFeed*, April 13, 2016, https://www.buzzfeednews.com/article/matthewzeitlin/the-digital-media-bloodbath-hundreds-of-jobs-lost.

26. Jeffrey M. Jones, "U.S. Media Trust Continues to Recover from 2016 Low," Gallup, October 12, 2018, https://news.gallup.com/poll/243665/media-trust-continues-recover-2016-low.aspx.

27. McCarthy, "Trust in Mass Media Returns to All-Time Low."

28. Robert W. McChesney, *The Problem of the Media: U.S. Communication Politics in the Twenty-First Century* (New York: Monthly Review Press, 2004). See also James R. Compton and Paul Benedetti, "Labor, New Media and the Institutional Restructuring of Journalism," *Journalism Studies* 11(4) (2010): 487–99.

29. Jill Lepore, "Does Journalism Have a Future?" *New Yorker*, January 21, 2019, https://www.newyorker.com/magazine/2019/01/28/does-journalism-have-a-future.

30. David Carr, "Risks Abound as Reporters Play in Traffic," *New York Times*, March 23, 2014, https://www.nytimes.com/2014/03/24/business/media/risks-abound-as-reporters-play-in-traffic.html.

31. Christin, *Metrics at Work*, 153.

32. Zamith, "Quantified Audiences in News Production."

33. See, e.g., Usher, "Al Jazeera English Online"; MacGregor, "Tracking the Online Audience"; Anderson, "Between Creative and Quantified Audiences"; Tandoc and Thomas, "The Ethics of Web Analytics"; Tandoc, "Journalism Is Twerking?"; Zamith, "Quantified Audiences in News Production"; Blanchett Neheli, "News by Numbers"; Hanusch, "Web Analytics and the Functional Differentiation of Journalism Cultures"; Christin, *Metrics at Work*; Valérie Bélair-Gagnon and Avery E. Holton, "Boundary Work, Interloper Media, and Analytics in Newsrooms: An Analysis of the Roles of Web Analytics Companies in News Production," *Digital Journalism* 6(4) (2018): 492–508; and Federica Cherubini and Rasmus Kleis Nielsen, *Editorial Analytics: How News Media Are Developing and Using Audience Data and Metrics*, Reuters Institute, February 29, 2016, https://reutersinstitute.politics.ox.ac.uk/our-research/editorial-analytics-how-news-media-are-developing-and-using-audience-data-and-metrics.

34. Boczkowski and Mitchelstein, *The News Gap*.

35. Tandoc and Thomas, "The Ethics of Web Analytics." See also Tandoc, "Journalism Is Twerking?"

36. In his study of Argentinian newspapers, Boczkowski found that metrics increase news homogeneity (Pablo Boczkowski, *News at Work: Information in an Age of Information Abundance* [Chicago: University of Chicago Press, 2010]). Studies relying on time-lagged content analyses of news sites provide some evidence to support the view that analytics are driving editorial agendas, though it is mixed. For instance, Lee, Lewis, and Powers found that popular stories (as represented by metrics) were slightly more likely to subsequently appear on a news site's home page; Zamith found a similar effect, though in both cases the magnitude of the effect was small (Lee, Lewis, and Powers, "Audience Clicks and News Placement"; Zamith, "On Metrics-Driven Homepages"). Bright and Nicholls found that popular articles were less likely to be removed from UK newspaper home pages than their less popular counterparts by about 25% and that the effect was similar for both "hard" and "soft" news items (Jonathan Bright and Tom Nicholls, "The Life and Death of Political News: Measuring the Impact of the Audience Agenda Using Online Data," *Social Science Computer Review* 32[2] [2014]: 170–81). In a study of Dutch

newspapers, Welbers et al. found that popular articles were more likely to receive follow-up coverage, which suggests that analytics are shaping longer-term editorial agendas as well as short-term home-page placement decisions (Kasper Welbers, Wouter van Atteveldt, Jan Kleinnijenhuis, Nel Ruigrok, and Joep Schaper, "News Selection Criteria in the Digital Age: Professional Norms versus Online Audience Metrics," *Journalism* 17[8] [2016]: 1037–53). In a different methodological vein, an experimental study found that Belgian journalists ranked hypothetical stories as deserving of more prominence if they saw metrics showing the stories were popular, as opposed to a control group who did not see metrics. However, the effect of popularity on perceptions of newsworthiness only held for "soft" news and was smaller in magnitude than other traditional news values, such as negativity (Kenza Lamot and Peter Van Aelst, "Beaten by Chartbeat?: An Experimental Study on the Effect of Real-Time Audience Analytics on Journalists' News Judgment," *Journalism Studies* 21[4] [2019]: 477–93).

37. See, e.g., Cherubini and Nielsen, *Editorial Analytics*.

38. Nikki Usher, "Why SEO and Audience Tracking Won't Kill Journalism as We Know It," *Nieman Lab*, September 14, 2010, https://www.niemanlab.org/2010/09/why-seo-and-audience-tracking-won%E2%80%99t-kill-journalism-as-we-know-it-2/.

39. Matthew Hindman, "Journalism Ethics and Digital Audience Data," in *Remaking the News: Essays on the Future of Journalism Scholarship in the Digital Age*, ed. Pablo J. Boczkowski and C. W. Anderson (Cambridge, MA: MIT Press, 2017), 192.

40. Christin, *Metrics at Work*. For more on metrics and institutional culture, see Anderson, "Between Creative and Quantified Audiences"; Usher, "Al Jazeera English Online"; and Hanusch, "Web Analytics and Functional Differentiation of Journalism Cultures." Other studies have found that factors such as organizational size and ownership structure influenced metrics usage: see Carly T. McKenzie, Wilson Lowrey, Hal Hays, Jee Young Chung, and Chang Wan Woo, "Listening to News Audiences: The Impact of Community Structure and Economic Factors," *Mass Communication and Society* 14(3) (2011): 375–95; Wilson Lowrey and Chang Wan Woo, "The News Organization in Uncertain Times: Business or Institution?" *Journalism & Mass Communication Quarterly* 87(1) (2010): 41–61. At the level of the individual journalist, Tandoc found that perception of competition in the media field and a perception of the audience as a form of capital influenced self-reported analytics usage (Edson C. Tandoc, "Why Web Analytics Click: Factors Affecting the Ways Journalists Use Audience Metrics," *Journalism Studies* 16[6] [2015]: 782–99).

41. Hanusch, "Web Analytics and Functional Differentiation of Journalism Cultures."

42. Critical journalism scholar Nicole S. Cohen has argued that "labor remains sidelined in journalism studies" and has called for more attention to labor relations and power dynamics in newsrooms ("At Work in the Digital Newsroom," 571). Henrik Örnebring concurs, noting that "journalism studies as a field has not paid much attention to journalism as labor" ("Technology and Journalism-as-Labour," 57). For exceptions, though, see Cohen, "Pink Slips to Pink Slime"; Nicole S. Cohen, "Cultural Work as a Site of Struggle: Freelancers and Exploitation," *Communication, Capitalism & Critique* 10(2) (2012): 141–55; Bunce, "Management and Resistance in the Digital Newsroom"; Christin, *Metrics at Work*, chap. 4; Edward Comor and James Compton, "Journalistic Labor and Technological Fetishism," *Political Economy of Communication* 3(2) (2015): 74–87; and Compton and Benedetti, "Labor, New Media, and the Institutional Restructuring of Journalism."

43. See, e.g., Pickard, *Democracy without Journalism?*; McChesney, *The Problem of the Media*; Edward S. Herman and Noam Chomsky, *Manufacturing Consent: The Political Economy of the Mass Media* (New York: Pantheon, 2010); and C. Edwin Baker, *Advertising and a Democratic Press* (Princeton: Princeton University Press, 1994).

44. Hesmondhalgh and Baker, *Creative Labour*, 17.

45. Ananny, *Networked Press Freedom*, 42.

46. Clio Chang, "How to Save Journalism," *New Republic*, July 11, 2019, https://newrepublic .com/article/154455/save-journalism.

47. Cohen and de Peuter, *New Media Unions*, vii–ix.

48. Notably, this shift is not limited to digital journalism. Cohen and de Peuter note a broader "turn to labor politics" by other groups of "white-collar and millennial workers, including adjunct professors, grad students, tech workers, and art and cultural workers" (ibid., 83).

49. Ibid., 74.

50. While this book focuses on full-time newsroom employees, freelancers make up a large and growing portion of the journalistic workforce (Bureau of Labor Statistics, "Occupational Outlook Handbook: Reporters, Correspondents, and Broadcast News Analysts," U.S. Department of Labor, 2019, https://www.bls.gov/ooh/media-andcommunication /reporters-correspondents-and-broadcast-news-analysts.htm). For an in-depth discussion of freelance journalism labor issues, see Cohen, *Writers' Rights*; Christin, *Metrics at Work*, chap. 4.

51. Alexis Sobel Fitts, "Can Tony Haile Save Journalism by Changing the Metric?" *Columbia Journalism Review*, March 11, 2015, https://www.cjr.org/innovations/tony_haile_chartbeat .php.

52. Chartbeat, "About Chartbeat," n.d., https://chartbeat.com/company/.

53. Chartbeat, "Chartbeat Announces New Funding to Fuel Growth," press release, July 25, 2018, https://www.businesswire.com/news/home/20180725005039/en/Chartbeat-Announces -New-Funding-Fuel-Growth.

54. Sobel Fitts, "Can Tony Haile Save Journalism by Changing the Metric?"

55. The company continued to undergo rapid expansion after I left the field, at one point growing to almost 90 employees and leasing a satellite office space. It has since contracted again, with approximately 60 employees at the time of this writing.

56. During the time of my fieldwork, there had never been a woman on the engineering staff. Women tended to occupy more client- and public-facing positions such as sales, marketing, and tech support.

57. Gay Talese, *The Kingdom and the Power: Behind the Scenes at the New York Times: The Institution That Influences the World* (New York: World Publishing Company, 1969), 6.

58. Daniel Okrent, "Paper of Record? No Way, No Reason, No Thanks," *New York Times*, April 25, 2004, https://www.nytimes.com/2004/04/25/weekinreview/the-public-editor- paper-of-record-no-way-no-reason-no-thanks.html.

59. Ibid.

60. Boczkowski, *Digitizing the News*, 79.

61. Usher, *Making News at the New York Times*, 5.

62. Josh Braun, David Hand, Kate Novack, Alan Oxman, and Adam Schlesinger (producers), Andrew Rossi (director), *Page One: Inside the New York Times* (2011).

63. Joshua Benton, "It Continues to Be Very Good to Be *The New York Times*," *Nieman Lab*, August 5, 2020, https://www.niemanlab.org/2020/08/it-continues-to-be-very-good-to-be-the -new-york-times/.

64. Ibid.

65. Usher, *Making News at the New York Times*.

66. New York Times Company, "The New York Times Company Enters the 21st Century with a New Technologically Advanced and Environmentally Sensitive Headquarters," press release, November 19, 2007, http://www.newyorktimesbuilding.com/docs/2007-Opening.pdf.

67. Ben Smith, "Why the Success of *The New York Times* May Be Bad News for Journalism," *New York Times*, March 1, 2020, https://www.nytimes.com/2020/03/01/business/media/ben-smith-journalism-news-publishers-local.html.

68. Philip B. Corbett, "News Clichés from All Over," *New York Times*, March 22, 2016, http:// afterdeadline.blogs.nytimes.com/?module=BlogMain&action=Click&region=Header&pgtype =Blogs&version=Blog%20Author&contentCollection=After%20Deadline.

69. For an argument about the irreducible exceptionalism of the *Times*, see C. W. Anderson, Emily Bell, and Clay Shirky, *Post-Industrial Journalism: Adapting to the Present*, Tow Center for Digital Journalism, 2014, https://academiccommons.columbia.edu/doi/10.7916/D8N01JS7, 16–17.

70. Leslie Horn, "Here's Every Product We Have in the Home of the Future," *Gizmodo*, May 19, 2014, https://gizmodo.com/heres-every-product-we-have-in-the-home-of-the-future -1573480551.

Chapter 2: The Traffic Game

1. Burawoy, *Manufacturing Consent*.

2. See, e.g., a meta-analysis by Tayana Panova and Xavier Carbonell, "Is Smartphone Addiction Really an Addiction?" *Journal of Behavioral Addictions* 7(2) (2018): 252–59.

3. Erin Griffith, "Stats-Addicted Editors Suffer from Chartbeat Withdrawal," *Adweek*, April 29, 2011, https://www.adweek.com/digital/stats-addicted-editors-suffer-chartbeat -withdrawal-131175/.

4. Craig Calderone, "Measure, Change, Measure, Repeat: Understanding Distributed Content," *Chartbeat blog*, July 21, 2016, http://blog.chartbeat.com/2016/07/21/measure-change -measure-repeat-understanding-distributed-content/.

5. Because tools that track uniques do so by installing cookies on users' internet browsers, they are an imperfect proxy for distinct individuals, which is why uniques are most accurately understood as "inferred users," rather than simply as "users" or "individuals." This method of tracking can lead measurements to be over- or underestimated: a single individual who visits a site on two different browsers in thirty days will count as two monthly uniques—someone who does so on both their laptop and their mobile phone will count as four. Meanwhile, two individuals who visit a site from the same browser and device will only count as one. Despite these flaws, however, uniques are generally considered preferable to pageviews as the key audience metric for online advertisers.

6. Bonuses were capped at 20 percent of the site's monthly budget, though some sites routinely surpassed their growth target by far more than 20 percent.

7. As noted earlier, the phenomenon of workplace games is not a new one: generations of organizational ethnographers and labor process scholars have found that workers employed in

repetitive jobs play games and pull pranks on each other to stave off boredom. (See, e.g., Donald Roy, "'Banana Time': Job Satisfaction and Informal Interaction," *Human Organization* 18[4] [1959]: 158–68; Burawoy, *Manufacturing Consent*; and Knights and Wilmott, *Labor Process Theory*.) Yet recent years have seen a rapid proliferation of workplace games initiated and instituted not by workers but by *management*, in a strategic attempt to increase productivity. A growing list of business books and technology start-ups promote "workplace gamification," usually in the form of software that tracks and displays measures of job performance and provides recognition (in the form of points, badges, company swag, or, more rarely, monetary rewards) to top performers. See Caitlin Petre, "Gamifying the Workplace," *Public Books*, September 1, 2016, https://www.publicbooks.org/gamifying-the-workplace/.

8. The concurrents count was used as a proxy for individual readers but it really measured the number of open browsing sessions to a site: that is, someone viewing a site from two browsers or two devices simultaneously would count as two concurrents, not one. See appendix B for more detail.

9. Angèle Christin made a similar observation about Chartbeat. Noting that she sometimes found herself transfixed by the real-time dashboard, she writes: "Articles with low numbers of readers seem to hide ashamedly at the bottom of the page, whereas popular articles move up, and up again, until they reach the top of the charts. The upward movement of successful articles fills the observer with a sense of joy and excitement: the outside world likes the piece! Online readers are clicking!" (Christin, *Metrics at Work*, 16).

10. For more on the quality of endlessness in addictive games, see Natasha Dow Schüll, *Addiction by Design: Machine Gambling in Las Vegas* (Princeton: Princeton University Press, 2012). Electronic gambling machines are designed to maximize what is known in that industry as "time-on-device." Indeed, Dow Schüll interviewed gamblers who did not care about winning money; they simply wanted to play for as long as possible.

11. See Mihaly Csikszentmihalyi and Stith Bennett, "An Exploratory Model of Play," *American Anthropologist* 73 (1971): 45–58.

12. See Schüll, *Addiction by Design*.

13. In a content analysis of a U.S. news site (pseudonymized as the *Notebook*), Christin found quantitative evidence to corroborate that this kind of work speed-up is occurring: between 2009 and 2013, average monthly article output more than doubled, and article count per author also increased (Christin, *Metrics at Work*, 69).

14. Christin found a similar strategy in place at the *Notebook*, the U.S. news site she studied. Writers distinguished between "fast Notebook," which consisted of short, reactive, aggregated posts, and "slow Notebook," long-form and carefully researched articles (Christin, *Metrics at Work*, 103–8).

15. Keith Burgun, *Game Design Theory: A New Philosophy for Understanding Games* (Boca Raton, FL: CRC Press, 2013), 48–49. Though he did not make an explicit reference to grinding, journalist Dean Starkman lamented the "hamster wheel" of digital news production for similar reasons: "The Hamster Wheel isn't speed; it's motion for motion's sake. The Hamster Wheel is volume without thought. It is news panic, a lack of discipline, an inability to say no. It is copy produced to meet arbitrary productivity metrics." Dean Starkman, "The Hamster Wheel: Why Running as Fast as We Can Is Getting Us Nowhere," *Columbia Journalism Review*, September/October 2010, https://archives.cjr.org/cover_story/the_hamster_wheel.php.

16. Brice Morrison, "A Necessary Evil: Grinding in Games," *Gamasutra*, February 11, 2011, https://www.gamasutra.com/blogs/BriceMorrison/20110211/88931/A_Necessary_Evil_Grinding _in_Games.php.

17. Ibid.

18. Hesmondhalgh and Baker, *Creative Labour*, 10–11. See also Bernard Miège, *The Capitalization of Cultural Production* (New York: International General, 1989).

19. Alexis C. Madrigal, "Prepare for the New Paywall Era," *The Atlantic*, November 30, 2017, https://www.theatlantic.com/technology/archive/2017/11/the-big-unanswered-questions -about-paywalls/547091/.

20. *Slate*, which implemented a metered paywall in 2020, is a notable exception to the general trend.

21. Christin, *Metrics at Work*, 58.

22. Franklin Foer, "When Silicon Valley Took Over Journalism," *The Atlantic*, September 2017, https://www.theatlantic.com/magazine/archive/2017/09/when-silicon-valley-took -over-journalism/534195/.

23. Ananny, *Networked Press Freedom*.

24. See Cohen, "From Pink Slips to Pink Slime"; Raul Ferrer-Conill, "Quantifying Journalism? A Study on the Use of Data and Gamification to Motivate Journalists," *Television & New Media* 18(8) (2017): 706–20.

25. Foer, "When Silicon Valley Took Over Journalism."

26. Other scholars who have studied journalists' habits with metrics have noted similar findings (see, e.g., Hanusch, "Web Analytics and the Functional Differentiation of Journalism Cultures," 1577).

27. For an extended analysis of how digital technologies facilitate the collapse of boundaries between work and other aspects of knowledge workers' lives, see Melissa Gregg, *Work's Intimacy* (Cambridge: Polity, 2011).

28. Andrea's and Kevin's tendency to blame themselves for how often they checked Chartbeat echoes other scholars' findings: in her study of labor in contemporary newsrooms, Nicole S. Cohen notes that almost all of her interviewees reported working outside of paid work hours; tellingly, they framed doing so as a "personal choice, reflecting the deep individualization and precarization of contemporary work" (Cohen, "At Work in the Digital Newsroom," 582). Similarly, Hesmondhalgh and Baker argue that creative workers' expectation of "autonomy and self-realization" in their work is in some sense ideological, since it obscures the power relationships in creative fields and contributes to workers' "self-exploitation and self-blaming" (Hesmondhalgh and Baker, *Creative Labour*, 75; see also Bunce, "Management and Resistance in the Digital Newsroom"). What has gone unremarked upon in these other studies, however, is the role of performance analytics tools like Chartbeat in facilitating both workers' relentless self-monitoring (in the form of constantly checking their metrics) and their tendency to blame themselves for this practice, as opposed to attributing it to managerial pressure and other structural factors.

29. Other studies on metrics in newsrooms have similarly found that editors are more focused on the data than are writers/reporters (see, e.g., Hanusch, "Web Analytics and the Functional Differentiation of Journalism Cultures"). This aligns with pre-digital studies showing that higher-ranking editors were generally more aware of commercial imperatives than are the

reporters they supervise. See, e.g., Randal A. Beam, "What It Means to Be a Market-Oriented Newspaper," *Newspaper Research Journal* 19(3) (1998): 2–20.

30. Chartbeat's user experience design also encourages what Edward Comor and James Compton call a "fetishization of digital technologies" in journalistic discourse. Because the journalist's daily experience of consulting Chartbeat is usually severed from an explicit managerial directive, the dashboard and metrics more generally come to be seen as "inherently powerful forces" acting upon journalism, as opposed to reflections of the broader political-economic context within which journalism is embedded. Comor and Compton, "Journalistic Labour and Technological Fetishism."

31. See Andrew Friedman, "Managerial Strategies, Activities, Techniques and Technology: Towards a Complex Theory of the Labour Process," in *Labor Process Theory*, ed. David Knights and Hugh Wilmott (Houndmills: Macmillan, 1990).

32. Gans, *Deciding What's News*, 177.

33. Espeland and Sauder, "Rankings and Reactivity."

34. For an extensive discussion of the sociology of commensuration, see Wendy Nelson Espeland and Mitchell L. Stevens, "Commensuration as a Social Process," *Annual Review of Sociology* 24 (1998): 313–43.

35. Many scholars of media work have remarked upon the difficulty of managing knowledge workers (sometimes referred to as creative or cultural workers) because of their specialized skills and their expectation of autonomy. For example, following Erik Olin Wright, Hesmondhalgh and Baker write that creative workers' "control over knowledge and skills makes it difficult to manage or control skilled employees," meaning that owners must often pay "a kind of skill rent" (*Creative Labour*, 68).

Chapter 3: Enchanted Metrics

1. This echoes other scholars' findings about the impact of metrics on journalists' emotions. For instance, in her study of Al Jazeera English, where metrics were present in the newsroom but not tied to any short-term economic pressure, Nikki Usher notes that journalists relied on Chartbeat for "personal validation" rather than to make editorial decisions ("Al Jazeera English Online," 346). Though see Christin, *Metrics at Work*, for a different perspective: at the U.S. news site Christin studied, journalists mainly viewed metrics as a technical phenomenon and did not become emotional about them (see, e.g., p. 11); by contrast, in the French newsroom Christin studied, journalists did become fixated on and emotional about metrics. Christin attributes this distinction partly to the fact that the French site had a flatter hierarchy than its U.S. counterpart, weaker specialization among editorial staff, and blurry internal boundaries—in these respects, it was similar to Gawker.

2. For in-depth discussions of how enterprise discourse individualizes blame and risk in knowledge-work fields, see Banks, *The Politics of Cultural Work*; Deuze, *Media Work*; Angela McRobbie, "Clubs to Companies: Notes on the Decline of Political Culture in Speeded Up Creative Worlds," *Cultural Studies* 16(4) (2002): 516–31; and Neff, *Venture Labor*. As Banks, drawing on McRobbie, writes, "In the enterprise-led economy the entrepreneur/worker has 'only themselves to blame' for the shortcomings of their business or occupational disaffection— it is the individual who is not creative, pushy, or talented enough, rather than an economic

system that can only ever provide a limited number of winners (and substantially more losers)" (*The Politics of Cultural Work*, 61–62).

3. Weber, "Science as a Vocation."

4. Distrust of market research has a long and amply documented history in media work. See, e.g., Gans, *Deciding What's News*, 231–34. Hesmondhalgh and Baker attributed the "deep distrust of marketing data" they observed among workers in the magazine, TV, and music industries to "a desire on the part of workers to protect their own creative autonomy" (*Creative Labour*, 202).

5. Carr, "Risks Abound as Reporters Play in Traffic."

6. Mary Clare Fischer, "The Pay-Per-Visit Debate: Is Chasing Viral Traffic Hurting Journalism?" *American Journalism Review*, March 27, 2014, http://ajr.org/2014/03/27/pay-per-visit -debate-chasing-viral-traffic-hurting-journalism/.

7. John Del Signore, "Jerry Seinfeld Is the Devil Who Hates Minorities, Women," *Gothamist*, February 4, 2014, https://gothamist.com/arts-entertainment/jerry-seinfeld-is-the-devil-who -hates-minorities-women.

8. Sobel Fitts, "Can Tony Haile Save Journalism by Changing the Metric?"

9. For discussions of journalists' growing acceptance of newsroom analytics over time, see Angèle Christin and Caitlin Petre, "Making Peace with Metrics: Relational Work in Online News Production," *Sociologica* 14(2) (2020): 133–56; Hanusch, "Web Analytics and Functional Differentiation of Journalism Cultures"; Blanchett Neheli, "News by Numbers"; and Zamith, "Quantified Audiences in News Production."

10. For example, print news audience research relied heavily on surveys in which researchers asked readers about their news consumption behaviors and information preferences. Such surveys were highly prone to what psychologists call social desirability bias: wanting to come across as worldly and well-informed to the researcher (and to themselves), respondents were likely to overestimate the amount of time they spent consuming news, as well as their interest in news about topics they believed to be important and serious, such as politics, economics, and international affairs. Analytics tools, by contrast, provide greater insight into what economists call "revealed preferences." Unlike the "expressed preferences" that are gleaned from surveys, revealed preferences can be inferred by observing behavior. For this reason, they have taken on a reputation for being more accurate representations of people's real desires. As *Atlantic* magazine writer Derek Thompson put it, analytics expose "the ugly truth" about news consumers: "Audiences are liars, and the media organizations who listen to them without measuring them are dupes." Derek Thompson, "Why Audiences Hate Hard News—And Love Pretending Otherwise," *The Atlantic*, June 17, 2014, http://www.theatlantic.com/business/archive/2014/06/news -kim-kardashian-kanye-west-benghazi/372906/.

Of course, it's likely that audiences have always spent less time consuming news than journalists might have hoped and that many have always favored lighter, lifestyle-oriented content over so-called "hard" news about political and social affairs. In his 1955 study of social control in the newsroom, Warren Breed offered a dim view of the audience's likelihood of demanding more interpretive, hard-hitting news: "Seen as a client of the press, the reader should be entitled to not only an interesting paper, but one which furnishes significant news objectively presented. . . . Readership studies show that readers prefer 'interesting' news and 'features' over penetrating analyses. It can be concluded that the citizen has not been sufficiently motivated by society (and its press) to demand and apply the information he needs, and to discriminate between worthwhile and spurious information, for the fulfillment of the citizen's role" (Warren Breed, "Social Control in the Newsroom: A Functional Analysis," *Social Forces* 33[4] [1955]: 326–35, 334–35). Still, analytics make the gap between journalists' editorial agendas and audience's preferences visible in new ways. See Boczkowski and Mitchelstein, *The News Gap*; Christin, *Metrics at Work*, 25; and Nadler, *Making the News Popular*. Christin and Nadler argue that when analytics tools started to be taken up by news organizations in the 1980s, journalists had a rather poor view of the audience's preferences, deeming them to be more interested in entertainment than "hard news."

11. See, e.g., Mayer-Schönberger and Cukier, *Big Data*.

12. The client testimonials on Chartbeat's site also employed language that emphasized the dashboard's usefulness for instrumental decision making. For example, a testimonial from a Gawker Media executive read, "By providing key information in real time, we have a more precise understanding of the traffic we must support."

13. Farhad Manjoo, "You Won't Finish This Article," *Slate*, June 6, 2013, http://www.slate.com /articles/technology/technology/2013/06/how_people_read_online_why_you_won_t _finish_this_article.2.html.

14. Gregg, *Work's Intimacy*, 175.

15. George Ritzer, *Enchanting a Disenchanted World: Continuity and Change in the Cathedrals of Consumption* (Los Angeles: Pine Forge Press, 2010), 71.

16. Schüll, *Addiction by Design*, 97.

17. Christin also found that journalists used spiritually inflected language to characterize Chartbeat, though often with a negative valence: for instance, one journalist she interviewed "described Chartbeat as 'hell,' a term that has a double meaning—one with a spiritual component, as the nether realm in which people suffer everlasting punishment, the other more secular, describing a state of misery and torment" (*Metrics at Work*, 91).

18. The numbers appearing here are pseudonumerals, not the client's actual metrics. Part of my access agreement with Chartbeat was that I would not disclose clients' names or data. The numbers I use here, however, are proportionally similar to the actual ones.

19. Arthur A. Leff, "Law and," *Yale Law Journal* 87(5) (1978): 989–1011, 1002.

20. Stuart Hall, "The Determination of News Photographs," in *The Manufacture of News: A Reader*, ed. Stanley Cohen and Jock Young (Beverly Hills, CA: Sage, 1973), 181. See also Michael Schudson, "The Sociology of News Production," *Media, Culture and Society* 11(3) (1989): 263–82.

21. Ida Schultz, "The Journalistic Gut Feeling: Journalistic Doxa, News Habitus and Orthodox News Values," *Journalism Practice* 1(2) (2007): 198.

22. Gaye Tuchman, "Objectivity as Strategic Ritual: An Examination of Newsmen's Notions of Objectivity," *American Journal of Sociology* 77(4) (1972): 672.

23. Abbott, *The System of Professions*. See also Schudson and Anderson, "Objectivity, Professionalism, and Truth-Seeking in Journalism"; Carlson, *Journalistic Authority*.

24. Matt Carlson, "Blogs and Journalistic Authority: The Role of Blogs in US Election Day 2004 Coverage," *Journalism Studies* 8(2) (2007): 264–79.

25. In addition to metrics, programs like Narrative Science that use algorithms to produce news stories have also been a subject of trepidation. See Matt Carlson, "The Robotic Reporter: Automated Journalism and the Redefinition of Labor, Compositional Forms, and Journalistic Authority," *Digital Journalism* 3(3) (2015): 416–31.

26. This manifestation of the performance of deference is similar to what Herbert Gans found in his ethnography, conducted in the 1970s, in magazine and TV newsrooms. Journalists were "suspicious of audience research" for several reasons—but chief among them was the fear that audience research represented a threat to their "news judgment and professional autonomy." At NBC, one group of audience researchers was able to overcome these suspicions and win journalists' trust by employing a strategy similar to what I observed more than thirty years later at Chartbeat: "the researchers restricted themselves to research and did not make recommendations; in addition, they eschewed studies intended to cast doubt on journalists' news judgments" (*Deciding What's News*, 234). This continuity between Gans's finding and mine supports Nadler's argument that digital newsroom analytics do not represent a rupture with the past but rather a continuation and intensification of audience-measurement trends and market pressures that began in the analog era (Nadler, *Making the News Popular*).

27. Guardian, "Making Social Data Profitable," *Changing Media Summit*, 2013, https://www.theguardian.com/media-network/video/2013/apr/04/social-data-profitable-video.

28. See, for example, Allie Kosterich and Philip M. Napoli, "Reconfiguring the Audience Commodity: The Institutionalization of Social TV Analytics as Market Information Regime," *Television & New Media* 17(3) (2016): 254–71.

29. Daniel C. Hallin and Paolo Mancini, *Comparing Media Systems: Three Models of Media and Politics* (Cambridge: Cambridge University Press, 2004).

30. For example, in 2014, the *Times*'s David Carr warned about the "hazards" of using analytics to inform the news reporting process—namely that analytics incentivized journalists to pursue "any number of gambits to induce clicks, from LOL cats to slide shows to bait-and-switch headlines" instead of "serious work" ("Risks Abound as Reporters Play in Traffic"). David Simon, creator of the HBO television series *The Wire* and former *Baltimore Sun* reporter, famously took a similar line, criticizing what he viewed as the click-driven culture of digital publications: "The day I run into a *Huffington Post* reporter at a Baltimore zoning board hearing is the day I will no longer be worried about journalism." See John Nichols, "David Simon, Arianna Huffington and the Future of Journalism," *The Nation*, May 11, 2009, https://www.thenation.com/article/david-simon-arianna-huffington-and-future-journalism/.

31. For further discussion of the ambiguity of the term "reader engagement"—and the gap between its conceptual and operational definitions in newsrooms—see Raul Ferrer-Conill and Edson C. Tandoc, "The Audience-Oriented Editor: Making Sense of the Audience in the Newsroom," *Digital Journalism* 6(4) (2018): 436–53; and Jacob L. Nelson, "The Elusive Engagement Metric," *Digital Journalism* 6(4) (2018): 528–44.

32. In a sense, Pete's comments echo a line of argument that emerged in 1980s newsrooms, when a subset of journalists who resisted the turn to market-driven journalism contended that "quality" journalism, rather than marketing research, would best boost the bottom line (see Nadler, *Making the News Popular*, 74–75).

33. Terri Walter, "The Results Are In: 2016's Most Engaging Stories," *Chartbeat blog*, 2017, http://blog.chartbeat.com/2017/01/24/the-results-are-in-2016s-most-engaging-stories/. See also Boczkowski and Mitchelstein, *The News Gap*.

34. Boczkowski and Mitchelstein, *The News Gap*.

35. Christin and Petre, "Making Peace with Metrics."

36. Sobel Fitts, "Can Tony Haile Save Journalism by Changing the Metric?" As was the case with Chartbeat's decision not to make recommendations, there is a historical analogue to Haile's argument here. In the 1980s, proponents of the "market-driven approach" to newspaper production justified it partly on the basis of "survival": "By this logic, anyone who accepted that newspapers were valuable to society, even someone leery about marketing, should embrace the marketing approach because it offered the only hope for saving newspapers from a catastrophic decline in readers" (Nadler, *Making the News Popular*, 64). Of course, this way of thinking assumes that greater commercialization is the only means to produce high-quality journalism (as opposed to, say, lobbying for more public funding of media).

37. Ken Doctor, "Newsonomics: The Halving of America's Daily Newsrooms," *Nieman Lab*, July 28, 2015, https://www.niemanlab.org/2015/07/newsonomics-the-halving-of-americas-daily -newsrooms/.

38. Gans, *Deciding What's News*, 232.

39. Boczkowski, *Digitizing the News*. See also Ananny, *Networked Press Freedom*.

Chapter 4: The Interpretive Ambiguity of Metrics

1. Michael Lewis, *Moneyball: The Art of Winning an Unfair Game* (New York: W. W. Norton, 2004), 90–91.

2. See, e.g., Andrew McAfee and Erik Brynjolfsson, *Machine, Platform, Crowd: Harnessing Our Digital Future* (New York: W. W. Norton, 2017); Ayres, *Super Crunchers*; and Mayer-Schönberger and Cukier, *Big Data*. For a critical take on this discourse, see Pasquale, "Professional Judgment in an Era of Artificial Intelligence and Machine Learning."

3. For more on the influence of the "big data phenomenon" on the journalism field, see Seth C. Lewis and Oscar Westlund, "Big Data and Journalism: Epistemology, Expertise, Economics, and Ethics," *Digital Journalism* 3(3) (2014): 447–66.

4. As an erstwhile *Guardian* data analyst put it, newsrooms are "doing this big data thing because we have seen it work to great effect in other industries." Stijn Debrouwere, "Cargo Cult Analytics," *Debrouwere*, August 27, 2013, http://debrouwere.org/2013/08/26/cargo-cult -analytics/.

5. For a discussion of the art-commerce relation, see Banks, *The Politics of Cultural Work*, 6.

6. Ibid., 8. For more on how journalists struggle to navigate their profession's multiple mandates, see Jacob L. Nelson and Edson C. Tandoc, "Doing 'Well' or Doing 'Good': What Audience Analytics Reveal about Journalism's Competing Goals," *Journalism Studies* 20(13) (2019): 1960–76. Based on two periods of fieldwork conducted in the same newspaper newsroom in 2013 and 2016, Nelson and Tandoc argue that journalists became more aware of the tension between doing "well" commercially and doing "good" for the public possibly because of the growing presence of analytics. They also found persistent "internal uncertainty within the newsroom about whether or not reaching a large audience and publishing public service journalism are incompatible goals" (1968). See also Nadler, *Making the News Popular*; Bunce, "Management and Resistance in the Digital Newsroom." Bunce argues that while conflicts between journalists' professional values and market pressures have long been present, they became more salient starting in the 1980s, when "the values and motivations of journalists increasingly clashed with media executives fresh from business school" (892).

7. Christin, *Metrics at Work*, 100.

8. See, e.g., Bright and Nicholls, "The Life and Death of Political News"; Lee, Lewis, and Powers, "Audience Clicks and News Placement"; Zamith, "On Metrics-Driven Homepages"; and Welbers et al., "News Selection Criteria in the Digital Age."

9. As noted above, a version of this conflict exists not only in journalism but in cultural work more broadly. See Cohen, "Cultural Work as a Site of Struggle"; Banks, *The Politics of Cultural Work*; and Ryan, *Making Capital from Culture*.

10. See, e.g., Herman and Chomsky, *Manufacturing Consent*; Baker, *Advertising and a Democratic Press*.

11. These alternative revenue generation strategies include native advertising (sometimes called branded content), in which in-house teams at media companies create advertising campaigns for clients that mimic the tone and aesthetic of the editorial publication; branded conferences such as the New Yorker Festival and the Atlantic Festival; and affiliate links, in which news sites that link to a product collect a referral fee when a reader purchases it. For an in-depth discussion of the issues raised by these tactics, see Matt Carlson, "When News Sites Go Native: Redefining the Advertising-Editorial Divide in Response to Native Advertising," *Journalism* 16(7) (2015): 849–65.

12. For a list of current and past Pulitzer Prize categories, see the Pulitzer Prizes, "Winners by Category," n.d., https://www.pulitzer.org/prize-winners-categories.

13. Espeland and Sauder, "Rankings and Reactivity," 17. Emphasis added.

14. Ibid., 17.

15. Robinson made these remarks at a 2014 panel that I moderated at the Columbia Journalism School called "Beyond Clickbait: How Are News Organizations Actually Using Analytics, and What Does It Mean for Content?" See https://www.youtube.com/watch?v=3EqiEmSny-8.

16. Wanda J. Orlikowski and Debra C. Gash, "Technological Frames: Making Sense of Information Technology in Organizations," *ACM Transactions on Information Systems* 12(2) (1994): 175.

17. Erika Shehan Poole, Christopher A. Le Dantec, James R. Eagan, and W. Keith Edwards, "Reflecting on the Invisible: Understanding End-User Perceptions of Ubiquitous Computing," in *UbiComp '08: Proceedings of the 10th International Conference on Ubiquitous Computing* (New York: Association for Computing Machinery, 2008), 192–201.

18. Dedre Gentner and Donald R. Gentner, "Flowing Waters or Teeming Crowds: Mental Models of Electricity," in *Mental Models*, ed. Dedre Gentner and Albert L. Stevens (Hillsdale, NJ: Lawrence Erlbaum Associates, 1983), 99–129.

19. Willett Kempton, "Two Theories of Home Heat Control," *Cognitive Science* 10(1) (1986): 75–90.

20. Tarleton Gillespie, "The Politics of 'Platforms,'" *New Media & Society* 12(3) (2010): 347–64.

21. For more on this subject, see Philip Napoli and Robyn Caplan, "Why Media Companies Insist They're Not Media Companies, Why They're Wrong, and Why It Matters," *First Monday* 22(5) (2017); and Emily Bell, "Technology Company? Publisher? The Lines Can No Longer Be Blurred," *The Guardian*, April 2, 2017, https://www.theguardian.com/media/2017/apr/02/facebook-google-youtube-inappropriate-advertising-fake-news.

22. Poole et al., "Reflecting on the Invisible."

23. Gentner and Gentner, "Flowing Waters or Teeming Crowds," 107.

24. Andrew Beaujon, "Reporters at the *Washington Post* Will Soon Be Able to Check Their Articles' Traffic," *Washingtonian*, June 4, 2015, http://www.washingtonian.com/blogs/capitalcomment/media/reporters-at-the-washington-post-will-be-able-to-check-their-articles-traffic.

25. See also Usher, "Al Jazeera English Online."

26. Chris Anderson, "The End of Theory: The Data Deluge Makes the Scientific Method Obsolete," *WIRED*, June 23, 2008, https://www.wired.com/2008/06/pb-theory/.

27. See, for example, Mayer-Schönberger and Cukier, *Big Data*.

28. Pasquale, "Professional Judgment in an Era of Artificial Intelligence and Machine Learning," 75.

29. Safiya Umoja Noble, *Algorithms of Oppression: How Search Engines Reinforce Racism* (New York: New York University Press, 2018).

30. Eric A. Meyer, "My Year Was Tragic: Facebook Ambushed Me with a Painful Reminder," *Slate*, December 29, 2014, https://slate.com/technology/2014/12/facebook-year-in-review-my-tragic-year-was-the-wrong-fodder-for-facebook-s-latest-app.html.

31. Christin, *Metrics at Work*, 79.

32. Because algorithms are both opaque and ubiquitous in contemporary social life, they have proved to be fertile ground for the formation of folk theories. An interview-based study examining users' understandings of the Facebook News Feed algorithm found that participants held a range of different (and sometimes contradictory) folk theories about what determined the contents of the News Feed: some believed their feed prioritized certain friends; others thought the algorithm boosted particular types of posts.

Folk theories affect not only how we form understandings and expectations about a particular technology but also how we interact with it. "Sometimes when I see someone on my News Feed who I don't often see, I might go and click in [their timeline] so I can see their stuff more often," explained one user. Another user, who also subscribed to the theory that the News Feed was based on users' level of personal engagement with their friends' posts, reported sometimes hiding posts after "liking" them, in an attempt to prevent a particular person's posts from showing up in their feed all the time (Motahhare Eslami, Karrie Karahalios, Christian Sandvig, Kristen Vaccaro, Aimee Rickman, Kevin Hamilton, and Alex Kerlik, "First I 'Like' It, Then I Hide It: Folk Theories of Social Feeds," *Proceedings of the 2016 CHI Conference on Human Factors in Computing Systems* [2016]: 2371–2882). Users also tailored their own posts to align more closely with the formats they believed the algorithm prioritized—by, for instance, writing text posts instead of posts with videos or images (Motahhare Eslami, Aimee Rickman, Kristen Vaccaro, Amirhossein Aleyasen, Andy Vuong, Karrie Karahalios, Kevin Hamilton, and Christian Sandvig, "I Always Assumed That I Wasn't Really That Close to [Her]: Reasoning about Invisible Algorithms in News Feeds," *Proceedings of the 33rd Annual ACM Conference on Human Factors in Computing Systems* [2015]: 153–62). For more on folk theories more generally, see, e.g., Kempton, "Two Theories of Home Heat Control"; Susan A. Gelman and Cristine H. Legare, "Concepts and Folk Theories," *Annual Review of Anthropology* 40(1) (2011): 379–98. For more on folk theories and algorithms, see Michael A. DeVito, Darren Gergle, and Jeremy Birnholtz, "'Algorithms Ruin Everything': #RIPTwitter, Folk Theories, and Resistance to Algorithmic Change in Social Media," *Proceedings of the 2017 CHI Conference on Human Factors in Computing Systems* (2017): 3163–74.

33. Existing literature on newsroom metrics often pits analytics against journalists' "editorial judgment" or "gut feeling" as though the latter is something endogenous to the journalist while

the former is fully external (see, e.g., Bunce, "Management and Resistance in the Digital News-room"; Schultz, "The Journalistic Gut Feeling"). But what Felix's comment makes clear is that an intuitive sense of what will "play" in terms of traffic is increasingly a component of the journalistic "gut feeling." However, a key difference between gut feelings about a story's potential traffic performance and gut feelings about a story's "newsworthiness" is that the former can be—and often are—empirically proven wrong by metrics after the fact. Seeing their traffic predictions repeatedly turn out to be wrong was a humbling and perplexing experience for many journalists in my study and contributed to their sense of traffic as mysterious and ungovernable.

34. Taina Bucher, "The Algorithmic Imaginary: Exploring the Ordinary Affects of Facebook Algorithms," *Information, Communication & Society* 20(1) (2016): 30–44. For more on how journalists formulate different understandings of metrics and algorithms depending on context, see Christin, *Metrics at Work*; Christin, "Counting Clicks."

35. Constance L. Hays, "What Wal-Mart Knows about Customers' Habits," *New York Times*, November 14, 2004, https://www.nytimes.com/2004/11/14/business/yourmoney/what-walmart-knows-about-customers-habits.html.

36. Mayer-Schönberger and Cukier, *Big Data*, 2.

37. Gans, *Deciding What's News*, 232.

38. As has been discussed in previous chapters, Gawker writers were eligible to receive bonuses based on group traffic targets, and those who persistently failed to meet "eCPM" benchmarks were in danger of being fired. While the *Times* did not make compensation or personnel decisions directly based on metrics (or at least, not openly), the organization has cut online features based on what was considered underwhelming traffic, such as the closing of the environment-focused "Green" blog in 2013. For a more extensive discussion of the closing of blogs at the *Times*, see chapter 5.

39. For recent studies in this area, see Robert Prey, Marc Esteve Del Valle, and Leslie Zwerwer, "Platform Pop: Disentangling Spotify's Intermediary Role in the Music Industry," *Information, Communication & Society* (2020), DOI: 10.1080/1369118X.2020.1761859; Annemarie Navar-Gill, "The Golden Ratio of Algorithms to Artists? Streaming Services and the Platformization of Creativity in American Television Production," *Social Media & Society* 6(3) (2020): 1–11.

Chapter 5: Clean and Dirty Data

1. A. J. Daulerio, "Gawker Will Be Conducting an Experiment, Please Enjoy Your Free Cute Cats Singing and Sideboobs," *Gawker*, January 23, 2012, https://gawker.com/5878065/gawker-will-be-conducting-an-experiment-please-enjoy-your-free-cute-cats-singing-and-sideboobs.

2. Andrew Phelps, "I Can't Stop Reading This Analysis of Gawker's Editorial Strategy," *Nieman Lab*, March 21, 2012, https://www.niemanlab.org/2012/03/i-cant-stop-reading-this-analysis-of-gawkers-editorial-strategy/.

3. Mary Douglas, *Purity and Danger* (New York: Routledge Classics, 2002 [1966]), 44–45. For a critical engagement with Douglas and a discussion of her work's contemporary relevance, see Caitlin Zaloom, "Mary Douglas: *Purity and Danger*," *Public Culture* 32(2) (2020): 415–22.

4. This finding is not limited to *Gawker*: scholars have found strikingly similar language used in other newsrooms. For instance, an editor at a French news site in Angèle Christin's study

referred to a place on the home page where they published popular articles as "the whore's spot." Christin notes that the use of this kind of metaphoric language had a gendered element: "most of the journalists developing the metaphors of trash, indecency, and prostitution were men, whereas many of the writers who covered popular but low-status beats (sex, gender, lifestyle, celebrities, and so on) were women" (Christin, *Metrics at Work*, 75).

5. See, e.g., Everett Hughes, "Good People and Dirty Work," *Social Problems* 10(1) (1962): 3–11; Blake Ashforth, Glen E. Kreiner, Mark A. Clark, and Mel Fugate, "Normalizing Dirty Work: Managerial Tactics for Countering Occupational Taint," *Academy of Management Journal* 50(1) (2007): 149–74.

6. Cf. Christin, *Metrics at Work*. At the U.S. news site she studied, Christin found similar symbolic boundaries, which expressed themselves through the organization of the office, staffing patterns, and even the design of the home page.

7. Carlson, *Journalistic Authority*.

8. In his landmark article on "boundary work," sociologist Thomas Gieryn examined scientists' efforts to rhetorically distinguish science from non-science. While others had approached the science/non-science boundary as an analytical problem—trying to identify the specific qualities of scientific practice that set it apart—Gieryn approached it as a practical and political one. His interest was not so much in pinpointing the special attributes of science; in fact, his argument left aside the question whether any such attributes existed. Rather, he was curious about the way scientists themselves *asserted* the uniqueness of scientific practice in public addresses and debates. Gieryn argued that scientists drew boundaries between science and non-science in whatever way afforded them the greatest number of practical advantages, including career opportunities, an edge in competition against rival occupational or intellectual groups (some of which they deemed "pseudoscientists"), and increased autonomy and intellectual authority. Thomas F. Gieryn, "Boundary-Work and the Demarcation of Science from Non-Science: Strains and Interests in Professional Ideologies of Scientists," *American Sociological Review* 48(6) (1983): 781–95. Other scholars have pointed out that boundary-drawing efforts need not be only rhetorical; they can also take structural forms and produce material consequences. For instance, sociologist Andrew Abbott has argued that professions inhabit a complex and interdependent system in which they are continually competing against each other for cultural and epistemic authority as well as structural advantages. See Abbott, *The System of Professions*.

9. As noted in previous chapters, rhetorical boundary-work is particularly important for establishing and maintaining journalistic authority in the U.S. context, given that the First Amendment precludes journalists from establishing a credentialing system or other structural closure mechanism of the type that professions like medicine and law have deployed.

10. For example, Matt Carlson has shown how journalists' collective condemnation of Stephen Glass, a writer who was fired from the *New Republic* magazine in 1998 for fabricating numerous articles, was an attempt to delineate between professional insiders and outsiders. Had Glass been a lawyer or doctor, he would likely have been disbarred or stripped of his medical license; lacking an equivalently official and enforceable mechanism of professional excommunication, journalists vocally condemned and shunned Glass in order to distance themselves—and the profession—from his actions. In doing so, they asserted themselves as a relatively cohesive "interpretive community" with a shared set of norms, values, and meanings. See Carlson, "Blogs and Journalistic Authority"; Carlson, *Journalistic Authority*.

11. Daniel C. Hallin, *We Keep America on Top of the World: Television Journalism and the Public Sphere* (New York: Routledge, 1994), 171.

12. While some native advertising campaigns have been celebrated in the industry as clever win-win partnerships (such as the *Onion*'s satirical article for H&R Block, "Woman Going to Take Quick Break after Filling Out Name, Address on Tax Forms"), others have damaged the reputation of the media organizations that produced them. For example, Gawker and other companies have been criticized for failing to clearly label native advertising as "sponsored" (which was interpreted as an attempt to trick readers into believing ads were actually editorial content), while the *Atlantic* faced a massive backlash after publishing a native advertisement for the Church of Scientology. See Carlson, "When News Sites Go Native."

13. Even as the rise of native advertising has stirred controversy about which styles and partners are appropriate, native advertisements are nearly always created by employees on the "business side" of news organizations. Both the *New York Times* and Gawker called their native advertising divisions "brand studios," a term meant to indicate, in part, that that these teams were entirely separate from the newsroom. Even in Gawker's small SoHo headquarters, the Gawker Brand Studio team worked on a different floor from the editorial staff.

14. Allie Van Nest, "A Closer Look at How Pageviews Have Evolved Over Time," *Mediashift*, March 9, 2016, http://mediashift.org/2016/03/a-closer-look-at-how-pageviews-have-evolved -over-time/. See also Napoli, *Audience Evolution*.

15. Joshua Benton (@jbenton), "Clickbait, noun: Things I don't like on the Internet," Twitter, November 6, 2014, 7:04 p.m. https://twitter.com/jbenton/status/530511085049495553.

16. Lexico, "Clickbait," *Lexico*, n.d., https://www.lexico.com/en/definition/clickbait.

17. Rossalyn Warren, "A Boy Makes Anti-Muslim Comments in Front of an American Soldier. The Soldier's Reply: Priceless," *Upworthy*, November 9, 2013, https://www.upworthy.com/a-boy -makes-anti-muslim-comments-in-front-of-an-american-soldier-the-soldiers-reply-priceless.

18. Ben Smith, "Why BuzzFeed Doesn't Do Clickbait," *BuzzFeed*, November 6, 2014, https:// www.buzzfeed.com/bensmith/why-buzzfeed-doesnt-do-clickbait.

19. James Hamblin, "It's Everywhere, the Clickbait," *The Atlantic*, November 11, 2014, https:// www.theatlantic.com/entertainment/archive/2014/11/clickbait-what-is/382545/.

20. Julia Greenberg, "Page Views Don't Matter Anymore—But They Just Won't Die," *WIRED*, December 31, 2015, https://www.wired.com/215/12/everyone-knows-page-views-dont -matter-but-they-just-wont-die/.

21. Chartbeat, *Why Publishers Are Killing Pageviews to Capitalize on Reader Attention*, n.d., https://next.prdaily.com/wp-content/uploads/2018/09/attention_white_paper.pdf.

22. See, e.g., Om Malik, "Data without Context Is Dirt," *GigaOm*, February 7, 2012, https:// gigaom.com/2012/02/07/data-without-context-is-dirt/; Henry Blodget, "Launching the Engage-O-Meter: See How Many People Are Reading Business Insider Right Now!" *Business Insider*, August 4, 2011, https://www.businessinsider.com.au/business-insider-reader-meter-chartbeat-2011-8.

23. Eric Ries, "Entrepreneurs: Beware of Vanity Metrics," *Harvard Business Review*, February 8, 2010, https://hbr.org/2010/02/entrepreneurs-beware-of-vanity-metrics. See also Debrouwere, "Cargo Cult Analytics."

24. Malik, "Data without Context Is Dirt."

25. Barbara Kiviat, "The Moral Limits of Predictive Practices: The Case of Credit-Based Insurance Scores," *American Sociological Review* 84(6) (2019): 1148.

26. For an extended discussion of how viral content is framed as a subsidy for the production of "serious" news, see Christin and Petre, "Making Peace with Metrics."

27. New York Times, "A Blog's Adieu," *New York Times*, March 1, 2013, https://green.blogs.nytimes.com/2013/03/01/a-blogs-adieu/.

28. Kyle Massey, "The Old Page 1 Meeting, R.I.P.: Updating a Times Tradition for the Digital Age," *New York Times*, May 12, 2015, https://www.nytimes.com/times-insider/2015/05/12/the-old-page-1-meeting-r-i-p-updating-a-times-tradition-for-the-digital-age/.

29. David Leonhardt, Jodi Rudoren, Jon Galinsky, Karron Skog, Marc Lacey, Tom Giratikanon, and Tyson Evans, "Journalism That Stands Apart: The Report of the 2020 Group," *New York Times*, January 2017, https://www.nytimes.com/projects/2020-report/index.html.

30. New York Times, "New York Times Media Kit: Newspaper," n.d., https://web.archive.org/web/20200128100547/http://nytmediakit.com/newspaper.

31. New York Times, "New York Times Media Kit: Digital," n.d., https://web.archive.org/web/20200128100549/https://nytmediakit.com/index.php?p=digital.

32. For more on the practice of "day-parting," see Hanusch, "Web Analytics and the Functional Differentiation of Journalism Cultures," 1580–81.

33. Laura Hazard Owen, "Get Rid of the Content No One Reads. Offer Surprises and 'Candy.' And Other Tricks for Retaining Subscribers," *Nieman Lab*, December 5, 2018, https://www.niemanlab.org/2018/12/get-rid-of-the-content-no-one-reads-offer-surprises-and-candy-and-other-tricks-for-retaining-subscribers/.

34. Ryan, *Making Capital from Culture*, 110–11.

35. In his interview study with Australian journalists, Hanusch found a similar dynamic, in which journalists professed a tendency to use analytics to "slightly adjust their stories" by changing a "headline, angle, or image." There was "general consensus that this was a good thing," Hanusch writes, "because it allowed journalists to hold on to traditional news values but . . . achieve better engagement or a wider audience" at the same time. Hanusch, "Web Analytics and the Functional Differentiation of Journalism Cultures," 1578.

36. Kevin G. Barnhurst and John Nerone, *The Form of News: A History* (New York: Guilford Press, 2001).

37. Joshua A. Braun, *This Program Is Brought to You By . . . : Distributing Television News Online* (New Haven, CT: Yale University Press, 2015), especially chap. 2.

38. See, e.g., Bell et al., "The Platform Press"; Tarleton Gillespie, "Facebook's Algorithm—Why Our Assumptions Are Wrong, and Our Concerns Are Right," *Culture Digitally*, July 4, 2014, https://culturedigitally.org/2014/07/facebooks-algorithm-why-our-assumptions-are-wrong-and-our-concerns-are-right/.

39. Benny Johnson, "The Story of Egypt's Revolution in 'Jurassic Park' Gifs," *BuzzFeed*, July 8, 2013, https://www.buzzfeednews.com/article/bennyjohnson/the-story-of-egypts-revolution-in-jurassic-park-gifs.

40. L. V. Anderson, "Is This the Worst Thing BuzzFeed's Ever Done?" *Slate*, July 8, 2013, https://slate.com/culture/2013/07/buzzfeed-egyptian-revolution-in-jurassic-park-gifs-oy.html.

41. Chris O'Shea, "BuzzFeed Explains Egyptian Revolution with *Jurassic Park* Gifs," *Adweek*, July 9, 2013, https://www.adweek.com/digital/buzzfeed-explains-egyptian-revolution-with-jurassic-park-gifs/.

42. Ben Cohen, "Buzz Feed Takes Journalism to New Low with Jurassic Park GIF Version of Egyptian Revolution," *Daily Banter*, July 9, 2013, https://thedailybanter.com/2013/07/buzz-feed-takes-journalism-to-new-low-with-jurassic-park-gif-version-of-egyptian-revolution/.

43. Later, the piece garnered yet more controversy when its author, Benny Johnson, was discovered to have repeatedly plagiarized text from Wikipedia.

44. Anderson, "Is This the Worst Thing BuzzFeed's Ever Done?"

45. The absence of universally accepted norms around the appropriate uses of metrics is partly the result of the data's relative novelty: over the next few decades, the field may coalesce around a set of taken-for-granted expectations and practices with regard to metrics, as it has around issues like interview ground rules, fact-checking, and plagiarism. In the meantime, however, journalists are left largely to their own devices when trying to make sense of metrics—and the way they do so has high stakes for their lived experience of work.

Chapter 6: The Struggle to Monopolize Interpretive Labor

1. Other scholars have found versions of this dynamic: Nadler explains that critics of the push toward market-driven journalism in the 1980s "argued that news managers and editors drawing lessons from market research have primarily used the research as justification to support preconceived notions about audience taste" (Nadler, *Making the News Popular*, 77). More recently, Christin encountered a similar phenomenon in her fieldwork at a U.S. news site where an editor used metrics as a "justificatory tool" for decisions he had already made (Christin, *Metrics at Work*, 7).

2. In her study of metrics at Al Jazeera English, Nikki Usher found a similar system of tiered access to metrics: while all staffers had access to Chartbeat, only editors could see Google Analytics. Using the Social Construction of Technology (SCOT) as her theoretical framework, Usher argues that editors thus established themselves as the "relevant social group" that "decided who would interpret what metrics." She notes that management made it seem like "Google Analytics [which reporters could not see] were most important, creating a hierarchical distribution of knowledge." Usher, "Al-Jazeera English Online," 346.

3. Örnebring, "Technology and Journalism-as-Labour," 63.

4. Usher, *Making News at the New York Times*.

5. This was because the most-emailed list was only able to capture instances where readers had used the *Times*'s built-in "email this story" feature. Younger readers were more likely to simply copy the story's URL from their browser window and paste it into the text of an email, and the list did not track stories that were emailed in this way.

6. This finding has been corroborated by other scholars of newsroom metrics. In interviews with analytics company employees, Valérie Bélair-Gagnon and Avery Holton found that during the initial rollout of newsroom analytics, editors only wanted the data provided to a "limited number of staff" so that they could "control the flow of analytics through the newsroom" (Bélair-Gagnon and Holton, "Boundary Work, Interloper Media, and Analytics in Newsrooms," 498). Similarly, Hanusch found that non-management staff working predominantly for a print news product were much less likely to access individual analytics (Hanusch, "Web Analytics and the Functional Differentiation of Journalism Cultures," 1577).

7. For an early analysis of this dynamic, see Shoshana Zuboff's 1988 book *In the Age of the Smart Machine*, which updated labor process theory to explore the adoption and impact of

information technologies in diverse work settings—including paper mills, a telecommunications company, and an insurance company. Zuboff defines an information technology as a tool that not only automates aspects of human labor but also "informates"—that is, "generates information about the underlying productive and administrative processes through which an organization accomplishes its work" (9). When managers and workers alike must interpret new forms of data generated by information technologies and make decisions based on these interpretations, work at all levels of the organization becomes more intellectual. As the workplace experience of workers and managers becomes increasingly similar, workers are more likely to question the legitimacy of managers' authority. Managers in Zuboff's study responded to this status threat in a manner similar to *Times* editors: that is, they took steps to control the circulation and interpretation of information provided by the new technologies. Shoshana Zuboff, *In the Age of the Smart Machine: The Future of Work and Power* (New York: Basic Books, 1988).

8. For more examples of the strategic disclosure of metrics, see Bunce, "Management and Resistance in the Digital Newsroom"; Christin and Petre, "Making Peace with Metrics."

9. For a comprehensive account of the *Times*'s laborious transition to digital formats and work rhythms, see Usher, *Making News at the New York Times.*

10. Jason Abbruzzese, "The Full New York Times Innovation Report," *Mashable*, May 16, 2014, http://mashable.com/2014/05/16/full-newyork-times-innovation-report/, p. 87. My interviews echoed this theme: Betsy recalled that when she was made a reporter in 2011, she asked to be judged "by my traffic rather than the number of stories I do or the number of stories I get on the front page. [But] in my annual review, even though I was an exclusively digital person who was supposed to be pioneering things, there was no mention made of anything other than the number of stories I had on page one." Josh, a blogger who had been recruited to report for the *Times* at a relatively young age specifically because of his digital media savvy, had a similar realization early in his tenure in the newsroom: "Even though they hired me to blog . . . I had to have a presence in the paper. So I really pivoted toward the paper, wrote mostly for the paper."

11. Looking at these examples, it becomes clear that when editors strategically disclosed particular metrics in order to motivate reporters or praise them for a job well done, they were not subordinating their editorial judgment to a commercial logic. Instead, in these moments they were temporarily transforming metrics into a signifier, not of economic capital but of journalistic prestige. When an editor congratulated a reporter for having earned especially high traffic or having made the most-emailed list, this did not make the approval of the "jury of your peers" any less important at the *Times*, because editors still controlled the circulation of metrics and unilaterally decided which numbers, at which times, were praiseworthy. Instead, editors' strategic disclosure of metrics indicated to reporters that traffic was an additional way to earn editors' approval.

12. Nick Denton, "Introducing Group Chats in Kinja," *Kinja Team blog*, 2014, https://product.kinja.com/thanks-normally-i-dont-care-if-people-hate-changes-to-1517639642.

13. Mary Clare Fischer, "Why the Verge Declines to Share Detailed Metrics with Reporters," *American Journalism Review*, March 19, 2014, http://ajr.org/2014/03/19/analytics-news-sites-grapple-can-see-data/.

14. Erik Olin Wright, *Class Counts: Comparative Studies in Class Analysis* (Cambridge: Cambridge University Press, 1997), 16, as quoted in Hesmondhalgh and Baker, *Creative Labour*, 68.

Chapter 7: The Autonomy Paradox

1. Peter Sterne, "The Gawker Boomerang," *Politico*, January 14, 2015, http://www.capitalnewyork.com/article/media/2015/01/8560066/gawker-boomerang.

2. Survey research indicates that this finding is not limited to Gawker: a 2015 survey of 343 self-selected Canadian journalists found that the majority felt pessimistic about their future in journalism. Still, when the researchers asked respondents about working conditions in their current jobs, only 6% said they had little or no autonomy. Comor and Compton, "Journalistic Labour and Technological Fetishism."

3. Lydia DePillis, "Why Internet Journalists Don't Organize," *Washington Post*, January 30, 2015, https://www.washingtonpost.com/news/storyline/wp/2015/01/30/why-internet-journalists-dont-organize/.

4. Rodney Benson and Erik Neveu, "Introduction: Field Theory as a Work in Progress," in *Bourdieu and the Journalistic Field*, ed. Rodney Benson and Erik Neveu (Cambridge: Polity, 2005), 4.

5. Rodney Benson, "Field Theory in Comparative Context: A New Paradigm for Media Studies," *Theory and Society* 28(3) (1999): 463–98.

6. For a detailed account of how journalists imagine their audiences in the print and digital eras, see Robinson, "The Audience in the Mind's Eye."

7. Ananny, *Networked Press Freedom*. See also Schudson, "Autonomy from What?"

8. Jia Tolentino, "Gawker's Essential Unevenness," *New Yorker*, August 20, 2016, https://www.newyorker.com/culture/jia-tolentino/gawkers-essential-unevenness/amp.

9. Craggs gave me permission to use his real name when quoting him.

10. Porter, *Trust in Numbers*.

11. Kevin Draper, "Presenting: The In-Progress Deadspin Style Guide," *Deadspin*, March 27, 2015, https://deadspin.com/presenting-the-in-progress-deadspin-style-guide-1691611039.

12. A. J. Daulerio, "Brian Williams Says Gawker Should Have Torched Lana Del Rey: 'One of the Worst Outings in SNL History,'" *Gawker*, January 16, 2012, https://gawker.com/5876450/brian-williams-says-gawker-should-have-torched-lana-del-rey-one-of-the-worst-outings-in-snl-history.

13. Erik Wemple, "Four Truths about Gawker–Brian Williams E-mail Thing," *Washington Post*, January 17, 2012, https://www.washingtonpost.com/blogs/erik-wemple/post/four-truths-about-gawker-brian-williams-e-mail-thing/2012/01/17/gIQAUktt5P_blog.html.

14. Unlike the private complaints, this tactic delivered rapid results: Gawker leadership implemented a number of changes to address the problem. Jessica Coen, "What Gawker Media Is Doing about Our Rape Gif Problem," *Jezebel*, August 13, 2014, https://jezebel.com/what-gawker-media-is-doing-about-our-rape-gif-problem-1620742504.

15. Dayna Evans, "On Gawker's Problem with Women," *Medium*, November 16, 2015, https://medium.com/matter/on-gawker-s-problem-with-women-f1197d8c1a4e.

16. The appeal of metrics as an alternative form of value was also present, albeit more muted, at the *Times*. In chapter 6, we saw that *Times* editors contained the spread of data in the newsroom in part to prevent reporters from marshalling metrics to challenge editors' assessments of newsworthiness and decisions about story assignment and placement.

17. Christin shows that this dynamic, in which the size of the quantified audience is an indicator of professional worth, is even more pronounced for freelance writers, for whom "digital

metrics can become proxies for reputational value and professional success in a competitive employment market" (*Metrics at Work*, 128).

18. See, e.g., Karin Wahl-Jorgensen, "The Construction of the Public in Letters to the Editor: Deliberative Democracy and the Idiom of Insanity," *Journalism* 3(2) (2002): 183–204; Gans, *Deciding What's News*.

19. Other digital journalism scholars have found similar attitudes toward commenters. See, e.g., Robinson, "The Audience in the Mind's Eye"; Jacob L. Nelson, "And Deliver Us to Segmentation: The Growing Appeal of the Niche News Audience," *Journalism Practice* 12(2) (2017): 204–19; Tandoc, "Journalism Is Twerking?"; and Anderson, "Between Creative and Quantified Audiences."

20. Anderson, "Between Creative and Quantified Audiences."

21. See also Christin, *Metrics at Work*. Christin found that staffers at the *Notebook*, an NYC-based site that competed with Gawker, also segmented the "algorithmic public" between loyal, returning readers and "strangers" who may have simply seen a headline on social media. But unlike at Gawker, *Notebook* staffers tended to value the former more than the latter.

22. Banks, *The Politics of Cultural Work*, 92.

23. See Friedman, "Managerial Strategies, Activities, Techniques and Technology"; Hesmondhalgh and Baker, *Creative Labour*; Ryan, *Making Capital from Culture*; and Banks, *The Politics of Cultural Work*.

24. Christin found that writers were more fixated on metrics in a "disciplinary" work context, which was defined by flatter organizational hierarchies and weak internal boundaries, than in a "bureaucratic" one in which power was hierarchical and roles were more clearly defined and specialized (*Metrics at Work*). For more on the dynamics of self-exploitation and self-blaming, see Banks, *The Politics of Cultural Work*.

25. E.g., see Banks, *The Politics of Cultural Work*: "Soft management adopts a non-traditional, de-Taylorized approach to workplace organization, disavowing formality, discipline and hierarchy and promoting 'mutuality' and cooperation as the keys to economic success" (12).

26. Ibid., 42.

27. See Knights and Wilmott, *Labor Process Theory*, 16.

28. Ananny, *Networked Press Freedom*, 17. Similarly, in their analysis of the working conditions of creative labor, Hesmondhalgh and Baker sought to understand how their respondents conceptualize autonomy in their work but also "interpret and triangulate their perspectives by examining the political, economic, and organizational forces shaping their experiences" (*Creative Labour*, 67).

29. Nadler, *Making the News Popular*, 37.

30. Ibid. See also Douglas Birkhead, "News Media Ethics and the Management of Professionals," *Journal of Mass Media Ethics* 1(2) (1986): 37–46; McChesney, *The Problem of the Media*; and Arthur J. Kaul, "The Proletarian Journalist: A Critique of Professionalism," *Journal of Mass Media Ethics* 1(2) (1986): 47–55.

31. Initially, I hypothesized that the backlash against the Kinja leaderboard was a result of its relative novelty compared to the Big Board, which had been a fixture in the Gawker offices for years. However, in the course of six months of fieldwork from February through July 2014, I did not observe even a marginal change in negative attitudes about the Kinja leaderboard.

32. In addition, as discussed in chapter 6, staffers (especially site leads and other editors) disliked the leaderboard's unit of analysis—individuals as opposed to sites or posts—because they felt it had a negative impact both on morale and, relatedly, on the kind of teamwork required to make the sites run smoothly.

33. Adrienne LaFrance, "Gawker Is Letting Readers Rewrite Headlines and Reframe Articles," *Nieman Lab*, July 25, 2013, https://www.niemanlab.org/2013/07/gawker-is-letting-readers-rewrite-headlines-and-reframe-articles/.

34. Kat Stoeffel, "Deadliest Klatsch: Nick Denton Gives Gawker's Drive-By Peanut Gallery a Promotion," *New York Observer*, June 27, 2012, http://observer.com/2012/06/deadliest-klatsch-nick-denton-gives-gawkers-drive-by-peanut-gallery-a-promotion.

35. Ibid.

36. E.g., in 2006, media scholar Jay Rosen published a post on his blog introducing "media people" to a group he called "the people formerly known as the audience," a group made up of "the writing readers. The viewers who picked up a camera. The formerly atomized listeners who with modest effort can connect with each other and gain the means to speak—to the world, as it were." Jay Rosen, "The People Formerly Known as the Audience," *Pressthink*, June 27, 2006, http://archive.pressthink.org/2006/06/27/ppl_frmr.html. Jeff Jarvis, another media blogger and author, made a similar argument: "The people we used to call consumers, readers, or viewers (let's call them citizens now) will take more and more control of what we used to call media (I don't know what new name to give it, but now it's as much about conversation as it is about consumption)." Jeff Jarvis, "Argue with Me," *Buzz Machine*, November 11, 2004, http://buzzmachine.com/2004/11/11/argue-with-me-c/. See also Napoli, *Audience Evolution*.

37. Stoeffel, "Deadliest Klatsch."

38. Jonathan Mahler, "Gawker's Moment of Truth," *New York Times*, June 12, 2015, https://www.nytimes.com/2015/06/14/business/media/gawker-nick-denton-moment-of-truth.html.

39. Wendy Nelson Espeland, *The Struggle for Water: Politics, Rationality, and Identity in the American Southwest* (Chicago: University of Chicago Press, 1998), 28.

40. Geoffrey C. Bowker and Susan Leigh Star, *Sorting Things Out: Classification and Its Consequences* (Cambridge, MA: MIT Press, 1999), 6.

41. Of the 107 Gawker staffers who cast votes (out of 118 eligible voters), 80 voted in favor of unionizing and 27 voted against. Gawker Media Staff, "Gawker Media Votes to Unionize," *Gawker*, June 4, 2015, https://gawker.com/gawker-media-votes-to-unionize-1708892974.

42. Noam Scheiber, "Gawker Media Employees Vote to Form a Union, and the Bosses Approve," *New York Times*, June 4, 2015, https://www.nytimes.com/2015/06/05/business/gawker-media-employees-vote-to-form-a-union-and-the-bosses-approve.html.

43. For more on the discourse of risk in high-tech workplaces, see Neff, *Venture Labor*.

44. Cohen and de Peuter, *New Media Unions*, xi.

45. Prasad, "An Organized Workforce Is Part of Growing Up."

46. Cohen and de Peuter, *New Media Unions*, 1.

47. Ibid., chaps. 1 and 2.

48. For a critique of professionalism along these lines, see Magali Sarfatti Larson, *The Rise of Professionalism: A Sociological Analysis* (Berkeley: University of California Press, 1977).

49. Cohen and de Peuter, *New Media Unions*, 20.

Conclusion

1. For a sustained discussion of the news media's vital civic role, see Schudson, *Why Democracies Need an Unlovable Press*.

2. See Baker, *Advertising and a Democratic Press*.

3. Pickard, *Democracy without Journalism?* 1.

4. Jessica Mahone, Qun Wang, Philip Napoli, Matthew Weber, and Katie McCollough, "Who's Producing Local Journalism: Assessing Journalistic Output across Different Outlet Types," *DeWitt Wallace Center for Media & Democracy*, August 2019, https://dewitt.sanford.duke.edu/wp-content/uploads/2019/08/Whos-Producing-Local-Journalism_FINAL.pdf.

5. For further discussion about journalism as a case of market failure, see Emily Bell, "The Cairncross Review Admits What America Won't about Journalism," *Columbia Journalism Review*, February 15, 2019, https://www.cjr.org/tow_center/the-cairncross-review.php; Victor Pickard, "Journalism's Market Failure Is a Crisis for Democracy," *Harvard Business Review*, March 12, 2020, https://hbr.org/2020/03/journalisms-market-failure-is-a-crisis-for-democracy.

6. Richard Fletcher, "Paying for News and the Limits of Subscription," Reuters Institute, May 24, 2019, http://www.digitalnewsreport.org/survey/2019/paying-for-news-and-the-limits-of-subscription/.

7. See, e.g., Chadwick Matlin, "A Faustian Bargain," *Columbia Journalism Review*, November/December 2010, https://archives.cjr.org/reports/a_faustian_bargain.php.

8. Nadler, *Making the News Popular*, 76.

9. For more on this theme, see the discussion of "overspelling" in Christin and Petre, "Making Peace with Metrics."

10. John Saroff, "A Chartbeat Evolution," *Chartbeat blog*, October 3, 2017, https://blog.chartbeat.com/2017/10/03/a-chartbeat-evolution/.

11. Shan Wang, "The New York Times Is Trying to Narrow the Distance between Reporters and Analytics Data," *Nieman Lab*, July 25, 2016, https://www.niemanlab.org/2016/07/the-new-york-times-is-trying-to-narrow-the-distance-between-reporters-and-analytics-data/. For an extended discussion of the creation of bespoke analytics tools at prestigious news publications, see Christin and Petre, "Making Peace with Metrics."

12. Wang, "The New York Times Is Trying to Narrow the Distance."

13. Matt Drange, "Peter Thiel's War on Gawker: A Timeline," *Forbes*, June 21, 2016, https://www.forbes.com/sites/mattdrange/2016/06/21/peter-thiels-war-on-gawker-a-timeline/#7f3322015c5.

14. Megan Greenwell, "The Adults in the Room," *Deadspin*, August 23, 2019, https://theconcourse.deadspin.com/the-adults-in-the-room-1837487584. Greenwell's objection to Spanfeller's plan as irrational and counterproductive is hardly the first time that workers have noted that technological innovations implemented by management to make the labor process more efficient sometimes do just the opposite. As Joan Greenbaum explains, "In the 1950s and 1960s . . . making office work fit a factory assembly-line model made it take longer to get some things done and resulted in clumsy computer systems. In the 1980s, office systems were supposed to bring about a paperless office, but by all accounts more and more paperwork was created. The rocky road of technical change is littered with proposals that highlight contradictions and clashes between management plans and workplace practice." Joan Greenbaum,

Windows on the Workplace: Technology, Jobs, and the Organization of Office Work (New York: Monthly Review Press, 2004), 31.

15. Barry Petchesky, "I Was Fired from Deadspin for Refusing to 'Stick to Sports,'" *New York Times*, November 11, 2019, https://www.nytimes.com/2019/11/11/opinion/deadspin-sports.html.

16. Cf. Usher, "Al Jazeera English Online."

17. Cohen and de Peuter, *New Media Unions*; Marc Tracy, "BuzzFeed News Is Part of a Union Wave at Digital Media Outlets," *New York Times*, June 18, 2019, https://www.nytimes.com/2019/06/18/business/media/buzzfeed-news-union-walkout.html.

18. Cora Lewis, "BuzzFeed Founder Jonah Peretti: 'I Don't Think a Union Is Right' for Staff," *BuzzFeed*, August 14, 2015, https://www.buzzfeednews.com/article/coralewis/buzzfeed-founder-jonah-peretti-i-dont-think-a-union-is-right#.wb48n8YQx.

19. See Max Besbris and Caitlin Petre, "Professionalizing Contingency: How Journalism Schools Adapt to Deprofessionalization," *Social Forces* 98(4) (2019): 1524–47; Christin, *Metrics at Work*, chap. 6.

20. See Cohen and de Peuter, *New Media Unions*; DePillis, "Why Internet Journalists Don't Organize."

21. Schiller, "Labor and Digital Capitalism," 14. Emphasis added.

22. E.g., as Banks wrote, "Perhaps it is now futile to expect any forms of organizing that might displace the ideological primacy now afforded creative autonomy in the flexible cultural workplace" (*The Politics of Cultural Work*, 65).

Appendix B: A Guide to the Chartbeat Publishing Dashboard

1. Chartbeat, "Understanding the Difference between Concurrents and Pageviews," n.d., https://help.chartbeat.com/hc/en-us/articles/210258697-Understanding-the-difference-between-concurrents-and-pageviews.

2. For Chartbeat's explanation of recirculation and other key metrics on the dashboard, see Chartbeat, "Guide to Real-Time," n.d., https://help.chartbeat.com/hc/en-us/articles/360017785694-Guide-to-Real-Time.

REFERENCES

Abbott, Andrew. 1988. *The System of Professions: An Essay on the Division of Expert Labor*. Chicago: University of Chicago Press.

Abbruzzese, Jason. 2014. "The Full New York Times Innovation Report." *Mashable*, May 16. http://mashable.com/2014/05/16/full-newyork-times-innovation-report/.

Ananny, Mike. 2018. *Networked Press Freedom: Creating Infrastructures for a Public Right to Hear*. Cambridge, MA: MIT Press.

Anderson, C. W. 2011. "Between Creative and Quantified Audiences: Web Metrics and Changing Patterns of Newswork in Local US Newsrooms." *Journalism* 12(5): 550–66.

Anderson, C. W., Emily Bell, and Clay Shirky. 2014. *Post-Industrial Journalism: Adapting to the Present*. Tow Center for Digital Journalism. https://academiccommons.columbia.edu/doi/10.7916/D8N01JS7.

Anderson, Chris. 2008. "The End of Theory: The Data Deluge Makes the Scientific Method Obsolete." *WIRED*, June 23. https://www.wired.com/2008/06/pb-theory/.

Anderson, L. V. 2013. "Is This the Worst Thing BuzzFeed's Ever Done?" *Slate*, July 8. https://slate.com/culture/2013/07/buzzfeed-egyptian-revolution-in-jurassic-park-gifs-oy.html.

Ashforth, Blake, Glen E. Kreiner, Mark A. Clark, and Mel Fugate. 2007. "Normalizing Dirty Work: Managerial Tactics for Countering Occupational Taint." *Academy of Management Journal* 50(1): 149–74.

Ayres, Ian. 2007. *Super Crunchers: Why Thinking-by-Numbers Is the New Way to Be Smart*. New York: Bantam Books.

Baker, C. Edwin. 1994. *Advertising and a Democratic Press*. Princeton: Princeton University Press.

Banks, Mark. 2007. *The Politics of Cultural Work*. Houndmills: Palgrave Macmillan.

Barnhurst, Kevin G., and John Nerone. 2001. *The Form of News: A History*. New York: Guilford Press.

Beam, Randal A. 1998. "What It Means to Be a Market-Oriented Newspaper." *Newspaper Research Journal* 19(3): 2–20.

Beaujon, Andrew. 2015. "Reporters at the *Washington Post* Will Soon Be Able to Check Their Articles' Traffic." *Washingtonian*, June 4. http://www.washingtonian.com/blogs/capitalcomment/media/reporters-at-the-washington-post-will-be-able-to-check-their-articles-traffic.

Beer, David. 2016. *Metric Power*. London: Palgrave Macmillan.

Bélair-Gagnon, Valérie, and Avery E. Holton. 2018. "Boundary Work, Interloper Media, and Analytics in Newsrooms: An Analysis of the Roles of Web Analytics Companies in News Production." *Digital Journalism* 6(4): 492–508.

Bell, Emily. 2017. "Technology Company? Publisher? The Lines Can No Longer Be Blurred." *The Guardian*, April 2. https://www.theguardian.com/media/2017/apr/02/facebook-google -youtube-inappropriate-advertising-fake-news.

———. 2019. "The Cairncross Review Admits What America Won't about Journalism." *Columbia Journalism Review*, February 15. https://www.cjr.org/tow_center/the-cairncross-review.php.

Bell, Emily J., Taylor Owen, Peter D. Brown, Codi Hauka, and Nushin Rashidian. 2017. "The Platform Press: How Silicon Valley Reengineered Journalism." *Columbia Journalism Review*, March 29. https://www.cjr.org/tow_center_reports/platform-press-how-silicon-valley -reengineered-journalism.php.

Benson, Rodney. 1999. "Field Theory in Comparative Context: A New Paradigm for Media Studies." *Theory and Society* 28(3): 463–98.

Benson, Rodney, and Erik Neveu, eds. 2005. *Bourdieu and the Journalistic Field*. Cambridge: Polity.

Benton, Joshua. 2020. "It Continues to Be Very Good to Be *The New York Times*." *Nieman Lab*, August 5. https://www.niemanlab.org/2020/08/it-continues-to-be-very-good-to-be-the -new-york-times/.

Besbris, Max, and Caitlin Petre. 2019. "Professionalizing Contingency: How Journalism Schools Adapt to Deprofessionalization." *Social Forces* 98(4): 1524–47.

Birkhead, Douglas. 1986. "News Media Ethics and the Management of Professionals." *Journal of Mass Media Ethics* 1(2): 37–46.

Blanchett Neheli, Nicole. 2018. "News by Numbers: The Evolution of Analytics in Journalism." *Digital Journalism* 6(8): 1041–51.

Blodget, Henry. 2011. "Launching the Engage-O-Meter: See How Many People Are Reading Business Insider Right Now!" *Business Insider*, August 4. https://www.businessinsider.com .au/business-insider-reader-meter-chartbeat-2011-8.

Boczkowski, Pablo J. 2005. *Digitizing the News: Innovation in Online Newspapers*. Cambridge, MA: MIT Press.

Boczkowski, Pablo, and Eugenia Mitchelstein. 2013. *The News Gap: When Information Preferences of the Media and the Public Diverge*. Cambridge, MA: MIT Press.

Bowker, Geoffrey C., and Susan Leigh Star. 1999. *Sorting Things Out: Classification and Its Consequences*. Cambridge, MA: MIT Press.

Braun, Joshua A. 2015. *This Program Is Brought to You By . . . : Distributing Television News Online*. New Haven, CT: Yale University Press.

Braverman, Harry. 1974. *Labor and Monopoly Capital: The Degradation of Work in the Twentieth Century*. New York: Monthly Review Press.

Breed, Warren. 1955. "Social Control in the Newsroom: A Functional Analysis." *Social Forces* 33(4): 326–35.

Bright, Jonathan, and Tom Nicholls. 2014. "The Life and Death of Political News: Measuring the Impact of the Audience Agenda Using Online Data." *Social Science Computer Review* 32(2): 170–81.

Brooks, Robert A. 2011. *Cheaper by the Hour: Temporary Lawyers and the Deprofessionalization of the Law*. Philadelphia: Temple University Press.

Bruell, Alexandra. 2018. "Rivals Chip Away at Google's and Facebook's U.S. Digital Ad Dominance, Data Show." *Wall Street Journal*, March 19. https://www.wsj.com/articles/rivals-chip -away-at-googles-and-facebooks-u-s-digital-ad-dominance-data-show-1521457321.

Bucher, Taina. 2016. "The Algorithmic Imaginary: Exploring the Ordinary Affects of Facebook Algorithms." *Information, Communication & Society* 20(1): 30–44.

Bunce, Mel. 2019. "Management and Resistance in the Digital Newsroom." *Journalism* 20(7): 890–905.

Burawoy, Michael. 1979. *Manufacturing Consent: Changes in the Labor Process under Monopoly Capitalism*. Chicago: University of Chicago Press.

Bureau of Labor Statistics. 2019. "Occupational Outlook Handbook: Reporters, Correspondents, and Broadcast News Analysts." *U.S. Department of Labor*. https://www.bls.gov/ooh/media-andcommunication/reporters-correspondents-and-broadcast-news-analysts.htm.

Burgun, Keith. 2013. *Game Design Theory: A New Philosophy for Understanding Games*. Boca Raton, FL: CRC Press.

Calderone, Craig. 2016. "Measure, Change, Measure, Repeat: Understanding Distributed Content." *Chartbeat blog*, July 21. http://blog.chartbeat.com/2016/07/21/measure-change-measure-repeat-understanding-distributed-content/.

Carlson, Matt. 2007. "Blogs and Journalistic Authority: The Role of Blogs in US Election Day 2004 Coverage." *Journalism Studies* 8(2): 264–79.

———. 2015a. "The Robotic Reporter: Automated Journalism and the Redefinition of Labor, Compositional Forms, and Journalistic Authority." *Digital Journalism* 3(3): 416–31.

———. 2015b. "When News Sites Go Native: Redefining the Advertising-Editorial Divide in Response to Native Advertising." *Journalism* 16(7): 849–65.

———. 2017. *Journalistic Authority: Legitimating News in the Digital Era*. New York: Columbia University Press.

Carr, David. 2014. "Risks Abound as Reporters Play in Traffic." *New York Times*, March 23. https://www.nytimes.com/2014/03/24/business/media/risks-abound-as-reporters-play-in-traffic.html.

Chang, Clio. 2019. "How to Save Journalism." *New Republic*, July 11. https://newrepublic.com/article/154455/save-journalism.

Chartbeat. N.d.a. *About Chartbeat*. https://chartbeat.com/company/.

———. N.d.b. *Why Publishers Are Killing Pageviews to Capitalize on Reader Attention*. https://next.prdaily.com/wp-content/uploads/2018/09/attention_white_paper.pdf.

———. N.d.c. "Understanding the Difference between Concurrents and Pageviews." https://help.chartbeat.com/hc/en-us/articles/210258697-Understanding-the-difference-between-concurrents-and-pageviews.

———. N.d.d. "Guide to Real-Time." https://help.chartbeat.com/hc/en-us/articles/360017785694-Guide-to-Real-Time.

———. 2015. *Media Kit*. https://static2.chartbeat.com/images/marketing_ng/media_kit/media_kit.pdf.

———. 2018. "Chartbeat Announces New Funding to Fuel Growth." Press release, July 25. https://www.businesswire.com/news/home/20180725005039/en/Chartbeat-Announces-New-Funding-Fuel-Growth.

Cherubini, Federica, and Rasmus Kleis Nielsen. 2016. *Editorial Analytics: How News Media Are Developing and Using Audience Data and Metrics*. Reuters Institute, February 29. https://reutersinstitute.politics.ox.ac.uk/our-research/editorial-analytics-how-news-media-are-developing-and-using-audience-data-and-metrics.

Christians, Clifford G., Theodore L. Glasser, Denis McQuail, Kaarle Nordenstreng, and Robert A. White. 2009. *Normative Theories of the Media: Journalism in Democratic Societies*. Urbana: University of Illinois Press.

Christin, Angèle. 2018. "Counting Clicks: Quantification and Variation in Web Journalism in the United States and France." *American Journal of Sociology* 123(5): 1382–1415.

———. 2020. *Metrics at Work: Journalism and the Contested Meaning of Algorithms*. Princeton: Princeton University Press.

Christin, Angèle, and Caitlin Petre. 2020. "Making Peace with Metrics: Relational Work in Online News Production." *Sociologica* 14(2): 133–56.

Clawson, Dan, and Richard Fantasia. 1983. "Beyond Burawoy: The Dialectics of Conflict and Consent on the Shop Floor." *Theory and Society* 12(5): 671–80.

Coddington, Mark. 2015. "The Wall Becomes a Curtain: Revisiting Journalism's News-Business Boundary." In *Boundaries of Journalism: Professionalism, Practices and Participation*, ed. Matt Carlson and Seth C. Lewis, 67–82. Abingdon: Routledge.

———. 2019. *Aggregating the News: Secondhand Knowledge and the Erosion of Journalistic Authority*. New York: Columbia University Press.

Coen, Jessica. 2014. "What Gawker Media Is Doing about Our Rape Gif Problem." *Jezebel*, August 13. https://jezebel.com/what-gawker-media-is-doing-about-our-rape-gif-problem-1620742504.

Cohen, Ben. 2013. "Buzz Feed Takes Journalism to New Low with Jurassic Park GIF Version of Egyptian Revolution." *Daily Banter*, July 9. https://thedailybanter.com/2013/07/buzz-feed-takes-journalism-to-new-low-with-jurassic-park-gif-version-of-egyptian-revolution/.

Cohen, Nicole S. 2012. "Cultural Work as a Site of Struggle: Freelancers and Exploitation." *Communication, Capitalism & Critique* 10(2): 141–55.

———. 2015. "From Pink Slips to Pink Slime: Transforming Media Labor in a Digital Age." *Communication Review* 18(2): 98–122.

———. 2016. *Writers' Rights: Freelance Journalism in a Digital Age*. Montreal: McGill-Queen's University Press.

———. 2018. "At Work in the Digital Newsroom." *Digital Journalism* 7(5): 571–91.

Cohen, Nicole S., and Greig de Peuter. 2020. *New Media Unions: Organizing Digital Journalists*. London: Routledge.

Comor, Edward, and James Compton. 2015. "Journalistic Labour and Technological Fetishism." *Political Economy of Communication* 3(2): 74–87.

Compton, James R., and Paul Benedetti. 2010. "Labor, New Media and the Institutional Restructuring of Journalism." *Journalism Studies* 11(4): 487–99.

Corbett, Philip B. 2016. "News Clichés from All Over." *New York Times*, March 22. http://after-deadline.blogs.nytimes.com/?module=BlogMain&action=Click&region=Header&pgtype=Blogs&version=Blog%20Author&contentCollection=After%20Deadline.

Csikszentmihalyi, Mihaly, and Stith Bennett. 1971. "An Exploratory Model of Play." *American Anthropologist* 73: 45–58.

Daulerio, A. J. 2012a. "Brian Williams Says Gawker Should Have Torched Lana Del Rey: 'One of the Worst Outings in SNL History.'" *Gawker*, January 16. https://gawker.com/5876450/brian-williams-says-gawker-should-have-torched-lana-del-rey-one-of-the-worst-outings-in-snl-history.

———. 2012b. "Gawker Will Be Conducting an Experiment, Please Enjoy Your Free Cute Cats Singing and Sideboobs." *Gawker*, January 23. https://gawker.com/5878065/gawker-will-be-conducting-an-experiment-please-enjoy-your-free-cute-cats-singing-and-sideboobs.

Debrouwere, Stijn. 2013. "Cargo Cult Analytics." *Debrouwere*, August 27. http://debrouwere.org/2013/08/26/cargo-cult-analytics/.

Del Signore, John. 2014. "Jerry Seinfeld Is the Devil Who Hates Minorities, Women." *Gothamist*, February 4. https://gothamist.com/arts-entertainment/jerry-seinfeld-is-the-devil-who-hates-minorities-women.

Denton, Nick. 2014. "Introducing Group Chats in Kinja." *Kinja Team blog*. https://product.kinja.com/thanks-normally-i-dont-care-if-people-hate-changes-to-1517639642.

DePillis, Lydia. 2015. "Why Internet Journalists Don't Organize." *Washington Post*, January 30. https://www.washingtonpost.com/news/storyline/wp/2015/01/30/why-internet-journalists-dont-organize/.

Deuze, Mark. 2007. *Media Work*. Cambridge: Polity Press.

DeVito, Michael A., Darren Gergle, and Jeremy Birnholtz. 2017. "'Algorithms Ruin Everything': #RIPTwitter, Folk Theories, and Resistance to Algorithmic Change in Social Media." *Proceedings of the 2017 CHI Conference on Human Factors in Computing Systems*, 3163–74.

DeWerth-Pallmeyer, Dwight. 2009 [1997]. *The Audience in the News*. New York: Routledge.

DiMaggio, Paul J., and Walter W. Powell. 1983. "The Iron Cage Revisited: Institutional Isomorphism and Collective Rationality in Organizational Fields." *American Sociological Review* 48(2): 147–60.

Doctor, Ken. 2015. "Newsonomics: The Halving of America's Daily Newsrooms." *Nieman Lab*, July 28. https://www.niemanlab.org/2015/07/newsonomics-the-halving-of-americas-daily-newsrooms/.

Douglas, Mary. 2002 [1966]. *Purity and Danger*. New York: Routledge Classics.

Dow Schüll, Natasha. 2012. *Addiction by Design: Machine Gambling in Las Vegas*. Princeton: Princeton University Press.

Drange, Matt. 2016. "Peter Thiel's War on Gawker: A Timeline." *Forbes*, June 21. https://www.forbes.com/sites/mattdrange/2016/06/21/peter-thiels-war-on-gawker-a-timeline/#7f3322015ic5.

Draper, Kevin. 2015. "Presenting: The In-Progress Deadspin Style Guide." *Deadspin*, March 27. https://deadspin.com/presenting-the-in-progress-deadspin-style-guide-1691611039.

duGay, Paul. 1995. *Consumption and Identity at Work*. London: Sage.

Eslami, Motahhare, Aimee Rickman, Kristen Vaccaro, Amirhossein Aleyasen, Andy Vuong, Karrie Karahalios, Kevin Hamilton, and Christian Sandvig. 2015. "I Always Assumed That I Wasn't Really That Close to [Her]: Reasoning about Invisible Algorithms in News Feeds." *Proceedings of the 33rd Annual ACM Conference on Human Factors in Computing Systems*: 153–62.

Eslami, Motahhare, Karrie Karahalios, Christian Sandvig, Kristen Vaccaro, Aimee Rickman, Kevin Hamilton, and Alex Kerlik. 2016. "First I 'Like' It, Then I Hide It: Folk Theories of Social Feeds." *Proceedings of the 2016 CHI Conference on Human Factors in Computing Systems*: 2371–2882.

Espeland, Wendy Nelson. 1998. *The Struggle for Water: Politics, Rationality, and Identity in the American Southwest*. Chicago: University of Chicago Press.

Espeland, Wendy Nelson, and Michael Sauder. 2007. "Rankings and Reactivity: How Public Measures Recreate Social Worlds." *American Journal of Sociology* 113(1): 1–40.

Espeland, Wendy Nelson, and Mitchell L. Stevens. 1998. "Commensuration as a Social Process." *Annual Review of Sociology* 24: 313–43.

———. 2008. "A Sociology of Quantification." *European Journal of Sociology* 49(3): 401–36.

Evans, Dayna. 2015. "On Gawker's Problem with Women." *Medium*, November 16. https://medium.com/matter/on-gawker-s-problem-with-women-f1197d8c1a4e.

Ferrer-Conill, Raul. 2017. "Quantifying Journalism? A Study on the Use of Data and Gamification to Motivate Journalists." *Television & New Media* 18(8): 706–20.

Ferrer-Conill, Raul, and Edson C. Tandoc. 2018. "The Audience-Oriented Editor: Making Sense of the Audience in the Newsroom." *Digital Journalism* 6(4): 436–53.

Fischer, Mary Clare. 2014a. "Why the Verge Declines to Share Detailed Metrics with Reporters." *American Journalism Review*, March 19. http://ajr.org/2014/03/19/analytics-news-sites-grapple-can-see-data/.

———. 2014b. "The Pay-Per-Visit Debate: Is Chasing Viral Traffic Hurting Journalism?" *American Journalism Review*, March 27. http://ajr.org/2014/03/27/pay-per-visit-debate-chasing-viral-traffic-hurting-journalism/.

Fletcher, Richard. 2019. "Paying for News and the Limits of Subscription." Reuters Institute, May 24. http://www.digitalnewsreport.org/survey/2019/paying-for-news-and-the-limits-of-subscription/.

Foer, Franklin. 2017. "When Silicon Valley Took Over Journalism." *The Atlantic*, September. https://www.theatlantic.com/magazine/archive/2017/09/when-silicon-valley-took-over-journalism/534195/.

Foucault, Michel. 1991. "Governmentality." In *The Foucault Effect: Studies in Governmentality*, ed. Graham Burchell, Colin Gordon, and Peter Miller, 87–104. Chicago: University of Chicago Press.

———. 2012. *Discipline and Punish: The Birth of the Prison*. New York: Random House.

Friedman, Andrew. 1990. "Managerial Strategies, Activities, Techniques and Technology: Towards a Complex Theory of the Labour Process." In *Labor Process Theory*, ed. David Knights and Hugh Wilmott, 177–208. Houndmills: Macmillan.

Fuchs, Christian. 2020. *Communication and Capitalism: A Critical Theory*. London: University of Westminster Press.

Gans, Herbert J. 2004 [1979]. *Deciding What's News: A Study of CBS Evening News, NBC Nightly News, Newsweek, and Time*. Evanston, IL: Northwestern University Press.

Gawker Media Staff. 2015. "Gawker Media Votes to Unionize." *Gawker*, June 4. https://gawker.com/gawker-media-votes-to-unionize-1708892974.

Gelman, Susan A., and Cristine H. Legare. 2011. "Concepts and Folk Theories." *Annual Review of Anthropology* 40(1): 379–98.

Gentner, Dedre, and Donald R. Gentner. 1983. "Flowing Waters or Teeming Crowds: Mental Models of Electricity." In *Mental Models*, ed. Dedre Gentner and Albert L. Stevens, 99–129. Hillsdale, NJ: Lawrence Erlbaum Associates.

Gieryn, Thomas F. 1983. "Boundary-Work and the Demarcation of Science from Non-Science: Strains and Interests in Professional Ideologies of Scientists." *American Sociological Review* 48(6): 781–95.

Gillespie, Tarleton. 2010. "The Politics of 'Platforms.'" *New Media & Society* 12(3): 347–64.

———. 2014. "Facebook's Algorithm—Why Our Assumptions Are Wrong, and Our Concerns Are Right." *Culture Digitally*, July 4. https://culturedigitally.org/2014/07/facebooks-algorithm-why-our-assumptions-are-wrong-and-our-concerns-are-right/.

Greenbaum, Joan. 2004. *Windows on the Workplace: Technology, Jobs, and the Organization of Office Work*. New York: Monthly Review Press.

Greenberg, Julia. 2015. "Page Views Don't Matter Anymore—But They Just Won't Die." *WIRED*, December 31. https://www.wired.com/215/12/everyone-knows-page-views-dont-matter-but-they-just-wont-die/.

Greenwell, Megan. 2019. "The Adults in the Room." *Deadspin*, August 23. https://theconcourse.deadspin.com/the-adults-in-the-room-1837487584.

Gregg, Melissa. 2011. *Work's Intimacy*. Cambridge: Polity.

Griffith, Erin. 2011. "Stats-Addicted Editors Suffer from Chartbeat Withdrawal." *Adweek*, April 29. https://www.adweek.com/digital/stats-addicted-editors-suffer-chartbeat-withdrawal-131175/.

Guardian. 2013. "Making Social Data Profitable." *Changing Media Summit*. https://www.theguardian.com/media-network/video/2013/apr/04/social-data-profitable-video.

Ha, Anthony. 2011. "'The New 'Aol Way': It's All about the Numbers." *Venturebeat*, February 1. https://venturebeat.com/2011/02/01/the-aol-way/.

Hacking, Ian. 1986. "Making Up People." In *Reconstructing Individualism: Autonomy, Individuality, and the Self in Western Thought*, ed. Thomas C. Heller, Morton Sosna, and David E. Wellbery, 161–71. Stanford: Stanford University Press.

Hall, Stuart. 1973. "The Determination of News Photographs." In *The Manufacture of News: A Reader*, ed. Stanley Cohen and Jock Young, 176–90. Beverly Hills, CA: Sage.

Hallin, Daniel C. 1994. *We Keep America on Top of the World: Television Journalism and the Public Sphere*. New York: Routledge.

Hallin, Daniel C., and Paolo Mancini. 2004. *Comparing Media Systems: Three Models of Media and Politics*. Cambridge: Cambridge University Press.

Hamblin, James. 2014. "It's Everywhere, the Clickbait." *The Atlantic*, November 11. https://www.theatlantic.com/entertainment/archive/2014/11/clickbait-what-is/382545/.

Hanusch, Folker. 2017. "Web Analytics and the Functional Differentiation of Journalism Cultures: Individual, Organizational and Platform-Specific Influences on Newswork." *Information, Communication & Society* 20(10): 1571–86.

Hardt, Hanno. 1990. "Newsworkers, Technology, and Journalism History." *Critical Studies in Media Communication* 7(4): 346–65.

Hartley, John. 1996. *Popular Reality: Journalism, Modernity and Popular Culture*. London: Arnold.

Hays, Constance L. 2004. "What Wal-Mart Knows about Customers' Habits." *New York Times*, November 14. https://www.nytimes.com/2004/11/14/business/yourmoney/what-walmart-knows-about-customers-habits.html.

Herman, Edward S., and Noam Chomsky. 2010. *Manufacturing Consent: The Political Economy of the Mass Media*. New York: Pantheon.

Hesmondhalgh, David, and Sarah Baker. 2011. *Creative Labour: Media Work in Three Cultural Industries*. London: Routledge.

Hindman, Matthew. 2017. "Journalism Ethics and Digital Audience Data." In *Remaking the News: Essays on the Future of Journalism Scholarship in the Digital Age*, ed. Pablo J. Boczkowski and C. W. Anderson, 177–94. Cambridge, MA: MIT Press.

Horn, Leslie. 2014. "Here's Every Product We Have in the Home of the Future." *Gizmodo*, May 19. https://gizmodo.com/heres-every-product-we-have-in-the-home-of-the-future-1573480551.

Hughes, Everett. 1962. "Good People and Dirty Work." *Social Problems* 10(1): 3–11.

Jarvis, Jeff. 2004. "Argue with Me." *Buzz Machine,* November 11. http://buzzmachine.com/2004/11/11/argue-with-me-c/.

Johnson, Benny. 2013. "The Story of Egypt's Revolution in 'Jurassic Park' Gifs." *BuzzFeed,* July 8. https://www.buzzfeednews.com/article/bennyjohnson/the-story-of-egypts-revolution-in-jurassic-park-gifs.

Jones, Jeffrey M. 2018. "U.S. Media Trust Continues to Recover from 2016 Low." Gallup, October 12. https://news.gallup.com/poll/243665/media-trust-continues-recover-2016-low.aspx.

Joshua Benton (@jbenton). 2014. "Clickbait, noun: Things I don't like on the Internet." Twitter, November 6, 7:04 p.m. https://twitter.com/jbenton/status/530511085049495553.

Kaul, Arthur J. 1986. "The Proletarian Journalist: A Critique of Professionalism." *Journal of Mass Media Ethics* 1(2): 47–55.

Kempton, Willett. 1986. "Two Theories of Home Heat Control." *Cognitive Science* 10(1): 75–90.

Kiviat, Barbara. 2019. "The Moral Limits of Predictive Practices: The Case of Credit-Based Insurance Scores." *American Sociological Review* 84(6): 1134–58.

Klinenberg, Eric. 2007. *Fighting for Air: The Battle to Control America's Media.* New York: Metropolitan Books.

Knights, David, and Hugh Wilmott. 1990. *Labor Process Theory.* Houndmills: Macmillan.

Kosterich, Allie, and Philip M. Napoli. 2016. "Reconfiguring the Audience Commodity: The Institutionalization of Social TV Analytics as Market Information Regime." *Television & New Media* 17(3): 254–71.

LaFrance, Adrienne. 2013. "Gawker Is Letting Readers Rewrite Headlines and Reframe Articles." *Nieman Lab,* July 25. https://www.niemanlab.org/2013/07/gawker-is-letting-readers-rewrite-headlines-and-reframe-articles/.

Lamot, Kenza, and Peter Van Aelst. 2019. "Beaten by Chartbeat?: An Experimental Study on the Effect of Real-Time Audience Analytics on Journalists' News Judgment." *Journalism Studies* 21(4): 477–93.

Larson, Magali Sarfatti. 1977. *The Rise of Professionalism: A Sociological Analysis.* Berkeley: University of California Press.

Lee, Angela M., Seth C. Lewis, and Matthew Powers. 2012. "Audience Clicks and News Placement: A Study of Time-Lagged Influence in Online Journalism." *Communication Research* 41(4): 505–30.

Leff, Arthur A. 1978. "Law and." *Yale Law Journal* 87(5): 989–1011.

Leidner, Robin. 1993. *Fast Food, Fast Talk: Service Work and the Routinization of Everyday Life.* Berkeley: University of California Press.

Leonhardt, David, Jodi Rudoren, Jon Galinsky, Karron Skog, Marc Lacey, Tom Giratikanon, and Tyson Evans. 2017. "Journalism That Stands Apart: The Report of the 2020 Group." *New York Times,* January. https://www.nytimes.com/projects/2020-report/index.html.

Lepore, Jill. 2019. "Does Journalism Have a Future?" *New Yorker,* January 21. https://www.newyorker.com/magazine/2019/01/28/does-journalism-have-a-future.

Lewis, Cora. 2015. "BuzzFeed Founder Jonah Peretti: 'I Don't Think a Union Is Right' for Staff." *BuzzFeed,* August 14. https://www.buzzfeednews.com/article/coralewis/buzzfeed-founder-jonah-peretti-i-dont-think-a-union-is-right#.wb48n8YQx.

Lewis, Michael. 2004. *Moneyball: The Art of Winning an Unfair Game*. New York: W. W. Norton.

Lewis, Seth C., and Oscar Westlund. 2014. "Big Data and Journalism: Epistemology, Expertise, Economics, and Ethics." *Digital Journalism* 3(3): 447–66.

Lexico. N.d. "Clickbait." *Lexico*. https://www.lexico.com/en/definition/clickbait.

Liu, Chang-de. 2006. "De-skilling Effects on Journalists: ICTs and the Labour Process of Taiwanese Newspaper Reporters." *Canadian Journal of Communication* 31(3): 695–714.

Lowrey, Wilson, and Chang Wan Woo. 2010. "The News Organization in Uncertain Times: Business or Institution?" *Journalism & Mass Communication Quarterly* 87(1): 41–61.

MacGregor, Phil. 2007. "Tracking the Online Audience: Metric Data Start a Subtle Revolution." *Journalism Studies* 8(2): 280–98.

Madrigal, Alexis C. 2017. "Prepare for the New Paywall Era." *The Atlantic*, November 30. https://www.theatlantic.com/technology/archive/2017/11/the-big-unanswered-questions-about-paywalls/547091/.

Mahler, Jonathan. 2015. "Gawker's Moment of Truth." *New York Times*, June 12. https://www.nytimes.com/2015/06/14/business/media/gawker-nick-denton-moment-of-truth.html.

Mahone, Jessica, Qun Wang, Philip Napoli, Matthew Weber, and Katie McCollough. 2019. "Who's Producing Local Journalism: Assessing Journalistic Output across Different Outlet Types." *DeWitt Wallace Center for Media & Democracy*, August. https://dewitt.sanford.duke.edu/wp-content/uploads/2019/08/Whos-Producing-Local-Journalism_FINAL.pdf.

Malik, Om. 2012. "Data without Context Is Dirt." *GigaOm*, February 7. https://gigaom.com/2012/02/07/data-without-context-is-dirt/.

Manjoo, Farhad. 2013. "You Won't Finish This Article." *Slate*, June 6. http://www.slate.com/articles/technology/technology/2013/06/how_people_read_online_why_you_won_t_finish_this_article.2.html.

Marjoribanks, Timothy. 2000. *News Corporation, Technology, and the Workplace: Global Strategies, Local Change*. Cambridge: Cambridge University Press.

Massey, Kyle. 2015. "The Old Page 1 Meeting, R.I.P.: Updating a Times Tradition for the Digital Age." *New York Times*, May 12. https://www.nytimes.com/times-insider/2015/05/12/the-old-page-1-meeting-r-i-p-updating-a-times-tradition-for-the-digital-age/.

Matlin, Chadwick. 2010. "A Faustian Bargain." *Columbia Journalism Review*, November/December. https://archives.cjr.org/reports/a_faustian_bargain.php.

Mayer-Schönberger, Viktor, and Kenneth Cukier. 2013. *Big Data: A Revolution That Will Transform How We Live, Work, and Think*. Boston: Houghton Mifflin Harcourt.

McAfee, Andrew, and Erik Brynjolfsson. 2017. *Machine, Platform, Crowd: Harnessing Our Digital Future*. New York: W. W. Norton.

McCarthy, Justin. 2014. "Trust in Mass Media Returns to All-Time Low." Gallup, September 17. http://www.gallup.com/poll/176042/trust-mass-media-returns-time-low.aspx.

McChesney, Robert. 2004. *The Problem of the Media: U.S. Communication Politics in the Twenty-First Century*. New York: Monthly Review Press.

McKenzie, Carly T., Wilson Lowrey, Hal Hays, Jee Young Chung, and Chang Wan Woo. 2011. "Listening to News Audiences: The Impact of Community Structure and Economic Factors." *Mass Communication and Society* 14(3): 375–95.

McRobbie, Angela. 2002. "Clubs to Companies: Notes on the Decline of Political Culture in Speeded Up Creative Worlds." *Cultural Studies* 16(4): 516–31.

Meyer, Eric A. 2014. "My Year Was Tragic: Facebook Ambushed Me with a Painful Reminder." *Slate*, December 29. https://slate.com/technology/2014/12/facebook-year-in-review-my -tragic-year-was-the-wrong-fodder-for-facebook-s-latest-app.html.

Meyer, John W., and Brian Rowan. 1977. "Institutionalized Organizations: Formal Structure as Myth and Ceremony." *American Journal of Sociology* 83(2): 340–63.

Miège, Bernard. 1989. *The Capitalization of Cultural Production*. New York: International General.

Mitchell, Dan. 2011. "The AOL Way: Broken, Battered, and Hopeless." *Fortune*, February 2. http://fortune.com/2011/02/02/the-aol-way-broken-battered-and-hopeless/.

Morrison, Brice. 2011. "A Necessary Evil: Grinding in Games." *Gamasutra*, February 11. https:// www.gamasutra.com/blogs/BriceMorrison/20110211/88931/A_Necessary_Evil_Grinding _in_Games.php.

Mosco, Vincent. 2009. *The Political Economy of Communication*. 2nd ed. London: Sage.

Mosco, Vincent, and Catherine McKercher. 2009. *The Laboring of Communication: Will Knowledge Workers of the World Unite?* Lanham, MD: Rowman & Littlefield.

Muller, Jerry. 2019. *The Tyranny of Metrics*. Princeton: Princeton University Press.

Nadler, Anthony M. 2016. *Making the News Popular: Mobilizing U.S. News Audiences*. Urbana: University of Illinois Press.

Napoli, Philip. 2011. *Audience Evolution: New Technologies and the Transformation of Media Audiences*. New York: Columbia University Press.

Napoli, Philip, and Robyn Caplan. 2017. "Why Media Companies Insist They're Not Media Companies, Why They're Wrong, and Why It Matters." *First Monday* 22(5).

Navar-Gill, Annemarie. 2020. "The Golden Ratio of Algorithms to Artists? Streaming Services and the Platformization of Creativity in American Television Production." *Social Media & Society* 6(3): 1–11.

Neff, Gina. 2012. *Venture Labor: Work and the Burden of Risk in Innovative Industries*. Cambridge, MA: MIT Press.

Nelson, Jacob L. 2017. "And Deliver Us to Segmentation: The Growing Appeal of the Niche News Audience." *Journalism Practice* 12(2): 204–19.

———. 2018. "The Elusive Engagement Metric." *Digital Journalism* 6(4): 528–44.

Nelson, Jacob L., and Edson C. Tandoc. 2019. "Doing 'Well' or Doing 'Good': What Audience Analytics Reveal about Journalism's Competing Goals." *Journalism Studies* 20(13): 1960–76.

New York Times. N.d.a. "New York Times Media Kit: Digital." https://web.archive.org/web /20200128100549/https://nytmediakit.com/index.php?p=digital.

———. N.d.b. "New York Times Media Kit: Newspaper." https://web.archive.org/web /20200128100547/http://nytmediakit.com/newspaper.

———. 2013. "A Blog's Adieu." March 1. https://green.blogs.nytimes.com/2013/03/01/a-blogs -adieu/.

New York Times Company. 2007. "The New York Times Company Enters the 21st Century with a New Technologically Advanced and Environmentally Sensitive Headquarters." Press release, November 19. http://www.newyorktimesbuilding.com/docs/2007-Opening.pdf.

Nichols, John. 2009. "David Simon, Arianna Huffington and the Future of Journalism." *Nation*, May 11. https://www.thenation.com/article/david-simon-arianna-huffington-and-future -journalism/.

Noble, Safiya Umoja. 2018. *Algorithms of Oppression: How Search Engines Reinforce Racism*. New York: New York University Press.

Norman, Jim. 2016. "Americans' Confidence in Institutions Stays Low." Gallup, June 13. https://news.gallup.com/poll/192581/americans-confidence-institutions-stays-low.aspx.

Okrent, Daniel. 2004. "Paper of Record? No Way, No Reason, No Thanks." *New York Times*, April 25. https://www.nytimes.com/2004/04/25/weekinreview/the-public-editor-paper-of-record-no-way-no-reason-no-thanks.html.

Orlikowski, Wanda J., and Debra C. Gash. 1994. "Technological Frames: Making Sense of Information Technology in Organizations." *ACM Transactions on Information Systems* 12(2): 174–207.

Örnebring, Henrik. 2010. "Technology and Journalism-as-Labour: Historical Perspectives." *Journalism* 11(1): 57–74.

O'Shea, Chris. 2013. "BuzzFeed Explains Egyptian Revolution with *Jurassic Park* Gifs." *AdWeek*, July 9. https://www.adweek.com/digital/buzzfeed-explains-egyptian-revolution-with-jurassic-park-gifs/.

Owen, Laura Hazard. 2018. "Get Rid of the Content No One Reads. Offer Surprises and 'Candy.' And Other Tricks for Retaining Subscribers." *Nieman Lab*, December 5. https://www.niemanlab.org/2018/12/get-rid-of-the-content-no-one-reads-offer-surprises-and-candy-and-other-tricks-for-retaining-subscribers/.

Panova, Tayana, and Xavier Carbonell. 2018. "Is Smartphone Addiction Really an Addiction?" *Journal of Behavioral Addictions* 7(2): 252–59.

Parse.ly. N.d. "Referral Trends in the Parse.ly Network." *Parse.ly blog*. https://www.parse.ly/resources/data-studies/referrer-dashboard/.

Pasquale, Frank. 2015. *The Black Box Society: The Secret Algorithms That Control Money and Information*. Cambridge, MA: Harvard University Press.

———. 2019. "Professional Judgment in an Era of Artificial Intelligence and Machine Learning." *boundary 2* 46(1): 73–101.

Petchesky, Barry. 2019. "I Was Fired from Deadspin for Refusing to 'Stick to Sports.'" *New York Times*, November 11. https://www.nytimes.com/2019/11/11/opinion/deadspin-sports.html.

Petre, Caitlin. 2016. "Gamifying the Workplace." *Public Books*, September 1. https://www.publicbooks.org/gamifying-the-workplace/.

———. 2018. "Engineering Consent: How the Design and Marketing of Newsroom Analytics Tools Rationalize Journalists' Labor." *Digital Journalism* 6(4): 509–27.

Phelps, Andrew. 2012. "I Can't Stop Reading This Analysis of Gawker's Editorial Strategy." *Nieman Lab*, March 21. https://www.niemanlab.org/2012/03/i-cant-stop-reading-this-analysis-of-gawkers-editorial-strategy/.

Pickard, Victor. 2019. *Democracy without Journalism? Confronting the Misinformation Society*. Oxford: Oxford University Press.

———. 2020. "Journalism's Market Failure Is a Crisis for Democracy." *Harvard Business Review*, March 12. https://hbr.org/2020/03/journalisms-market-failure-is-a-crisis-for-democracy.

Poole, Erika Shehan, Christopher A. Le Dantec, James R. Eagan, and W. Keith Edwards. 2008. "Reflecting on the Invisible: Understanding End-User Perceptions of Ubiquitous Computing." In *UbiComp '08: Proceedings of the 10th International Conference on Ubiquitous Computing*, 192–201. New York: Association for Computing Machinery.

Porter, Theodore. 1995. *Trust in Numbers: The Pursuit of Objectivity in Science and Public Life.* Princeton: Princeton University Press.

Prasad, Revati. 2019. "An Organized Work Force Is Part of Growing Up: Gawker and the Case for Unionizing Digital Newsrooms." *Communication, Culture and Critique* 12(3): 359–77.

Prey, Robert, Marc Esteve Del Valle, and Leslie Zwerwer. 2020. "Platform Pop: Disentangling Spotify's Intermediary Role in the Music Industry." *Information, Communication & Society*, 1–19. DOI: 10.1080/1369118X.2020.1761859.

Pulitzer Prizes. n.d. "Winners by Category." https://www.pulitzer.org/prize-winners-categories.

Ries, Eric. 2010. "Entrepreneurs: Beware of Vanity Metrics." *Harvard Business Review*, February 8. https://hbr.org/2010/02/entrepreneurs-beware-of-vanity-metrics.

Ritzer, George. 2010. *Enchanting a Disenchanted World: Continuity and Change in the Cathedrals of Consumption.* Los Angeles: Pine Forge Press.

Robinson, James G. 2019. "The Audience in the Mind's Eye: How Journalists Imagine Their Readers." *Tow Center for Digital Journalism*, June 26. https://www.cjr.org/tow_center_reports/how-journalists-imagine-their-readers.php.

Rosen, Jay. 2006. "The People Formerly Known as the Audience." *Pressthink*, June 27. http://archive.pressthink.org/2006/06/27/ppl_frmr.html.

Roy, Donald. 1959. "'Banana Time': Job Satisfaction and Informal Interaction." *Human Organization* 18(4): 158–68.

Ryan, Bill. 1991. *Making Capital from Culture: The Corporate Form of Capitalist Cultural Production.* Berlin: DeGruyter.

Salcetti, Marianne. 1995. "The Emergence of the Reporter: Mechanization and Devaluation of Editorial Workers." In *Newsworkers: Towards a History of the Rank and File*, ed. Hanno Hardt and Bonnie Brennen, 48–74. Minneapolis: University of Minnesota Press.

Saroff, John. 2017. "A Chartbeat Evolution." *Chartbeat blog*, October 3. https://blog.chartbeat.com/2017/10/03/a-chartbeat-evolution/.

Scheiber, Noam. 2015. "Gawker Media Employees Vote to Form a Union, and the Bosses Approve." *New York Times*, June 4. https://www.nytimes.com/2015/06/05/business/gawker-media-employees-vote-to-form-a-union-and-the-bosses-approve.html.

Schiller, Dan. 2016. "Labor and Digital Capitalism." In *The Routledge Companion to Labor and Media*, ed. Richard Maxwell, 3–17. New York: Routledge.

Schlesinger, Philip. 1978. *Putting "Reality" Together: BBC News.* London: Routledge.

Schudson, Michael. 1989. "The Sociology of News Production." *Media, Culture and Society* 11(3): 263–82.

———. 2005. "Autonomy from What?" In *Bourdieu and the Journalistic Field*, ed. Rodney Benson and Erik Neveu, 214–23. Cambridge: Polity.

———. 2008. *Why Democracies Need an Unlovable Press.* Cambridge: Polity.

Schudson, Michael, and Chris Anderson. 2009. "Objectivity, Professionalism, and Truth-Seeking in Journalism." In *The Handbook of Journalism Studies*, ed. Karin Wahl-Jorgensen and Thomas Hanitzsch, 88–101. New York: Routledge.

Schultz, Ida. 2007. "The Journalistic Gut Feeling: Journalistic Doxa, News Habitus and Orthodox News Values." *Journalism Practice* 1(2): 190–207.

Smith, Ben. 2014. "Why BuzzFeed Doesn't Do Clickbait." *BuzzFeed*, November 6. https://www.buzzfeed.com/bensmith/why-buzzfeed-doesnt-do-clickbait.

———. 2020. "Why the Success of *The New York Times* May Be Bad News for Journalism." *New York Times*, March 1. https://www.nytimes.com/2020/03/01/business/media/ben-smith-journalism-news-publishers-local.html.

Sobel Fitts, Alexis. 2015. "Can Tony Haile Save Journalism by Changing the Metric?" *Columbia Journalism Review*, March 11. https://www.cjr.org/innovations/tony_haile_chartbeat.php.

Starkman, Dean. 2010. "The Hamster Wheel: Why Running as Fast as We Can Is Getting Us Nowhere." *Columbia Journalism Review*, September/October. https://archives.cjr.org/cover_story/the_hamster_wheel.php.

Sterne, Peter. 2015. "The Gawker Boomerang." *Politico*, January 14. http://www.capitalnewyork.com/article/media/2015/01/8560066/gawker-boomerang.

Stoeffel, Kat. 2012. "Deadliest Klatsch: Nick Denton Gives Gawker's Drive-By Peanut Gallery a Promotion." *New York Observer*, June 27. http://observer.com/2012/06/deadliest-klatsch-nick-denton-gives-gawkers-drive-by-peanut-gallery-a-promotion.

Sullivan, Margaret. 2020. *Ghosting the News: Local Journalism and the Crisis of American Democracy*. New York: Columbia Global Reports.

Talese, Gay. 1969. *The Kingdom and the Power: Behind the Scenes at the New York Times: The Institution That Influences the World*. New York: World Publishing Company.

Tandoc, Edson. 2014. "Journalism Is Twerking? How Web Analytics Is Changing the Process of Gatekeeping." *New Media & Society* 16(4): 559–75.

———. 2015. "Why Web Analytics Click: Factors Affecting the Ways Journalists Use Audience Metrics." *Journalism Studies* 16(6): 782–99.

Tandoc, Edson C., and Ryan J. Thomas. 2015. "The Ethics of Web Analytics: Implications of Using Audience Metrics in News Construction." *Digital Journalism* 3(2): 243–58.

TechCrunch. 2011. "Paul Miller and the Five Rules of Stunt Resignation." February 19. https://techcrunch.com/2011/02/19/aol-way-or-the-highway/.

Thompson, Derek. 2014. "Why Audiences Hate Hard News—And Love Pretending Otherwise." *The Atlantic*, June 17. http://www.theatlantic.com/business/archive/2014/06/news-kim-kardashian-kanye-west-benghazi/372906/.

Tolentino, Jia. 2016. "Gawker's Essential Unevenness." *New Yorker*, August 20. https://www.newyorker.com/culture/jia-tolentino/gawkers-essential-unevenness/amp.

Tracy, Marc. 2019. "BuzzFeed News Is Part of a Union Wave at Digital Media Outlets." *New York Times*, June 18. https://www.nytimes.com/2019/06/18/business/media/buzzfeed-news-union-walkout.html.

Tuchman, Gaye. 1972. "Objectivity as Strategic Ritual: An Examination of Newsmen's Notions of Objectivity." *American Journal of Sociology* 77(4): 660–79.

Ureneck, Lou. 1999. "Newspapers Arrive at Economic Crossroads." *Nieman Lab*, June 15. https://niemanreports.org/articles/newspapers-arrive-at-economic-crossroads/.

Usher, Nikki. 2010. "Why SEO and Audience Tracking Won't Kill Journalism as We Know It." *Nieman Lab*, September 14. https://www.niemanlab.org/2010/09/why-seo-and-audience-tracking-won%E2%80%99t-kill-journalism-as-we-know-it-2/.

———. 2013. "Al Jazeera English Online: Understanding Web Metrics and News Production When a Quantified Audience Is Not a Commodified One." *Digital Journalism* 1(3): 335–51.

———. 2014. *Making News at the New York Times*. Ann Arbor: University of Michigan Press.

Van Nest, Allie. 2016. "A Closer Look at How Pageviews Have Evolved Over Time." *Mediashift*, March 9. http://mediashift.org/2016/03/a-closer-look-at-how-pageviews-have-evolved -over-time/.

Wahl-Jorgensen, Karin. 2002. "The Construction of the Public in Letters to the Editor: Deliberative Democracy and the Idiom of Insanity." *Journalism* 3(2): 183–204.

Walter, Terri. 2017. "The Results Are In: 2016's Most Engaging Stories." *Chartbeat blog.* http:// blog.chartbeat.com/2017/01/24/the-results-are-in-2016s-most-engaging-stories/.

Wang, Shan. 2016. "The New York Times Is Trying to Narrow the Distance between Reporters and Analytics Data." *Nieman Lab*, July 25. https://www.niemanlab.org/2016/07/the-new -york-times-is-trying-to-narrow-the-distance-between-reporters-and-analytics-data/.

Warren, Rossalyn. 2013. "A Boy Makes Anti-Muslim Comments in Front of an American Soldier. The Soldier's Reply: Priceless." *Upworthy*, November 9. https://www.upworthy.com/a-boy -makes-anti-muslim-comments-in-front-of-an-american-soldier-the-soldiers-reply -priceless.

Weber, Max. 1991 [1917]. "Science as a Vocation." In *From Max Weber: Essays in Sociology*, ed. H. H. Gerth and C. Wright Mills, 129–58. Abingdon: Routledge.

———. 2002 [1905]. *The Protestant Ethic and the "Spirit" of Capitalism*. New York: Penguin.

Welbers, Kasper, Wouter van Atteveldt, Jan Kleinnijenhuis, Nel Ruigrok, and Joep Schaper. 2016. "News Selection Criteria in the Digital Age: Professional Norms Versus Online Audience Metrics." *Journalism* 17(8): 1037–53.

Wemple, Erik. 2012. "Four Truths about Gawker–Brian Williams E-mail Thing." *Washington Post*, January 17. https://www.washingtonpost.com/blogs/erik-wemple/post/four-truths -about-gawker-brian-williams-e-mail-thing/2012/01/17/gIQAUktt5P_blog.html.

Wright, Erik Olin. 1997. *Class Counts: Comparative Studies in Class Analysis*. Cambridge: Cambridge University Press.

Zaloom, Caitlin. 2020. "Mary Douglas: *Purity and Danger*." *Public Culture* 32(2): 415–22.

Zamith, Rodrigo. 2018a. "On Metrics-Driven Homepages: Assessing the Relationship between Popularity and Prominence." *Journalism Studies* 19(8): 1116–37.

———. 2018b. "Quantified Audiences in News Production: A Synthesis and Research Agenda." *Digital Journalism* 6(4): 418–35.

Zeitlin, Matthew. 2016. "The Digital Media Bloodbath: Hundreds of Jobs Lost." *BuzzFeed*, April 13. https://www.buzzfeednews.com/article/matthewzeitlin/the-digital-media -bloodbath-hundreds-of-jobs-lost.

Zuboff, Shoshana. 1988. *In the Age of the Smart Machine: The Future of Work and Power*. New York: Basic Books.

———. 2019. *The Age of Surveillance Capitalism: The Fight for a Human Future at the New Frontier of Power*. New York: Public Affairs.

INDEX

Page numbers in *italics* refer to illustrations.

257